P9-EDA-057

ML   Pahlen, Kurt, 1907-.
400
P2413 Great singers, from
1974   the seventeenth
       century to the
       present day

DATE			
DEC 1 75			
JAN 5 76			
MAR 25 '76			
JAN 20 '77			

COLLEGE OF MARIN LIBRARY
COLLEGE AVENUE
KENTFIELD, CA 94904

© THE BAKER & TAYLOR CO.

GREAT SINGERS

GREAT SINGERS

From the seventeenth century to the present day

KURT PAHLEN

Translated by Oliver Coburn

STEIN AND DAY / *Publishers* / New York

First published in the United States of America by
Stein and Day/*Publishers* in 1974
Copyright © Bertelsmann 1971, 1972
Copyright © English Translation W. H. Allen 1973
Library of Congress Catalog Card No. 73-93033
All rights reserved
Printed in the United States of America
Stein and Day/*Publishers*/Scarborough House, Briarcliff Manor, N.Y. 10510
ISBN 0-8128-1698-6

Contents

Translator's Acknowledgments

I should like to express my appreciation of the very extensive help and careful advice I have had from Mr Charles Lewis, a young singer and actor, who has given me the benefit of his technical expertise, going through my translation chapter by chapter. I gratefully acknowledge, too, the help of Mr R. W. S. Mendl, a music-lover of long experience and writer of six books on musical subjects, who contributed the short section in Chapter 7 on the British oratorio tradition (which the author felt should certainly be included but did not feel qualified to write himself). Thanks to Mr Mendl also for various additions and amendments he has suggested for this edition, especially in connection with British singers and opera.

I

In the Beginning was Song

THE first human mother used song to lull her baby to sleep. All round her the birds were singing, as they had done before Man appeared on the scene. For millions of years, according to ancient belief, the stars had been singing in space. With his first cry – a sound, but not yet a word – Man began to express his feelings, to communicate with his fellows and make himself understood.

Then came the word, and with it he learnt to form thoughts. He became chieftain, king, tyrant over other human beings. But it was a singer who tamed wild beasts, quietened raging torrents, moved even rocks and trees. To us he is known as Orpheus; he has a hundred other names in the myths and epics of other civilisations, from the Babylonian Gilgamesh to the Mayan Popol-Vuh. Whatever he is called, the highest power attributed to a human in sagas and legends, power over nature, is given not to the orator, the poet or the prince, but to the music-maker. For his sake, indeed, the gods abolished the one law which seemed immutable – restoring the dead to life. Orpheus, the 'lyric' singer (song and lyre went together), was allowed to lead his beloved Eurydice back into the world from the realm of the shades; from the past into the present. A singer could recall the irrevocable – time.

Enchantment by song is as old as the hills; from Man's first cry to *bel canto* there is a continuous line. For people of the remote past, song penetrated to the depths of their being, as it does for the few primitive tribes left today. This is not surprising, but the sound of a glorious voice can still give moments of insight and awareness, serenity and even inspiration, to the harassed inhabitants of an age of computers, atomic power and space travel; which is good evidence for the eternal validity of the Orpheus saga, for the power of song, the undying spell of the human voice.

It has given rise to this book, a tiny twig on the mighty tree of musical magic.

The Present

Every evening – or rather, at every hour of the day, since it is always evening somewhere – curtains are going up on thousands of operas and operettas and musicals. A stream of sound swells from the orchestras beneath conductors' batons, and then ten thousand voices pour over the footlights into theatres filled with audiences a hundred times that number.

Somewhere in the world there are also a thousand singers on concert platforms. They have a hundred thousand hearts swaying with them to the rustle of the lime tree outside the gate, or the flow of the millstream with a boy wandering along its banks. They make these hearts share the lament of two grenadiers for an Emperor who rises impressively out of the lifeless pages of the history books.

We are already talking of singers in their tens of thousands, audiences in their millions. Such figures are remarkable enough, but they pale beside those most clearly characteristic of today's musical life. In addition to the audience who feel the direct impact of song in opera-house and concert-hall, there are the unnumbered thousands more who experience it through records, radio and television. Perhaps popular song has degenerated; you often hear people bemoaning the fact. There may be fewer people than a century ago who know how to give full vent to their feelings in song and so relieve their burdened hearts, but beyond all doubt the number of people with a real love of singing has risen steeply in our age.

We live in 'unmusical' times – another common complaint. Technology rules the day, while the arts lead a shadowy existence in the background. There is a terrifying spread of materialism, which threatens to stifle all spiritual values. Yet, I would repeat, the number of music-lovers in our day has vastly increased, with technology acting not as Demon King but as Fairy Godmother. For besides clearing the way to the stars, technology has given music a fantastic new impetus, taking it into the huts and cottages of the poorest, to the beds of the sick and lonely in all corners of the earth.

If we cast a glance today at one of the hundreds of music colleges where singing is taught to the highest standards, it is astonishing to find such a mass of good material, so many fine and often glorious voices, so much determination to succeed in one of the most difficult of all careers, so much willing dedication to a profession which offers no easy rewards, so much faith in a vocation and hope of being given the chance to fulfil it.

Compare singing with some other professions – teaching, say, or medicine. The great majority of those trained at colleges of education will be able to obtain teaching posts, most medical students who qualify will find jobs as doctors, and it is the same with all other professions and trades where demand exceeds supply. To that extent, students and apprentices can look forward with some confidence to earning a livelihood in their own field. Anyone training as a singer, however, is taking a step into the unknown. For his career there are only possibilities, no certainties. He can only cherish the hope and dream of one day standing out in the bright lights of fame. Meanwhile he must work tirelessly day after day to perfect his art, with an intensity perhaps known only to artistic and creative people. But he has no choice, for anyone who can choose is not an artist.

Good Singers and Great Singers

Rossini, asked what was needed to become a professional singer, answered 'Only three things; voice, voice and again voice.' Was this the *bon mot* of an intellectual mocker, or the attitude of a country and a particular period?

'A great talent is the first thing a singer must possess. Also, of course, very great industry. But you must have a fair amount of intelligence as well.' So wrote Lilli Lehmann about a century later – and she was not only a great singer but initiated countless young people into her art. Other authorities may have expressed it a little differently, but most agree in principle that the singing profession represents a synthesis of natural ability and hard work.

What is this 'talent' required by Lilli Lehmann? It is significant that she did *not* say 'voice'. On the other hand, Toscanini, her mighty contemporary, maintained the Italian faith in voice. Introducing Marian Anderson into the world of her future triumphs, he said she had a voice 'such as appears only once in a century', while Renata Tebaldi had '*la voce d'un angelo*', his way of acclaiming supreme quality in a human voice. But Lilli Lehmann's 'talent' is more than Rossini's and Toscanini's 'voice'. Grillparzer, Austria's great dramatic poet, who loved music and was closely connected with it all his life, wrote of Jenny Lind, the 'Swedish Nightingale', who has today become a legend, 'Here is no body, scarcely even sound; I listen to your soul' – which brings up a central point in the problem. For singing talent, or genius, as we should no doubt have to say in this case, is an ability to express the soul with the highest vocal resources. The singer's true mission is to reveal the soul in sound. For it is only his soul's vibrations that will carry over distance and make other souls vibrate in harmony. Souls tuned to the same frequency, naturally, as vibrating strings produce sympathetic vibrations from other strings. That is a physical law. Why should the same not apply in the immaterial world of souls?

When Caruso died, his larynx was dissected. Of course nothing was found which could have explained anatomically his incredible singing powers. For these did not consist in his having an exceptional larynx. There *are* exceptional larynxes, of course, which might be worth examining. They do not necessarily make a great singer, even though they lead to a 'freak' voice; like Antonia Bernasconi's, for instance (described rather ironically by Mozart), with its vocal range of four octaves; or the *Bastardella's*, for whom Mozart designed coloratura passages, for the full enjoyment of the acrobatic facility of that 'extraordinary throat'; or, to come to our own time, the voice of Yma Sumac, the Peruvian Indian who trilled in rivalry with the birds in her native high Andes (before she was 'commercialised' and ruined by Hollywood); or the voices of Miliza Korjus and Erna Sack. In such cases there may well be abnormalities in the structure of the larynx. But it is clear that freak voices and artistry have nothing in common, and artistry cannot be anatomically observed or proved.

Lilli Lehmann's second point, 'very great industry', is undisputed. Although normally it cannot replace vocal talent, some great singers (I shall be speaking of them in due course) by sheer will-power and strength of character have made a quite ordinary voice the basis for a brilliant career. There are, indeed, exceptions also to the rule about hard work; some outstanding singers have been lucky enough to be able to achieve fame without working at all hard on either their voices or their rôles.

On Lilli Lehmann's third point, too, exceptions have been known. The 'fair amount of intelligence' required of the singer sometimes represents a pipe-dream of singing teachers, conductors and directors, rather than an essential condition for success, which has often been attained without it. In his *Collected Works* Leo Slezak, most humorous among the great singers of our century, tells an old story about the man who sent his brain to be repaired because it wasn't functioning properly, and then forgot to collect it, because meanwhile his tenor voice had been discovered, so that for the rest of his life the brain wasn't needed any more.

We need not be quite as scathing as that. In fact a singer is scarcely conceivable today without more than 'a fair amount of intelligence'. Contemporary music, above all, sets very difficult problems for its interpreters, and the time is past for the 'purely emotional' singer or the 'prodigy'. If singers in prominent positions had their IQs assessed, they would probably be found to have a very high average. A glorious voice may reduce a deficit in intelligence, but can scarcely wipe it out. It is possible, in fact, to become a good singer where not all of three Lilli Lehmann's preconditions are fulfilled. But for a great singer they are indispensable.

Can a definite line be drawn, though, between a good singer and a great one? Today we have an unprecedented number of good singers, for which there are several reasons. The new media of records, radio and television have killed off the merely 'provincial' singers who used to flourish in the towns of Europe. Even on smaller stages remote from the important centres, inferior productions are no longer acceptable. The public in their own homes have possibilities of comparison undreamt-of in former times. Good singing, or at least great vocal ability, is needed today in the provincial towns as well. This is in one way a gain, for the general level of opera has without doubt risen steeply; but on the other hand it means a dangerous loss for young artists, the loss of what are in practice 'try-out' theatres. This has made it hard to come gradually to maturity. Today the young singer appears on the operatic stage in rivalry not only with his colleagues, but with the great ones on record, a rivalry he has not intended or challenged. He cannot avoid being compared to and judged against them. From the moment he starts his career, a high level of performance is demanded of him. Anyone who can produce it will be on his way up, and today, through the increased possibilities of the media, there are chances of quicker advancement than there used to be. Anyone who 'cannot make it' is eliminated, not only from a star's career, as formerly – when he at least had the comfort of being able to work in the provinces all his life – but from the very profession of a singer. This harsh alternative leads to immense efforts and so to greater achievements than in earlier times. Hence the number of good singers is increasing.

It is also increasing because their 'reservoir' is no longer geographically limited as in the past. For centuries the new generation of opera-singers naturally came from the 'opera countries', among which Italy was supreme. It was rare for young singers from other countries to succeed in joining Italian opera companies. Meanwhile France, Germany and Austria were expected to supply new singers for their own opera. The German-speaking music-schools trained their students for performance in theatres in their own area, where *Carmen* and *Traviata* were sung in German.

But today the world has become more closely connected and unified. This has often led, for better or worse, to productions of all works in their original language. The operatic students of most countries today learn to sing Verdi and Puccini in Italian, Gounod and Massenet in French, Weber, Wagner and Richard Strauss in German. So there are new singers emerging from a wider area, from Britain to the Balkans, from Spain to Scandinavia, and a big stream of them from the United States and Latin America. Nor, any longer, are there any limitations even in race or colour. Three hundred years ago opera was international because Italian opera reigned supreme for the world. Today it is far more international for the opposite reason; opera is a closely linked cultural field, dazzling in its variety and with new shoots constantly coming up from new ground. So singing talents can be discovered all over the world, and in many countries they can even be trained and brought to maturity. This produces a reserve corps of young singers in vast numbers, one of the most astonishing phenomena of artistic life today. It is no longer a rarity for young singers from twenty countries to appear at auditions in any theatre, and they often give remarkable performances.

In 1957, when a Maria was wanted for the original production of Leonard Bernstein's *West Side Story*, two thousand girls auditioned. Only two or three 'possibles' were found – so what happened to the rest? An immense number of young singers, male and female, are waiting and working for their big chance and the competition has become fiercer than ever. The access of new blood from classes, countries and races which used to have no contact with the singer's career, has forced the standard of talent sharply upwards. There are more good singers than in past ages, but comparatively few will get their chance.

Not that the demand for good singers and fine voices has dropped; it is as great as it has always been. The magic of the voice is a heritage from earlier centuries which still casts its spell even in our down-to-earth age. Over a generation ago Max Graf, Viennese musicologist, wrote 'Like melodious bells, fine voices are real works of art, and like all works of art which combine nature and spirit, something very rare and unforgettable.' This is still true.

In the last third of the twentieth century a fine voice and a singer's acting ability are as highly valued and as highly paid as in the times of pure *bel canto* and in the era of the prima donna. The technological age has not been able to banish the singer's art, indeed has greatly expanded its base, increased the demand for it, and made possible its spread round the whole world.

Does the increase in quantity automatically lower the quality, as is so often asserted? Is everything today simply expanded, transposed for the mass market, levelled out, with the heights of achievement surrendered? Is there really a perceptible decline in singing, as many connoisseurs complain?

No one can give a clear answer, for we are without any possibilities of comparison. Today, when there are electronic and stereophonic high-fidelity recordings, reproductions and sound-tracks, the standards are set for all time. But there is no sound-track back into previous centuries. We have only the descriptions of contemporaries, and even the most exalted and expressive words will not take us back to the actual sound. You can as little communicate clearly to the reader what a scent or a shade of light or colour is like as you can testify in words to a voice which on a remembered evening has carried you away from humdrum reality to a different world.

Adelina Patti and Nellie Melba were certainly great singers, but we cannot help being disappointed, even a little amused, by their recordings. What of Caruso? If you listen intently, you can still register the nobility of phrasing, the shattering force of a dramatic stress, the laughter and sobbing in his voice, all the things which must have made it a unique experience to hear him sing. But even with that genius of song, defective recording technique is still a serious handicap to full appreciation.

So we cannot properly compare the gods and goddesses of the past with those of today. In my opinion, Maria Callas, 'last of the prima donnas', operatic superstar of our era, shows utter perfection of voice, technique and intellect when she sings the great rôles from the *bel canto* period, which were written for the most brilliant divas of a particularly brilliant age: rôles such as Norma, Amina in *La Sonnambula* and Aminta in *I Puritani* by Bellini – who like Rossini and Donizetti might have composed specially for 'acrobats of the larynx'. Did Pasta and Grisi and Malibran sing these parts better than Callas? Idle questions, to which there can never be an answer. Quality, where it cannot be statistically calculated or proved, is a matter of comparison. Perhaps Caruso was not 'better' than Tamagno or Jean de Reszke, who sang before him. But he was the greatest of his time; and has since remained a symbol of the 'great' singer. Surely with justice, even though it cannot be demonstrated through recordings that he surpassed present-day singers.

In this book I am not trying to make such comparisons, still less to disparage the singing of our time over and against other ages, as is sometimes done. Our age, as I have said, can boast a very large number of good singers. Does it also possess the same number of great singers which brought the highest glory to earlier ages? This brings up again the crucial and perhaps insoluble question of where the boundary lies between the good and the great singer.

It can scarcely be in the purely vocal field. Nor in the technical either, or not in that alone. A great singer must of course be in perfect control of his voice, capable of making it produce all the subtlest nuances, so that he can draw everything there is from an operatic rôle or a song. But if it were only that, many would be 'great'. Does greatness lie in the personality? Here we are closer to an answer. The great singer has a special radiance which puts a spell on his audience. It emanates from him like hypnotic power; it is inexplicable. Either a singer has it or he hasn't. Call it perhaps an elemental process – or merely say that the great singer is a magician. The French boulevard author André Roussin produced a pleasant saying, which I can adopt complete by changing the word 'actor' to 'singer': 'The distance which separates a good singer from a great one is immense; the little finger of God.'

That would make a good ending to the chapter – but some afterthoughts come to mind. Good singers may turn into great singers in the exaltation of a single evening, carried by the indefinable atmosphere of a 'red-letter' night, whether at the side of a great partner, or under the impact of a direct spiritual experience, or borne on the wave of audience enthusiasm. Singers considered merely very good before, asked to step in on the withdrawal of a great singer, have in that moment of time become great themselves. I think of some words by Arthur Schnitzler, the Austrian dramatist and novelist: '. . . I felt then as if outside I could hear the call of life itself, as I had longed for it and in all its splendour, and as if it were waiting only on this one night and never again. . . .' Perhaps it is the same with such singers: only on this one night and never again. But for that one night they did 'achieve greatness'.

That is why my book will not be dealing only with the handful of indisputably great singers, who have surmounted the last ridge and now stand on the pinnacle of fame. It will speak also of those who perhaps were great for one evening because they had the potential for it - and because for them, too, God may just once have crooked His little finger.

II

Mainly Prima Donnas

TODAY'S great singers have an ancestry that goes back into legendary times. Orpheus sang to his lyre, beneath the clear skies of Greece, in the depths of the country – for his wife Eurydice, for himself, his flocks, for the gods. It was a happy touch of incongruity for Offenbach to present him as Director of the Theban Conservatoire. Then there were the sirens, against whose temptations Odysseus had himself tied down and his crew put wax in their ears; and the Lorelei, 'a maiden from olden times', who lured sailors with her singing on to the rocks of the Rhine. In the German heroic sagas Horand the singer, who charmed everyone with his songs, had learnt the loveliest of them from a mermaid who 'sang more sweetly than all human kind'. In the legends, fairy-tales and sagas of many countries the other-worldly, supernatural origin of music and singing is brought up again and again.

The Rise of the Prima Donna

Singing clearly played a part in the great age of the Greek theatre, but our ideas about it are mainly guesswork. The Olympic Games certainly gave an important part to singing, among other contests and public festivities. But Western Christianity banished these pagan, sensual songs. The Gregorian chants stand at the opposite pole, reflecting in their austerity the religious doctrines derived from Jewish worship at the Temple in Jerusalem. It was only gradually that young

Europe began to enjoy secular music again. Perhaps the pleasure in it had been kept alive through folk-song and folk-dance, however much the Church decried them. At any rate, directly Europe's first romantic spring dawned, the knights who rode from castle to castle were all at once singing songs of human love. Lyric-writer, composer and singer were one and the same person.

In the cities song grew into an art-form with very strict rules. If you had a thorough grasp of these rules, could make words and music fit them, and on top of that could give a pleasing 'rendering', you were called a 'master-singer'. In Wagner's opera the young knight Stolzing has grown up in feudal surroundings, his soul filled with the simple melodies of the minstrel Walther von der Vogelweide; when he comes to Nuremberg, the apprentice David makes a ponderous joke of telling him the hundred complications of a master-singer's art. So there were already many forms of coloratura and tone-colouring, grace-notes and staccati and slurs, as they were refined over a century later to *bel canto* – literally beautiful or fine singing – developed by the Italians to its highest mastery and for a long time held up as an ideal for singing throughout the world.

Bel canto and the Renaissance are closely connected, for it was the Renaissance which created the great art-form of opera, and with its creation discovered the singers for it. The Florentine *camerata*, breeding-ground for musical drama, which was later to take the name 'opera', showed an enthusiasm for the art of singing probably unknown till then. This art, through a finely trained and nobly produced voice, could express the stirrings of the soul in wide sweeps of melody. Orpheus was chosen as its symbol and ideal and he became the hero, both romantic and tragic, of many early works of musical drama; Orpheus, who by his singing and playing was master over man and beast, and at one time even over death.

The *camerata* period was the end of the sixteenth and the beginning of the seventeenth century. Since then generations of prima donnas, following hard on each other's heels, put their mass audiences into frenzies of excitement, made musical history and filled the gossipcolumns of the day. Much has changed in the course of time. The operas of today have scarcely anything in common with those of three centuries ago, except the framework of the stage; but the magic exercised by great singers has continued without a break. All of them – from Archilei, Basile, Cuzzoni, Mara, Todi, Malibran, Sontag, Lind, Patti, to Jeritza, Lotte Lehmann, Claudia Muzio – are the ancestors of Callas, Tebaldi and Schwarzkopf, Price and Sutherland.

Vittoria Archilei, Adriana Basile, Leonora Baroni, Catarina Martinelli were perhaps the earliest prima donnas. Originally the title simply meant that its bearer was the 'first lady' in an opera company. But these first ladies who sang the title rôle soon became all-powerful; they not only dictated terms to the theatrical impresario, they told the composer and the librettist just what kind of rôle they wanted to sing and the vocal embellishments required. In time they formed round them such an aura of scandal and selfishness, pride and caprice, extravagant displays of temperament and demands for fees, that the term 'prima donna' took on a new and derogatory meaning. But in fact the prima donnas included a wide variety of different characters, and their exceptional positions were achieved through outstanding personality and extremely hard work, often indeed through great sacrifices and self-denial.

The four ladies mentioned above worked partly at the luxury-loving court of Mantua, where the princely house of the Gonzagas is inseparably linked with the earliest great age of opera, and partly in Venice, then queen of the seas and mistress of the world. It was at Venice that the young art-form first took the decisive step from being an aristocratic preserve to reaching the general public, which soon enough developed an intense passion for it.

Two prima donnas, both born in Italy in the year 1700, were bitter rivals, especially in Dresden, then the centre of German opera. Faustina Bordoni, who married a well-known composer called Hasse, and Francesca Cuzzoni were completely opposite characters. Faustina led an existence of complete respectability, had a model family life, was accepted and esteemed in the highest circles. Francesca caused scandal after scandal, became involved in wild adventures, and in Holland she was actually thrust into a debtors' prison. They let her out every evening under strict guard to give her performance at the opera.

Despite the hazards and agitations – or perhaps because of them? – singing seems then to have been a very healthy occupation. (This should make us think, since correct singing is based on breathing correctly, which in turn is a basis for good health in general and something every child should be able to learn.) At any rate Faustina Bordoni-Hasse lived until she was eighty-one, Cuzzoni to seventy and their younger rival Regina Minotti to as old as eighty-six. The contralto Vittoria Tesi, born also, by the way, in the 'prima donna year' of 1700, not only lived to the age of seventy-five, but was still singing when well into her seventies. All this was in an era where the average expectation of life was only half as high as today and people 'grew old' far sooner.

To pursue for a moment the question of age, Adelina Patti's triumphant career spanned no less than forty-five years; while Lilli Lehmann was forty before she ventured on rôles like Fidelio, Norma, Isolde and Brünnhilde, and for her first Traviata was almost sixty! At the Salzburg Festival, which she helped to found, she sang Donna Anna at the age of sixty-two. Can we imagine such a thing today? It is very exceptional, despite the fact that we have pushed the frontiers of age a long way back. Far more than any earlier time, our era demands what the French call *le physique du rôl*; a substantial conformity in appearance between the ideal conception of the part and its portrayer.

But no rule can be derived from what has just been said. These examples and many others of long and late mastery of particular parts can be contrasted with others of amazingly early maturity. Mozart's first Pamina (in Vienna in 1791, the year of the composer's death) was seventeen. The legendary Maria Malibran burst on New York a year younger as Desdemona in Rossini's *Otello*. Jenny Lind sang Agathe in *Der Freischütz* at seventeen, and Schröder-Devrient was that age in 1822 when she took over the highly dramatic rôle of Fidelio and at last, after so many failures, brought the opera to full triumph – to Beethoven's joy and the young Wagner's inspiration. If the question is again asked, whether there are any parallels today, the answer is that they are very rare. Anja Silja, for instance, was only fifteen on her first engagement (at Brunswick), when she sang Rosina (*Barber of Seville*), Micaela (*Carmen*), Zerbinetta (*Ariadne at Naxos*); at eighteen in Stuttgart she was already singing Leonora in *Trovatore* and the Queen of the Night in *The Magic Flute*.

To follow this train of thought a little further, a singer's situation is fundamentally different from that of a violinist, who probably does not reach the peak of his ability till he is fifty, or a pianist, who often gives his most accomplished performances at sixty, not to mention a conductor, who may achieve a position as undisputed master in his seventies. All these may then continue their activities and preserve their energies for a good decade more. But with singers, vocal and psychological maturity do not always go hand in hand; they are bound to experience one of the sad frustrations of growing old. When they are mature enough as people to portray complete characters on the stage, their voices will often show the traces of long wear and tear.

For singing is a strenuous physical process, quite apart from the mental concentration needed. Good physical condition is as indispensable for singers as for sportsmen. The elasticity of muscle and sinews, as well as their strength, is a basic condition for good singing. The powerful holding of high notes, especially with big voices, demands enormous tension, of which only bodies in the best condition are capable; and with technical refinements like crescendi, pianissimo effects and long legato phrases, success is almost unthinkable without complete physical suppleness.

Certainly for singers, among others, mind may rule body and will-power extract amazing physical achievements. But such energies should be called on only in emergencies, like sudden indispositions, for instance. I shall have occasion later to refer to tragic cases where serious illnesses were overcome for a period through almost superhuman energy; Richard Tauber, whose physical impediments became more and more severe; Marjorie Lawrence, crippled from childhood; Axel Schiötz, who had to undergo a brain operation.

A correct placing of the voice guarantees that it will have as few demands made on it and therefore as little wear and tear as possible. Anyone who from youth onward sings with 'power' instead of with air and resonance, loses his voice, or rather its lustre, sooner than the well-trained singer. Voices that are well-placed remain intact longer. But the voice's volume, too, plays a part in this process; heavy, 'voluminous', big, strong voices generally wear out more quickly than small ones, which need a minimum expenditure of energy in their use. Soubrettes, theoretically, can sing much longer than dramatic sopranos; only they do not remain soubrettes. The law of life turns the youthful, playful soubrette, the lightly skipping, mischievous comedy character, into the lyrical singer, full of warmth and depth, and finally the dramatic or even 'high dramatic' singer. Male voices, of course, go the same way; from the buffo to the lyrical and perhaps right up to the heroic tenor.

All that was as valid and true with the early singers as it is today. For the foundations of singing have not changed, in fact cannot change. They are based on anatomy, combined with skilful training and deep knowledge about the potentialities for maximum achievement. Let us return to the prima donnas, who dominated the brilliant panorama of opera at the end of the eighteenth century and the beginning of the nineteenth.

For the first time a singer who became world-famous was born north of the Alps; Elisabeth Schmeling, who achieved her fame, however, under the name of La Mara. She was in fierce competition with the equally outstanding Luiza Todi from Portugal. They confronted each other in Paris, where not only the clash of different ideas of opera, but also the emergence of such musical rivals, led to brawls and riots more frequently than anywhere else. There was Pergolesi's *La Serva Padrona*, and the conflict arising from it over a French national opera; there was Gluck with ideas of reform, which he championed in person in the Paris theatres against his Italian adversary, Piccini; there was the emergence of the first generation of piano virtuosi, when groups of fanatical supporters gathered round Thalberg, Herz, Liszt, Kalkbrenner and Chopin. So too with the duel of the prima donnas Luiza Todi and Elisabeth Schmeling-Mara, 'Todists' and 'Maratists' fought each other bitterly.

Both ladies died in 1833, strangely enough, but before that, when they had already retired from the scene, they watched the rise of a new star, who held a city in thrall to an almost unprecedented degree. Angelica Catalani, 'voice of the *ancien régime*' (Honolka), more than the re-established Bourbons, was the real ruler of Paris. She had a supreme ability in coloratura – as always in such cases, it was said to be quite unique – and the imposing appearance of a queen. Ludwig Rellstab, Berlin's leading critic and the author of poetry immortalised by Schubert's music, wrote of Catalani: '. . . a dignity and nobility, indeed a majesty, which in my judgment defies comparison . . .' Yet if we are to believe reports, although she was also manager of the Théâtre Italien, she remained rather uneducated. Sitting next to Goethe at table, she didn't know anything about his work, and only remembered his name from a parody making fun of him. This is less surprising, however, than the view of some authorities that her voice was merely above average, and by no means outstanding. So it must have been sheer personality which made her the prima donna she was.

The great age of the prima donnas had started. They held absolute sway over the opera stage both in Italy and in Paris, now rising fast in prominence. They had just overcome and destroyed their first dangerous rivals – the *castrati*.

The Age of the Castrati – and 'Sex Changes'

What magnificent performances they must have given, these unfortunate *castrati*, robbed of their virility by an operation performed on them as children. In an era of over-refined artificiality they represent an aberration carried through with the utmost pomp.

It was first performed on a boy just about to reach puberty, probably some time at the end of the sixteenth century, at an Italian prince's court. No doubt the boy had a splendid voice, which had been very specially trained, and the intention was to preserve it for life. The cruelty this involved was not condemned by the Church. After the model of ancient Judaism a boy's voice in the liturgy was the only substitute for the 'sensual' and therefore forbidden woman's voice. So its preservation could not be a work unpleasing to God, especially as this surgery would also protect the voice's possessor from many of the worst snares of the Devil, in a world that was becoming daily more depraved. Nature was anyhow rather suspect, so it was less serious that the practice violated natural law.

A boy may reach puberty at any age from ten to fourteen, depending on race, climate and personal development. When he does, his voice breaks, thus giving him one basic distinction from a girl of the same age. In a few months or years his vocal apparatus, a sexual characteristic, grows to double its size, resulting in a voice which has deepened by a whole octave, and has also lost its suppleness.

Castration is a relatively simple operation. Animals, of course, have been 'doctored' millions of times without scruple. Performed on a boy, it 'saved' the voice, keeping it at boyish pitch and with its former suppleness. The body, however, continued its normal development, except that it almost always put on weight or even became bloated. This led to a strange disproportion between physical build and vocal apparatus, a boy's voice in a man's body. The boy's voice, though, was much stronger, because he now had much larger resonance spaces in his whole body. So the voice remained supple, adapted as before to runs, leaps in pitch and coloraturas, but at the same time gained strength. With the breathing powers of a man, it acquired tremendous new potentialities. So the eunuch became a rival to the woman singer.

In the woman there is a natural relation between the vocal apparatus and the parts of the body forming resonance, head space and above all chest space. But with the *castrati* this proportion was distorted so as to create favourable conditions for exceptional vocal acrobatics. A normal man's breathing, strengthened by intensive exercises, and helped by the eunuch's usual fatness, carried a voice of childish lightness, amplified by incongruously large resonance spaces – to the extent achieved today by microphone and loudspeaker. It was as light as a small boat carried by the sea.

The amazing vocal powers of the *castrati* were paid rapturous homage by a decadent aristocratic society, interested only in new pleasures, experiences and sensations. They apparently found nothing to offend their taste in the unnatural phenomenon, which was just one of the refinements of an age of luxury. These virtuoso singers were 'bred', like new breeds of animal, without any regard for the creatures so produced. But animals could do nothing to get their revenge; the eunuchs could. They dominated society, extracted immense sums of money from it, and by sheer force of voice, despite or because of their emasculation, fought ruthlessly and triumphantly for personal recognition and power. Their psychological state must have been complex in the extreme. They would over-compensate for their feelings of inferiority, and this, combined with frustration and the desire to get their own back, led to explosions beside which the escapades and extravagances of the prima donnas often seemed like harmless caprice.

Nevertheless, among the prominent *castrati* there were many whose names must be familiar to connoisseurs of the art of singing. Senesino (really Francesco Bernardini) was discovered in 1720 by Handel, who took him to London to perform in opera there. Gaetano Majorano, who called himself Cafarelli, also became very famous and extremely rich in London, where he drove through the streets amidst cheering crowds in a flower-bedecked carriage; in old age he built himself a palatial mansion in Naples. His contemporary, Farinelli, really Carlo Broschi (from Bologna), became the most celebrated singer in the world. In 1737, at the age of fifty-two, he retired from the stage, and obeying a call from the melancholy King Philip V, went to the Spanish court. Philip would summon him late at night to sing four arias, always the same ones. By this therapy he succeeded in alleviating the King's depression for a time, and got him attending to affairs of state, from which Philip had long withdrawn. Farinelli became Knight of Calatrava, a Prince, the most influential man at the mighty court; after Philip's death he was also a favourite of Ferdinand VI and his wife. He too built a 'fairy castle' for his old age – in Bologna, his home town – but had no enjoyment from it. He succumbed to the melancholy which had afflicted his royal masters.

There were many other important *castrati*, while the numbers who remained unknown cannot be established even approximately, but must run into tens of thousands. For a time this operation, which opened up for a boy the possibility of a brilliant singing career at the cost of his manhood, was an almost daily occurrence in Italy anywhere that boys' choirs flourished.

The French Revolution, among its many other consequences, started to close down the *castrati* business, although one of the last of them, Girolamo Crescentini, often sang for the pleasure of Napoleon, who took him back from Vienna to Paris. But before his fall the Emperor had issued a decree making castration an offence punishable by death. This ordinance reflected a current of opinion which had long been gaining ground. The age of Cafarelli and Farinelli was coming to an end in Italy as well. For several decades the prima donnas could once more reign supreme in opera, which made up most of the musical life of the time. This supremacy was not challenged again until the rise to power of the *primi uomini*, above all the tenors, who in the Romantic Age expressed the conception of exalted and heroic manhood.

While the *castrati* still flourished, however, they added a further complication to the 'sex-changes' which were an accepted convention of the early days of opera.

In many plays from Shakespeare to the present, disguises, often involving transvestism, are an important element in the plot. That those disguised are not recognised generally seems most improbable, and from any realistic point of view makes the desirable suspension of disbelief very difficult. Such an element is also common in operas and operettas, even in modern times. In Richard Strauss's *Rosenkavalier*, for instance, the Princess conceals Oktavian, her lover, by dressing him in woman's clothes, and also shows her 'cousin' Baron Ochs von Lerchenau the portrait of Oktavian, who is her suggestion for carrying out the presentation of the silver rose to Sophie. Ochs is surprised at the picture's likeness to the supposed chambermaid, whom he found with the Princess in the early hours of the morning. In the third act all is revealed; 'Mariandl' the chambermaid is a man – Oktavian, Count von Rofrano. That clears things up for the plot, but the audience still have a layer of transvestism left; for Oktavian is what used to be called a 'breeches part', a male character to be played by a woman.

These 'breeches parts' were the simplest type of sex-change. Mozart wrote his delightful Cherubino in *The Marriage of Figaro* for a girl; the mercurial and immature boy, enjoying his flirtations and love play, seemed to be better expressed by a woman's voice than by a light tenor. The casting of Gluck's Orpheus is more debatable. It used to be taken by a contralto, and so was technically a breeches part – even though the heroes of Greek mythology did not wear breeches! So the contralto voice, which does not get all that many good arias assigned to it, was enriched with the gem, 'What is life to me without thee?' (*Che farò senza Eurydice?* or *J'ai perdu mon Eurydice* in the original languages.) But the composer himself intended the part for a man, and today it is generally sung by a baritone – or sometimes a tenor. This seems to us more appropriate because more natural; past ages of opera were less concerned with realism.

So women sang men's parts. But it also happened, especially where
the influence of the Church made it difficult or impossible for
women to appear, that men sang women's parts. *Castrati* sang men's
parts; their masculine dress contradicted the feminine pitch of their
voice, for technically it was always that, however much they tried to
give the parts masculine strength and expression, the voices remained
soprano, mezzo-soprano or contralto, and could never turn into
tenor, baritone or bass.

But the mixing of sexes is far from complete with the above
examples. Sometimes prima donnas took over men's parts they
fancied. Sopranos had a craving for tenor parts, contraltos sang bass
parts. Who would think it possible today that the proud and very
virile Tamino in *The Magic Flute* could be played in Mozart's time
by women? In 1808, seventeen years after his premature death, two
famous prima donnas were fighting for the part; the victory went to
Anna Milder-Hauptmann. It was for her indeed that Beethoven
wrote the unfeminine part of Leonore in *Fidelio*, who also has to
change into a man's clothes. But this was to deceive a tyrant, not the
audience, who were intended to see her as the model of the loving
and self-sacrificing wife. In *La Clemenza di Tito*, the commissioned
work of the last summer of his life, Mozart, following the fashion of
his time, wrote two parts for *castrati*; but at the last moment filled
them with two women in men's clothes. A few decades later two of
the most famous prima donnas worked closely together. To offer the
public such a unique partnership for that period, they sang the leads
in Rossini's *Otello*; Henriette Sontag was Desdemona, Giuditta Pasta
the Otello!

Such anomalies often led to grotesque situations. The *castrati* in their
peak period were so much sought after and so highly paid that women
with fine voices sometimes pretended to be *castrati*. For instance, a certain Bellino turned up. He was extremely successful, travelled from
city to city, and gathered in plenty of money and honours. Casanova,
however, declared that the singer in question was really Bellina, and
this was something he was naturally well placed to find out.

The *castrati* are a phenomenon very remote from us today, and
some of the transvestism of earlier times may seem almost as fantastic
and absurd. But clearly both male and female impersonations still
have a big appeal for both performers and audiences, and no doubt –
though with different conventions from the past – will continue to
do so, aided by the current fashion for more or less unisex clothes and
hair-styles. As far as opera is concerned, however, the process will
always be limited at least by the lack of a unisex voice.

The Romantic Age

The twenties of the last century started a new great age for prima donnas, among whom Guiditta Pasta must have a special place. Before her, they had generally not cared much which works they performed in, but she inspired a brilliant composer, Vincenzo Bellini, and launched many of his works. At first she refused the 'unsingable' aria *Casta Diva*, the magnificent invocation to the chaste moon-goddess in *Norma*, but later became its first and for a long time its unsurpassed interpreter. Many prima donnas of the dramatic type were to follow her in the part, and *Casta Diva* is still a supreme test of personality and technique nearly a century and a half later – right up to singers such as Callas or Sutherland. It will no doubt remain so as long as great singing can be demonstrated by such touchstones.

At the première of *Norma* another great singer sang with Pasta – her best pupil, Giulia Grisi, whose performance in the part of Adalgisa started her on a world-wide career. Connoisseurs of opera would naturally assume she sang as a mezzo-soprano, for Adalgisa is one of the classic, and most difficult, rôles for that voice. But in those days such trivialities as type of voice meant little to prima donnas. Most of them sang soprano parts as perfectly as contralto ones, incredible as we may find it today. Musicologists, of course, have long recognised that the voice range of rôles in older operas is much wider than is generally demanded by more recent composers. Today there is very detailed specialisation in everything, singing included, and it was largely unknown in singing in the first half of the last century. Nor does this apply only to the women; we shall come later to men who could master both tenor and bass rôles.

In London a new rising star appeared with Pasta, Henriette Sontag from Coblenz. She was a *tedesca* – the Italian word for a German woman – previously a term of contempt in the world of singers, since the real art of singing always came from Italy, never from Germany. There had been well-thought-of German singers before, like Schmeling, or La Mara (mentioned earlier), Marianne Pirker and Aloysia Weber (Mozart's first love and later his sister-in-law), but despite their reputation in Germany they never achieved European fame. Henriette Sontag, however, broke through all barriers of language and country. In 1823, at the age of seventeen, she became Weber's first Euryanthe. At the end of that year, accompanied by her colleague, Caroline Unger, who was the same age, she was in Vienna, knocking a little nervously at Beethoven's door. The story of this meeting has been told and retold many times. Beethoven was a

revered, rather terrifying, solitary figure, notoriously inaccessible.
Yet when the two girls tried to kiss his hand, he would not let them
but offered his mouth instead, and then gallantly invited them to
stay for a meal. But the really astonishing thing is that he entrusted
them with the soprano and contralto solo parts in the original performance of his Ninth Symphony on 7th May 1824. He must surely
have had some instinctive recognition of their genius.

In 1825 we find Sontag in Leipzig and Berlin, and in 1826 she was
the rage of Paris. Soon her name was echoing throughout Europe.
But despite her fame, as a stage artist she was by no means considered a suitable wife for a count, neither for Count Clam-Gallas
from Prague, whom she had to renounce in her teens, nor for Count
Carlo Rossi from Piedmont. But this time love proved too strong;
there was a secret wedding, even a secret child (which died as a
baby), and in 1830 she gave up her meteoric career. She was only
twenty-four, and now she wanted to be known to the world as the
Countess Rossi, retiring into a feudal existence suitable to her new
status and emphasised by her husband's diplomatic dignity. The
revolutionary events of 1848/49 cost the couple their position and
fortune, but luckily, Henriette's voice was still intact. Impelled by
anxiety for her children, she returned to singing. Europe was gripped
by a second 'Sontag fever' as infectious as the first, but this time the
Old World was not enough for her. Jenny Lind, 'The Swedish
Nightingale', had recently revealed the possibilities of triumphant
tours of America. Sontag, apparently in full possession of her technique and voice at forty-eight, made a victorious progress through
the United States. She went on to Mexico, still a very wild country,
to which Manuel Garcia had brought opera for the first time a
quarter of a century before, and she died there on 17th June 1855,
one of the victims of a cholera epidemic.

The daughter of this Manuel Garcia, Maria Malibran, once appeared before an audience with Sontag. The scene was a Paris salon,
and there was great tension beforehand. Here were two tigresses
suddenly confined in a small cage; surely they would tear each other
to pieces. Not at all. Each recognised that in a Europe richly endowed with prima donnas, she had met her worthiest rival. They
kissed one another, and went on to alter the expected programme by
singing duets together. It must have been a remarkable occasion.

To fully appreciate its flavour, we must go back to the year 1816,
when two bachelor musicians, a composer and a singer, were living
together in a studio apartment in Rome. Gioachino Rossini was a
rising composer, who had already achieved repeated successes in

opera and was just writing a new comic opera entitled *Il Barbiere di Seviglia*. His singer friend was Manuel Garcia, born in Seville, and the story is that Rossini turned to Garcia, asking him to sing a Spanish tune which would at once establish the right atmosphere as an introductory piece to the new opera. Garcia produced a delightful song, more his own invention than authentic folk-song, and Rossini made it into the entrance serenade for the love-sick Count Almaviva.

Garcia led a very vigorous existence as singer, impresario, teacher and composer. He took the first complete opera company to America and, in New York in 1825, sang Mozart's *Don Giovanni* for the first time in the New World – in the presence of Mozart's librettist, the 'Abbé' Lorenzo da Ponte, by then an old man, who was delighted with the performance. Garcia then took a company through Mexico, where their coaches were attacked on a lonely path. He was not a man to admit defeat. He stood forth, announced his name, and sang a few arias as requested by the bandits – who promptly returned half their loot. That is how the tale goes in Garcia's rather romanticised memoirs, though it can also be read in today's accounts of the early history of opera.

One evening in New York, when Rossini's *Otello* was being performed, the Desdemona fell sick at the last moment. Garcia's daughter Maria, then just sixteen, had undergone training as a singer from her father. 'Undergone' is the *mot juste*, for Manuel had been more free with his blows than with encouragement. Now he summoned her, made her quickly put on the costume and whispered to her that if she did not sing well he would genuinely strangle her in the last act. As he sometimes came fairly near to it in singing lessons, Maria thought this quite possible. But Garcia didn't need to carry out his threat. From her first notes he recognised immediately that it was the break-through of an extraordinary talent. He could scarcely have guessed, however, at the world-wide fame his daughter would achieve; though not under his name, celebrated as that was. She escaped from that name at the first opportunity, married a man much older than herself, a banker who after various corrupt deals went bankrupt, whereupon she left him almost at once. But by an irony of fate his name was immortalised, for she continued to call herself Maria Malibran; perhaps the most brilliant among many dazzling names of that age.

In love with singing, ecstatic over her successes, she received the adoration of the world with child-like delight. There were torchlight processions, scenes of frenzied enthusiasm wherever she appeared or her carriage passed. She was paid fantastic fees, by the side of which the fees for great stars today seem quite small beer. So Maria Malibran rode in triumph through towns and countries, theatres and concert-halls, through life itself. One day she was riding her horse, a favourite occupation, over some English moors, when it stumbled and threw her. She managed to drag herself to the evening's concert, for she had never let down an impresario or broken a promise to her public. Only a few people in the audience noticed that while singing she had to cling desperately to the piano. Then she collapsed and died. She was only twenty-eight. The whole world mourned her, especially the only man she had loved, the Belgian violinist Charles de Bériot.

Garcia's genius was passed on to more than one of his children. His son, also Manuel, became an excellent singer, but still more famous as a teacher. Generations of singers learnt their art from him. He also invented the larynx-mirror, which for the first time enabled singers to watch their vocal cords in full activity. He lived to celebrate his one-hundred-and-first birthday, still in very good fettle, surrounded by large numbers of his former pupils.

Maria's sister Pauline, fifteen years younger, became the prima donna at the Paris Opéra; superb as Gluck's Orpheus and a magnificent Fides in Meyerbeer's *Le Prophète*, which was being rapturously received just then. By the time her name became famous, Maria's was already a legend of the past. Pauline married a strange Monsieur Viardot, called herself Pauline Viardot-Garcia, and ran a lavish bourgeois house in the Paris of the Second Empire. She had children and was on friendly terms with important people like the King of Prussia and Bismarck. For decades the great Russian author, Ivan Turgenev, lived under her roof as an accepted friend of the household and doubtless as her lover, so free were morals in the last century, or else it was an extraordinary concession to an extraordinary artist.

The 'Singing Actress' Appears

As a singer Pauline Viardot-Garcia was perhaps not so brilliant and entrancing as the *prima donna assoluta*, Maria Malibran, had been. But in Maria's day prima donnas were 'singers only'. Thirty years after her death, in a musical world which had changed a good deal, her sister Pauline established for good the new type of 'singing actress', creator of real characters.

She had one great predecessor, the German Wilhelmine Schröder-Devrient, of whom it was sometimes unkindly said that she was technically inadequate in the field of pure bel canto, and that was why she made a virtue of thorough characterisation on the opera stage. This was, of course, untrue, or only partly and accidentally true, for the fact is a new period had started. Baroque and rococo had come to an end, full-bottomed wigs and crinolines had disappeared. Idealised figures of gods and heroes had departed from the stage, and instead there was a desire to see real human beings and what happened to them. The intellectual and psychological foundations of bel canto were thereby removed as well; artistic accomplishment in a rôle took second place to its reality, and vocal acrobatics disappeared from the musical theatre. An opera-singer began to find it his most important task to 'express the soul', and to thrill audiences by presenting un-usual lives at their dramatic climax.

This process did not take place overnight, of course, it was a gradual development. Bel canto continued for decades, simply be-cause many works written in its spirit also continued to appeal to public taste – indeed they have recently come back strongly into favour in our own time – so it is not really true to say that the bel canto age was over. It would be more accurate to say that from the first half of the nineteenth century there were two schools which, although apparently mutually exclusive, had in fact connections with each other. Weber, for instance, was bred on *Singspiel*, dialogue interspersed with songs (perhaps *The Beggar's Opera* is the nearest English equivalent), and German naturalism; in *Der Freischütz* he seems far from bel canto. But later, in *Euryanthe* and *Oberon*, where he abandons ordinary humans for heroes and supernatural beings, he provides singing with more pathos and coloratura, a completely natural consequence of this change of setting. His Italian contem-poraries did not abandon bel canto at all. For Rossini, Donizetti and Bellini, the vocal line, with the finest artistic decoration, was above any demand for realism. North of the Alps, however, realism made a decisive break-through with Wagner, who found the bel canto style superficial and looked for dramatic profundity instead of decoration. Then in the South, Verdi achieved a balance. Without renouncing pure melody which obeys only aesthetic principles, he succeeded in giving his characters more human and psychological depth. At first sight (or hearing) it may look as if he deliberately came nearer Wagner's style with advancing age, but this is a mistake. Verdi's development is as logical and individual as Wagner's, and just as much adapted to his tradition and environment.

The first operas which broke with the bel canto style were, under-standably, the so-called rescue operas, which exactly corresponded to the postulates of the French Revolution. To understand this development, we have only to compare *The Marriage of Figaro* with *Fidelio*. Mozart's opera belongs completely to the aristocratic age, with music and book pure rococo, perfect in form and yet deep in humanity because it came from a genius to whom nothing human or artistic was alien. Less than twenty years later, in the same city, Beethoven wrote his 'rescue opera' which offers vital evidence of historical development through musical drama. There seems a whole abyss between the two masterpieces, the abyss of the French Revolution, the end of an epoch and the beginning of a new one.

It is not surprising that Wilhelmine Schröder-Devrient, perhaps the first great actress on the opera stage, became the finest Leonore in *Fidelio*. Her potential lay in Leonore's shattering, tragic humanity, no longer in the perfectly rendered arias of the old era. She had no concern for trills and *messa-di-voce* tricks, for sparkling runs of refined evenness or amazing staccati in the highest and therefore the 'unnatural' position. It was no wonder, either, that she made an extremely deep impression on the young Wagner, indeed was a major factor in showing him the path he must take. Without his yet realising it, she was the artist of his dreams, the tragic actress-singer who knew all the secrets of the human heart, who aspired to the re-creation of authentic experience, to dramatic expressiveness, deep sensitivity and psychological power.

The new era now dawning brought with it a new principle of character-portrayal, without which our operatic acting of today could never have developed. The principle is not exactly defined by the terms 'realistic' and 'naturalistic'. Although today we see Wilhelmine Schröder-Devrient as its first representative, that does not mean, of course, that all the prima donnas previously mentioned had no feel for realism in their parts. Pasta and Malibran certainly tried to be 'true to life' and in their performances, above all in recitative, they often attained strong dramatic effect. But they still regarded singing as supreme and directly an aria came, the climax for which the audience was eagerly waiting, they too, like all the singers of that era, came forward to the footlights and concentrated wholly on vocal achievement. In the earlier operas recitative was there to give scope for acting; we have only to think of Mozart. But with the arias the director's problem was almost insoluble, he had to move his company with as much variety and realism as possible within a rigid framework. So the opera-writers of the nineteenth century worked hard to end the split between recitative and arias, between animated film sequence, as it were, and fixed tableaux.

For the modern actor-singer, singing is no longer all-important.

He tries to bring dramatic and musical elements into complete harmony, not to inhibit or even interrupt for a moment the flow of theatrical action, not even to hold a high note for a specially long time. Whether this new dramatic principle has brought with it a decline in pure singing is quite another matter. At any rate perfection in bel canto and life-like dramatic acting are very rarely to be found together, only in opera-singers of real genius.

One thing is clear. The change from the emphasis on singing alone in the pre-revolutionary musical theatre to the music-drama of the post-revolutionary era was firmly based on the circumstances of the time. The works changed and with them the singers who had to present them on the stage. Schröder-Devrient became great and famous because the period needed an embodiment of the new style. The word 'truth' now appeared in the vocabulary of the actor and singer. Not that their art was 'untrue' before. In relation to its age it was just as true and correct as the later style was to its own period. But the rococo age was not looking for the truth which the post-revolutionary artists aimed at. Inevitably 'truth' and 'beauty' would one day come into conflict, but the time for that was not yet. The age of Schröder-Devrient became drunk with 'truth' and brought it into harmony with beauty; or at least tried hard to do so, as we know from many observations of the time.

'Truth and nature have disappeared, especially in the art of character-portrayal, and the only aim chased after is a full purse, regardless of the means by which it is filled. Mostly the theatrical artists of today are hypocrites on the stage as much as off it. And where there is no truth in life, there is no truth either in art.' This is not a plaintive cry from our own day, it was written in about 1850 by Schröder-Devrient. Did she believe her principle was being destroyed? If so, she was mistaken in making deductions from the false artists, who have always existed, which did not apply to the true ones.

Her ideas were along the same lines as Verdi's. Around the same time he wrote, 'In art as in life one must above all be sincere.' As the nineteenth century went on, sincerity and truth came to be demanded above all in the musical theatre. Victor Maurel, one of the century's great singers, first to sing Iago and Falstaff, gave this judgment on the basic difference between his own age and the bel canto time, by then almost legendary but still repeatedly mourned for its passing: 'At the time of the bel canto school probably no singing teacher talked about expression in singing; all that audiences expected from an opera-singer was that he should sing as beautifully as possible.'

Now something else was expected. Music-drama was born. And it called imperiously for the dramatic singer, the singing actor and actress.

From Jenny Lind to Lilli Lehmann

Where does the legendary Jenny Lind, the Swedish Nightingale, fit in? She was neither the pure song-bird of the old Italian bel canto days nor the dramatic heroine of the Schröder-Devrient stamp. She was the opposite of the prima donna type, a 'priestess of music' (Honolka), one of the purest, most ingenuous beings who ever appeared on a stage. She scarcely changed from part to part, for 'pretence' was alien to her; the person she presented to the audience was always herself. She lived far from all the intrigues and love affairs that pervaded the lives of most famous singers of the age. Envy was a word completely unknown to her. Indeed, she knew nothing of ambition, except the ambition of singing well; and even that was not for worldly fame but for the glory of God and to alleviate distress among the poor. For she earned vast sums, but used nearly all for charitable purposes. Seldom if ever has so much money come to so unworldly a person, or has an artist so indifferent to all externals generated such tremendous enthusiasm. She never sang in Italy, but for the rest of Europe and also for America, the rising land of music, she was the only singer. Jubilant crowds unharnessed the horses from her carriage in order to pull their idol themselves, and on one occasion, after she had used a coach, students pushed it into the river so that no other traveller could 'desecrate' it.

Jenny Lind's singing career was brief. At twenty-nine she retired from the stage, perhaps disgusted by such worldly activity, or it may have been to fulfill a vow she is supposed to have made. After that she would sing only at charity concerts, preferably in religious oratorios. She had made her début in Stockholm as Agathe in *Der Freischütz*, but soon afterwards decided to break off; she was so dissatisfied with her performances that she felt she must start her training all over again. She went to Paris to work with Manuel Garcia (the son), who told her she did not have an especially good singing voice. He devoted great energy to her training, however, and it must have been largely through him that she became one of the most renowned singers of all time. The training started with a complete ban on singing and talking for two months, which suggests she had overstrained her vocal apparatus, above all the vocal cords; a typical case, no doubt, of singing too much too early without adequate technique. Eduard Hanslick, the perceptive Viennese critic who had boundless admiration for her artistic personality, spoke of her voice as 'chronically veiled', so the defect may have lasted. Even so, her fame was unassailable. After her work with Garcia she sang in all the main cities of Europe, appearing before a London audience for the first time in 1847. Here too she had splendid success, was soon a popular heroine, grew attached to Britain and in 1859 became a naturalised British subject. But it was in America that she found her most rapturous reception.

A Viennese broadsheet of 1850 contains a caricature of Jenny Lind's American tour showing the bizarre forms which enthusiasm could take, the vast sums offered for the chance of getting in to hear her. Farmers are seen selling houses, farms and even wives, in order to obtain a ticket; and there is a golden cage in which the impresario shuts the Swedish Nightingale every evening. Here we have the old cultural centre poking contemptuous fun at the uncouth *parvenu* country, but in fact new perspectives had been opened up which were acted on increasingly in the next decades. Jenny Lind had blazed a trail to the West, and by the end of the century a trip to the United States became obligatory as a confirmation of success in any great singing career. It was not only for the precious dollars; there was something even more rewarding in the New World – an unsophisticated, if sometimes also uneducated public, with an immense capacity for devotion and homage.

Jenny Lind's existence was enriched by valuable friendships. The great story-teller Hans Christian Andersen was a close friend and admirer – in fact he nearly married her. Mendelssohn composed the soprano solo for her in his oratorio *Elijah*, and Schumann the song *O Sonnenschein* which so perfectly fitted her character. Meyerbeer, uncrowned king of French and German opera, brought her to Berlin, where she was overwhelmed with signs of favour from kings, princes and dukes, and idolised by the public. Grillparzer exalted her in the verse already quoted, but the poet Heine felt she lacked the erotic charm common to most prima donnas. Yet the portraits of her show an inner radiance, and it may have been like this with her voice; without achieving any sensuous effect, it contained a warmth that was from the heart.

Musicians have special reason to be grateful to Jenny Lind. The singers of her age were incredibly indifferent to artistic demands and paid no regard to the composer's intentions. But she insisted on singing Mozart's scores as he had written them. What that meant only becomes clear by comparison with the arbitrary ways of her con-

temporaries. One of them, for instance, the prominent tenor Theodor
Wachtel, even introduced an 'artistic' cadenza into Walther's prize-
song in *Die Meistersinger*!

Jenny Lind lived on as a legend long after giving up her career, and
in 1867 she died on her English estate. This strange antithesis of the
usual prima donna was the first world-famous singer from Europe's
far north. Others were soon to follow: Christine Nilsson, Kirsten
Flagstad, Karin Branzell, Birgit Nilsson, and the great male singers
John Forsell, Lauritz Melchior and Jussi Björling.

But the supreme prima donna of the next period, until the first
decade of the new century, came once more from Southern Europe;
the Spaniard, Adelina Patti, undisputed mistress of opera in both Old
World and New. Opera-houses had now reached their greatest
splendour, for besides La Scala at Milan and the Teatro Fenice at
Venice, there were the new dazzling music temples of Vienna and
Paris. Audiences from the bourgeois liberal world, wearing their
finest clothes, bedecked in jewellery and wrapped in furs, sat in
gleaming red stalls and boxes. Going to the opera had become a
luxurious pleasure for a new upper crust of aristocrats and patricians,
among whom genuine love of music was inextricably linked with
snobbery.

Unlike Lind, Patti was a true prima donna in the new sense, with
fits of temperament which drove her partners, impresarios and all
those around her to distraction; she was ostentatious, vindictive and
had the arrogance of a divine-right queen. Scandals followed her
everywhere, she married a French Marquis, deceived him with a
nonentity of a fellow-singer and finally lost herself to a lover thirty
years her junior. But none of this could reduce her fame; if anything,
it was further enhanced by each of her affairs, in an age where publicity was becoming more and more important. Where people feel
incapable of deep personal experience, they are all the keener to
share by proxy in the experience of more exciting personalities, and
Patti provided excellent material for newspaper and magazine gossip
as well as society conversation.

She did not lose her fortune, like so many singers of her day, nor
her fame, and certainly not her voice. Even at an advanced age she
still had a special lightness of voice and a complete confidence in
attack (this can be heard on her recordings, though they are far from
reflections of her real gifts); she could still produce those effortless
phrases, perfectly controlled and with a wonderful sweetness of
sound, which made the hearts of two generations of opera-lovers
beat faster. At sixty-five she retired from the opera stage and the

concert-hall, but in October 1914, at the age of seventy-one, she sang for the last time in public at a St John's Ambulance Association concert for British soldiers. In 1898 she married a Swedish Baron called Cederström, her last marriage, and spent her final years with him in their castle, Craig-y-Nos, in Wales. She died in 1919, aged seventy-six.

Patti's admirers called her 'the last prima donna'. But although she was for Verdi his 'true Gilda' and 'the only Gilda' (*Rigoletto*), she had rivals who for many connoisseurs were not far behind her; notably Pauline Lucca, Marcella Sembrich, Desirée Artôt and, above all, Nellie Melba.

Although the famous sweet 'Peach Melba' was later to be called after her, Melba was not her real name. She was born Helen Porter Mitchell, near Melbourne in 1861, and in 1882 married Charles Armstrong. In 1886 she came to take lessons, first in London then in Paris with the celebrated Madame Marchesi. She soon appeared in one of Marchesi's matinées with the stage name of Madame Melba derived from her home town. Her début in opera was as Gilda the following year in Brussels, but during the nineties she continued to study with Marchesi. From 1899, after her first appearance at the Paris Opéra, her record was of constantly growing popularity. During the First World War she raised over £100,000 for the soldiers, and was made a Dame of the British Empire. Like Patti she went on singing until she was quite old, giving farewell appearances in Australia and at Covent Garden in 1924. She was a coloratura singer with a voice of great range, purity and evenness; but she had limited dramatic depth and quite early on abandoned attempts to become a Wagnerian singer. She died in 1931. Although several recordings of her singing are available, they give no real idea of her voice, still less of her personality in performance. As Jenny Lind was the first Scandinavian among the world's great singers, Melba was the first Australian. She has been followed by Marjorie Lawrence, tragically stopped in a brilliant career by the onset of poliomyelitis, and by Joan Sutherland, who today seems a likely candidate for the Callas succession.

Pauline Lucca was an Italian but brought up in a suburb of Vienna, acquiring there a very low-class accent and dialect which she never lost. She started in the chorus, sang herself to stardom as a girl, had a great many affairs, broke her contract with the Berlin opera, which meant she could not appear at all in Germany for ten years, went to America, was eventually 'amnestied' and soon afterwards was fêted in Berlin once more. Despite her plebeian speech and her inability to assimilate any sort of education, she married a Baron; but for many opera-lovers in Berlin and Vienna the Baroness was simply 'Lucca', a higher accolade for a singer. She died in 1908, aged sixty-seven.

Marcella Sembrich took her mother's maiden name, because her own, Praxede Marcelline Kochanska, did not sound euphonious enough for a star's career. She started as a concert pianist and violinist; it was Liszt who brought her to the fore as a singer. In only six years she climbed to the highest positions. In 1884 she sang in the first season of the New York Metropolitan Opera and remained a celebrated member of that company until her retirement from the stage in 1909. She was very much in demand as a teacher in Berlin, Lausanne and the United States. She died in 1935 at the age of seventy-seven.

Desirée Artôt acquired European fame in the sixties. In 1868, when she was appearing as a guest star in Moscow, a young professor of harmony, Peter Ilyich Tchaikovsky, was in the stalls. Despite his shyness, he was so enchanted by her that he came to see her after a performance and made a clumsy proposal of marriage, which she declined. Soon afterwards she married a Spanish baritone, Padilla, in Warsaw, and their daughter Lola became equally famous as a singer. For over twenty years Lola Artôt-Padilla was one of the great favourites of Berlin's opera-houses; she died in 1931.

At the turn of the century Berlin and Vienna were at their operatic peak, turning the limelight on to a brilliant new generation of singers. Most of these will appear in a later chapter, but separate mention must be given to two of them, Ernestine Schumann-Heink and Lilli Lehmann.

The former was married three times and retained the names of her first two husbands in her stage name. She was probably the greatest contralto of the time in the German-language area. Born near Prague, she had tremendous success in Berlin and Hamburg, was guest star at Covent Garden under Gustav Mahler, for many years a member of the Bayreuth Festival and in 1899 made her first appearance at the New York Metropolitan Opera House as Ortrud in *Lohengrin*. On 25th January 1909, at the historic première of Richard Strauss's *Elektra*, she was the first Klytämnestra, giving the part a demonic force and vocal power which long remained an unapproachable model. In 1932 she gave farewell performances at the New York Met in the *Ring* cycle, but three years later at the age of seventy-five, made a surprisingly successful film in Hollywood.

Lilli Lehmann was one of those who added a new intellectual dimension to opera – a further development of the dramatic heroine à la Schröder-Devrient. By tireless hard work she became not only a superb singer but the artistic representative of a generation which found real psychological insight in opera instead of the often sketchy and simplified relationships presented until then.

Born in 1848 in Würzburg, she made her début in Prague at the age of nineteen, sang in Danzig and Leipzig and in 1870 went to Berlin, where she quickly achieved a big reputation. Her memoirs, called *Mein Weg* (My Way), are still worth reading; she went on that way 'with the lofty star of art before her eyes' (to write in the style of her time), fighting against abuses in her profession as well as wrong attitudes to life. She could never tolerate lies or hypocrisy, and in the theatre worked on rôle after rôle with the same alert senses and critical understanding. In contrast to those who can develop and exercise their natural gifts with no great labour, Lilli Lehmann was an artist for whom nothing came easily, who struggled hard throughout her life to achieve the perfection to which she aspired. Not that she had more difficulty than others in solving the technical problems of singing in general or of each rôle; but once the externals were mastered, she still needed to look behind them, to dis-cover a new, different and unknown world.

In 1876 she took part in the first Bayreuth Festival, though only as one of the Rhine-maidens and one of the Valkyries, with her sister Marie (three years younger) as one of the Norns. Twenty years later Lilli was singing Brünnhilde at Bayreuth, and now she had no rival in the high dramatic field. In between she had had triumphant American tours, besides conquering Europe, although like Lucca she was in breach-of-contract trouble at Berlin. In 1891, however, she was brought back there on the orders of Kaiser Wilhelm II himself. As the years went by, she became an outstanding personality in the cultural life of the day. Apart from her exceptional achievements in singing itself, she was a magnificent actress, an ingenious producer, a perceptive writer about music, a wise but kind teacher, an initiator and organiser whose name is very closely bound up with the early Salzburg Mozart Festivals of 1901 and 1910, as well as the founding of the annual festivals there, which soon became world-famous.

She was also one of the last prima donnas from the pre-cinema age, of 'imposing' build, as it was then called; few men could successfully play heroic parts opposite her, as she was at least a head taller than most of her partners and a good deal broader as well. Yet her figure was shapely enough, and even beautiful. L. Andro has described her thus: 'A tall figure nobly formed, tranquil in movement. A queen's hands; a neck of incredible beauty, and a way of carrying her head with a perfection seen otherwise only in noble animals. Snow-white hair, not trying to hide anything of its owner's age; dark eyes of piercing sharpness, a proud nose, a severe mouth, though when it smiles the stern face lights up with a golden sun of friendly confidence, indulgence and even mischievousness . . .'

At sixty-two she could still sing Donna Anna in *Don Giovanni*, when the brilliant Antonio Scotti, nearly twenty years her junior, was playing the title rôle. But apparently she was completely convincing; no one considered her an old woman, and she was still a wonderful singer. Almost a legendary figure in her lifetime, she died in 1929. It seemed like the end of an epoch.

Women Singers and Society

'If a woman hopes to keep her virtue in a stage career,' Pope Clement XI observed at the beginning of the eighteenth century, 'it is like making her jump into the Tiber and expecting her not to get wet.' How did the connection arise between women singers and 'loose morals'?

Most of the renaissance courts put a premium on sensual enjoyment. Duke Vincenzo Gonzaga at Mantua was a cultivated nobleman of high intellectual standing, friend of Torquato Tasso, Rubens and the greatest composer of the day, Monteverdi. But any woman who wanted to become a highly paid singer at his palace had to accept the Duke as lover; and it was no different at other courts. This seems very demeaning to us today, but it must be remembered that, for all the preferential treatment they often received, women singers were still basically members of the servant class. As in Mozart's *Marriage of Figaro* they still had to give their lord and master his *jus primae noctis*. Figaro is trying to settle a score against 'his' Count, not to overcome class divisions. Personal happiness is the main concern of the opera, not an extension of the class war.

The renaissance courts, it is true, were great patrons of the arts, and therefore of artists; and feminine beauty was valued much more than feminine virtue. This often masked the singer's inferior status. She rode and danced and had meals with her lord, so that outwardly her position was nearer a great lady's than a servant's. But she knew the realities of the situation, which had altered little over the centuries.

Attempts have sometimes been made to show that the lower

classes have a special flair for singing. Certainly up until our own time they have produced a surprisingly large number of important singers. But appearances are deceptive here. For a very long time the idea of a stage career was completely out of the question for the upper classes. Art was one of the social graces. A girl would learn to play the lute and accompany some little songs, so as to gratify the company during soirées at home. Later, she learnt the piano, thereby enhancing her possibilities of a successful marriage. It was an accomplishment which raised her cultural level, though – to be fair – it no doubt gave her pleasure and fulfilment as well.

But to make a career of music was quite a different matter. Nannerl Mozart, the composer's sister, may have been little less of a genius than her brother. Their father took them both as children on a European tour, including England. But as soon as she grew up, it was taken for granted that the world's attention should be concentrated on Wolfgang, while she was left at home in Salzburg like any other girl, to wait for a good marriage. This was even to be repeated more than a century later in the Mendelssohn family; the sister had to retire into the background, leaving brother Felix to tread the path of fame alone.

So it is not surprising that we find many girls with a poor background among the singers from the first centuries of opera. They had nothing to lose, they could only go up in the world. Instead of staying in their class, if they had the power to break out of it, they could win wealth and glory and so they were very ready to exploit their natural talent.

But even then the 'difference of station' derived from feudal society persisted. The singer could be honoured on the stage, but in life she belonged to a lower stratum. It was very exceptional for a singer to marry an aristocrat, and even Henriette Sontag, as we have seen, had to have a secret wedding with her Count. Fêted and idolised in the theatre, she was there a princess; outside her own sphere, she was not worthy to be a nobleman's bride. It was very wounding to a singer's pride, and the injury must have rankled all the more, perhaps unconsciously, for being apparently in the natural, God-given order of things. It might be merely a matter of the position at table, where the most insignificant courtier would take precedence over the finest singer or musician; the latter were simply inferiors by birth, a fact of life which could never be altered. Especially in the nineteenth century, this added a bitter note, even in the hour of their greatest triumphs.

As the century went on, the social barriers gradually came down.

The middle classes, many of them risen by their own efforts to prominent positions, willingly paid homage to artistic talent or genius. In the *salons* of the bourgeoisie, actors and singers, both men and women, could at last be found sitting as equals with millionaires and the new gentry. To our own age, whatever its faults, the idea that artists are socially inferior by birth would seem very strange.

Was Catalani an exception in the earlier days? She came from the very poorest background, yet at the peak of her fame 'bought herself' a French aristocrat. But he was an aristocrat who had come down in the world; indeed, he nearly succeeded in squandering her massive fortune. Also, the marriage took place in Paris, where the French Revolution had broken down the old standards. In Britain or Austria, let alone Russia or Spain, such a misalliance would have been quite out of the question for many more decades.

An aristocrat could marry a girl from the bourgeoisie, as Count Almaviva married Rosina in Beaumarchais's original *Barber of Seville*; in *Figaro*, with an irony seldom noticed, Mozart makes her behave with more nobility than her husband. In Hofmannsthal's libretto for *Der Rosenkavalier*, Baron Ochs von Lerchenau, wanting to marry the bourgeois girl Sophie Faninal in order to escape from his debts, finds it necessary to offer long explanations and excuses to his cousin from the high nobility, the Marschallin, Princess Werdenberg. Had they been actresses or singers, such marriages would have been considered impossible.

In contrast with the Far East, the theatre in Europe took its image from clowns, harlequins, sword-swallowers and jugglers. They were not only mountebanks but gypsies – because in those days there were no court or town theatres, no long-term contracts, let alone permanent appointments with pension attached. The performers had to move from place to place, for audiences in a small town were quickly exhausted, and in a bigger one that time would come not much later. If the ordinary public would not go to the theatre, which it very seldom did in earlier centuries, theatre had to go to the public. This meant that those involved with it never acquired respectability. They were often regarded as little better than prostitutes; and if they tried to settle down anywhere, the authorities would keep an eye on them as suspicious characters.

So the first opera-singers radiated an aura of licentiousness, which ruled them out for normal social intercourse but made them the more attractive to the type of man eager for amorous adventure, because they were so different from any women he knew in his ordinary life. The atmosphere of the theatre which surrounded them, often combined with genuine enthusiasm for their performances, enhanced by the magic of the different parts they played, proved a spur to erotic desire. Of course some actresses and singers deliberately led men astray or turned their heads – sometimes because they were very lonely and longed for a man's love. But in most of the associations formed the women were the hunted, not the hunters.

The love affairs of theatrical and operatic stars have always been a source of excitement for the man in the street. They provided gossip for the coffee-houses, as today they make front-page stories in the papers. But before these stars reached the top, they were exposed to the lusts of conductors, composers, impresarios, even of politicians and princes. Men of power and wealth would not only seduce them, but use all kinds of blackmail, against which the singers were more or less defenceless – short of resorting to the dagger, like Tosca in the opera, which is not every woman's style. So when they became prima donnas, they took revenge – on behalf of their whole profession. They wrecked composers' works, threw out conductors, cheated impresarios, flouted the politicians and even the princes. It was rather unfair that the world then made the term 'prima donna' into a synonym for temperamental arrogance.

As for morals in the narrower sense, a fair judge would have to allow mitigating circumstances. Here were women who won rapturous applause every evening, who had the duty of showing off their voice, figure and movements, who were under the limelight of constant publicity. Hundreds of eyes savoured their charms, and many of the parts they played had a strongly erotic flavour. When they took off the costume of Delilah or Lulu after the final curtain – or for that matter when a man had been playing Don Giovanni – it was easy enough to stay in character, keeping the impulses and excitement which the part demanded.

Wilhelmine Schröder-Devrient thought that if the public found her extraordinary because she did things on the stage which they could not imitate, and if they were thrilled by her performances, they could not expect her to stay within 'the barriers of their boring life, for in such a life there is nothing to feed my art'. But she would surely have jumped those barriers even if she had not been a great singer, and her remarks assume that a singer is a special type of person. That, of course, is not the case; the characters of great singers are as infinitely varied as in any other field of human activity.

III

Early Primi Uomini

IN his letters Mozart talked about many of the male singers of his time, often having digs at them. This applies, for instance, to the tenor Anton Raaff, who, no doubt after a distinguished career, was nearly sixty when he sang the title rôle in the first production of *Idomeneo*. If he was too old, the opposite could perhaps be said of Luigi Bassi, only just twenty when he sang the Count in the notable first production of *Figaro* at Prague and shortly afterwards became the first Don Giovanni. He was thus a prototype for the great interpreters of the part through nearly two centuries, from Garcia and d'Andrade to Pinza and Siepi, London and Wächter.

It is said that Josef August Röckel, Beethoven's first Florestan in *Fidelio*, had never studied singing, nor indeed appeared on the stage, before he was given this rôle, which today only the best-trained and most experienced tenors would dare tackle. We do not know how well or badly he carried it off.

It was not until the age of the *castrati* ended that the *primi uomini*, male equivalents to the prima donnas, began to spread the glory of the male voice on Europe's stages. One of the first and most famous was Battista Rubini, although Wagner – who heard Rubini in his sad Paris days after the flight from Riga – was disgusted by this Italian tenor's affected style of singing. The French tenor Adolphe Nourrit was in the company at the Grande Opéra with Rubini. At nineteen Nourrit had taken over his father's important position there; he became a great favourite of Paris audiences, but he began to suffer from increasingly severe attacks of melancholia, and at the age of thirty-seven he committed suicide by jumping out of a window. A number of French operas were composed for him, successful at the time and some of them still performed. He was also one of the early Lied singers, the first to sing Schubert's Lieder in France.

Antonio Tamburini (1800–76) was probably the most important baritone of those days, and the greatest bass was Luigi Lablache (1794–1858), a Frenchman, though with an Italian mother. Both sang mostly in Paris, which in the eighteen-twenties was emerging as the opera centre of the world. Its celebrities included Enrico Tamberlick (1820–99), partner of many of the prima donnas mentioned in the last chapter. Starting from Italy, he conquered the whole of Europe and was one of the first tenors who crossed the Atlantic to sing in America.

Francesco Tamagno (1851–1905) partnered Patti on many evenings which must have been unforgettable to audiences of the time. He made musical history as Verdi's first Otello, although his voice apparently had been little trained. But it was a powerful and beautiful tenor, which won him ovations everywhere in countless cities of both Europe and America. His most serious rival in the rôle of Otello was José Oxilia (1865–1919), Uruguayan by birth and perhaps the first Latin American male singer to achieve international repute.

For several decades the best Don Giovanni, it is said, was the Portuguese Francesco d'Andrade. This, like any such superlative, may be unfair to others who sang the part, but certainly d'Andrade had an unusual radiance. You can catch something of it in the portraits of him painted by a fine artist, Max Slevogt. Born in Lisbon in 1859, d'Andrade studied law, but gave this up at the age of twenty-two and began to take intensive singing lessons; he made his début in San Remo only a year later, as Amonasro in *Aida*. In 1886 he was already singing at Covent Garden, and in 1889 he conquered Berlin, which he liked so much that he made it his permanent home. At the Salzburg Mozart Festival in 1901, early precursor of today's festivals, he was naturally Don Giovanni. Finally he travelled half round the world, slipping into the same costume, that of the great seducer, in a different city every evening. He retired at sixty, and died two years later.

A similar type – also extremely like him in voice, some say – was the great Swedish baritone John Forsell. He too made a dazzling Don Giovanni and was still singing the part at the age of seventy. Born in Stockholm in 1868, he died there after fifteen years as director of the city's opera. Before that he had sung in Berlin, Vienna,

Amsterdam, London, Salzburg and fifteen other important centres, not to mention his visits to smaller ones.

The period, then, was full of great male voices. The prima donna no longer reigned supreme on the opera stage; in fact her glory was sometimes dimmed by the tenor, vocal symbol of masculinity, though his voice exercised its seductive fascination over the men as well as the women in his audiences. The magic also carried over to the baritones and basses, despite the fact that composers often gave them little scope for character study or else made them the villains of the piece.

This development is interesting from the social angle as well. In the first centuries of opera the crucial people in the audience were men – the king, prince, duke or aristocratic gentlemen, who saw operatic productions as an essential part of their display and their lavish pleasures. Naturally women were therefore given the most important parts on the stage. The emergence of the *castrati* is also understandable in such a social order. Just as the Arab sheikh appointed eunuchs in his harem, the European prince was quite happy to employ *castrati* in his theatre, since they could not be considered rivals for the prima donna's favours.

By the end of the nineteenth century women's emancipation was making swift progress. Before, women only went to the opera as guests of socially important men; now they achieved a firm place as members of the audience, while men, conversely, became more important on the stage. The women needed a hero to worship. 'Men's Lib' in opera started the age of magnificent male voices and correspondingly magnificent parts. Or perhaps it was the other way round, for with such interaction it is hard to know which came first. Wagner and Verdi wrote singing parts for heroes, in which vocal power and brilliance are combined with the noblest virtues or with a fascinating character. By way of Lohengrin's knightly splendour, Wagner reached Tristan, love symbol of an era, and finally the ideal hero Siegfried. Verdi created a whole gallery of splendid males and gave them melodies of heroic quality, from Ernani and Manrico to Otello.

It was Verdi who made Victor Maurel into one of the most prominent baritones of his generation, with d'Andrade and Forsell. Born in Marseilles in 1848, Maurel at twenty was already singing at the Paris opéra. Two years later he sang in the original production of the Brazilian opera *Il Guarany* at the Scala, Milan. Then he began his collaboration with Verdi, becoming the first Italian Marquis of Posa in *Don Carlos*, and in New York in 1873 singing Amonasro in the first American production of *Aida*. Half Italian, half French, he had a triumphant progress from Cairo to Moscow, from Madrid to Naples, and besides his vocal qualities he was a gripping actor, so Verdi entrusted him with the first Iago in *Otello* and finally with the first Falstaff. He was also the first Tonio in Leoncavallo's *Pagliacci*. Few other singers can have had so big a hand in the launching of operas like these. In 1904 he retired, publishing various works on singing and also an autobiography (*Dix ans de carrière*). He died in New York in 1923.

Jean and Edouard de Reszke were an unusual pair of brothers. Often in the history of opera there have been families of singers. We have already met the incredible Garcias, four of whom became world-famous, father Manuel, son Manuel, daughters Maria Malibran and Pauline Viardot-Garcia. Lilli Lehmann and Patti, and in our own day Astrid Varnay and Christa Ludwig have also belonged to 'singer families'. There can be very little doubt that singing talent is often inherited, although how heredity works in this field is hard to establish. A tenor may have a son who is a bass, but the son more often turns out to be a tenor too, and in general the type of voice as well as the talent is inherited, even where the sex is different. A tenor's daughter, for instance, is more likely to be a soprano, a bass's daughter a contralto.

To return to the de Reszkes; both brothers achieved fame all over the world, one as tenor, the other as bass, and a sister also proved a notable singer. Jean de Reszke was perhaps the most celebrated tenor before Caruso – though he started as a baritone in Venice's Teatro Fenice, calling himself Giovanni di Reschi (he was born in Warsaw in 1850, his original name being Jan Mieszislaw). After this he resumed his studies of singing, to start again with another change of name, now only a minor one, from di Reschi to de Reszke. A brilliant career followed. Audiences in Europe and America went mad over him, and for many people he was the greatest tenor of his time, even if this accolade is always rather freely bestowed. In the eighties he dominated Parisian musical life, and was the most highly prized and coveted guest star in Vienna, London, Russia and Italy. In 1890 he reached the New York Met. His voice acquired a more dramatic quality, so that he could now sing Wagner rôles as well. This meant that by the end of his career he had an unusually wide repertoire; the French operas (he sang the title rôle in the original production of Massenet's *Le Cid*), the Italian operas and some of the German ones. The press of the day gave him royal treatment, and when he was singing with Melba or Patti, it was doubtful whether he was the prima donna's partner or she his. As Caruso's star began to come into the ascendant, the younger generation said Jean de Reszke was 'leading up to Caruso', while older people said that Jean de Reszke's unsurpassable glory had fallen on the young Italian. No doubt the same thing happens with all generations, as one great artist succeeds another. Unfortunately, we can only hear Jean de Reszke's voice on a few inadequate recordings. He died in 1925 at his *château* in Nice.

His brother Edouard, also born in Warsaw, was five years younger. Jean discovered his voice and helped him forward in his career. Edouard took his famous brother's stage name (as did the sister, Josephine, when she decided on a stage career). He sang in Warsaw in 1875, the following year in Paris (in Verdi's presence), in 1879 at La Scala and in 1880 at Covent Garden. From 1891 to 1905 he was first bass at the New York Met, where he partnered brother Jean on many evenings. In 1909 he returned to Poland. His estate being near the border, he lost most of his money and was in personal danger when the Germans invaded the country in 1914. He died during the war, in 1917.

There may be many music-lovers still alive today who had the good fortune to hear Mattia Battistini, 'King of Baritones', in person. For although born in 1856, he was still singing until shortly before his death in 1928. The German professional term for his type of voice is *Kavaliersbariton*, and in manner as well as voice he certainly suggested the elegant, courtly cavalier. When he mounted the platform in a concert-hall, he first gave a long, serene look round, as if reviewing his subjects and their readiness to listen to him with due reverence; very, very slowly he would draw his white kid gloves off his well-formed hands and place them with solemnity on the piano. When he began to sing, a mist of bel canto magic enveloped the hall. His breathing powers seemed infinite, and he had an extremely sweet and melodious voice, which could produce continual new modulations. Today we have little time for what is merely playful and decorative; few would even know the names of the various bel canto effects in which Battistini excelled, *eg*; *messa di voce* – notes which begin like a breath, slowly swell to a thunderous forte, then just as gradually die away again to nothing; or *mezzavoce* phrases in a sweep of weightless song with 'half voice', held together in an impeccable legato.

Battistini started in 1878 at the Teatro Argentino in Rome, his home town. Ten years later he was singing at La Scala. Every year he went to Russia, but in keeping with his feudal way of life he never visited North America. In 1927 he was still giving recitals, an object for wondering reverence, like a relic from another world. He died the following year at his princely residence near Rieti. The time of the white kid gloves was past, perhaps for ever, the time of pure bel canto, of singing for singing's sake, not for expression and the message. Battistini was a big, portly man – how else could a true bel canto singer manage his long breathing? – but he was not thought of as fat. All great singers were well-covered, and at the time of Battistini's peak the highest achievements would not have been expected of the under-sized specimens who today would be regarded as having the best figures for performance.

I should mention here the baritone Ernest van Dyck, whom we shall be meeting again in the next chapter. He was born in 1861 in Antwerp, gave his first recital in Paris in 1883, sang the following year in opera in Amsterdam, in 1887 became the first Lohengrin in Paris and sang Parsifal at Bayreuth from 1888 to 1901. During his ten years in Vienna he created Massenet's Werther there. From 1898 on he worked at the New York Met, until 1906, when he returned to Antwerp, dying there in 1914.

Antonio Scotti was an Italian baritone of world stature. Born in Naples in 1866, he sang Amonasro in *Aida* at Malta when he was twenty-three, and quickly graduated to the opera-house at Rome, which was then still called Teatro Costanzi. By 1899 he had been guest star at all the opera-houses of Europe. Then he went to the New York Met, where he remained in the company until 1933, an unusually long period for a singer. He was one of Caruso's best partners, and their duets produced tumultuous enthusiasm. In the Mozart Festival at Salzburg in 1910 he was d'Andrade's successor as Don Giovanni, with Lilli Lehmann still singing Donna Anna. Returning to Italy in his old age, he died at Naples in 1936 in terrible poverty.

The very fine French bass, Marcel Journet, was born in 1867; he is known above all as the classic Méphistophélès in Gounod's *Faust*. He had an engagement at La Scala, where he sang in important first productions; but divided his months away from Milan between many other cities, especially Paris, Brussels and Monte Carlo. From 1900 to 1908 he was at the New York Met, and his dark sonorous bass voice remained until he was in his sixties. He died in 1933 at the age of sixty-six.

Allessandro Bonci must have been one of the last of the bel canto tenors. Born at Cesena in 1870, he was a shoemaker's apprentice and sang in church choirs. Then followed a brilliant break-through to stardom in the great opera-houses, although he was extremely short and no doubt partly as a result of this, extremely shy. He must have had a sweet-sounding and perfectly controlled lyric voice, which made him a fine tenor for Rossini, Bellini and Donizetti works, an excellent Duke in *Rigoletto* and an attractive Rodolfo in *La Bohème*. Once when he and Caruso were singing in London at the same time, *The Times* said 'It is quite unnecessary to make comparisons between these two distinguished singers, as our fanatical opera-lovers are doing today ... If Signor Caruso possesses the more powerful voice, Signor Bonci's is sweeter in quality. Both are outstanding actors.' This comparison with Caruso is enough to show Bonci's stature as a singer. When he went to the United States, he became in 1906 the star of the Manhattan Opera House, while Caruso reigned at the nearby Met (with another half dozen magnificent tenors to be heard besides). In the end the Met got rid of a rival by engaging Bonci too. During the war he volunteered for the Italian Air Force, then after the war he sang for several more years, finally in Rome. After a further stay in New York, where he taught singing, he returned home for good and died near Rimini in 1940.

1873 saw the birth of the two unique singers who left their mark on a whole era. Anyone who wants to understand present-day singing must know about Enrico Caruso and Fedor Chaliapin. After a look at Central Europe at the turn of the century, I shall be giving these two giants their own chapter.

IV

Singing at the Turn of the Century

GUSTAV Mahler was, of course, a conductor of genius; but more important for this book, he devoted much of his immense energy to creating and maintaining a company of brilliant singers. His ten years (1897–1907) as director of Vienna's Court Opera are therefore a model for such an institution, which no longer exists today.

It would, however, be unfair and a mistake to attribute to Mahler alone the leading position of Viennese opera at the beginning of the twentieth century. When he was appointed at the age of thirty-seven after a meteoric career, there were already plenty of excellent singers there, from the era of the two celebrated conductors, Hans Richter and Wilhelm Jahn. The heroic tenor Hermann Winkelmann, born in Brunswick in 1849, after the usual start in provincial towns, had gone to Hamburg and from there to international stardom, acquiring his highest fame in 1882 as the first Parsifal at Bayreuth. He had been in the company at Vienna since 1883, and remained there under Mahler (he also retired at the same time as Mahler). At the first Viennese production of Verdi's *Otello* Winkelmann sang the Moor, with Theodor Reichmann a magnificent Iago. Both had risen to the heights of popularity in Vienna; there were Hermann fans and Theodor fans, each roaring applause in their idol's honour, so that both fan clubs went home on such evenings hoarse but happy.

The women stars included Amalie Materna, Wagner's best Brünnhilde, and Marie Wilt. The former started in a very small way, as a soubrette in operettas, earning forty guineas a month. After a life full of success she died in 1918, strangely enough in great poverty. She was one of the last all-rounders; besides Wagner heroines, she made a splendid Amneris (but not Aida), and enhanced dramatic rôles with a powerful voice which could reach low contralto notes. Marie Wilt was quite phenomenal; her fortissimo, it was claimed, could shake the walls of the opera-house. She was extremely fat, a target for malicious Viennese wits – they said, for instance, that her partners had to go 'round the Wilt in eighty days' – and crude caricatures. Bitter and disappointed, one day she jumped out of a window to her death, the end of one of the most glorious voices of all time. Pauline Lucca, mentioned earlier, was called a 'demonic wild-cat', not least for her primitive Carmen.

In the lyrical field the 'great lovers' were the Belgian Ernest van Dyck and Marie Renard. The latter sang Massenet's Manon with matchless sweetness, created his Charlotte in *Werther* and had an extremely varied repertoire extending even to Carmen. In 1900 she retired, and at her farewell performance her frenzied admirers sent the curtain up over a hundred times, to catch one more glimpse of their adored star – who was marrying a Count. Although such a marriage was now possible, as we have seen, to her own sadness and that of countless thousands, it still meant the end of her stage career.

Besides these singers, who regularly brought lustre to the opera-house, there were visits from guest artists of international fame. Patti delighted Vienna as she did the whole world. Mascagni brought his *Cavalleria Rusticana*, then quite new, with the original cast from Milan including Roberto Stagno and Gemma Bellincioni. Victor Maurel came with Verdi's *Falstaff*. Wilhelm Heš arrived in a company from Bohemia; director Jahn persuaded him to stay in Vienna, write his name the German way (as Hesch), and made him one of the best basses of his time. Jahn ran a really brilliant opera-house. It was an assembly point for the finest voices, every evening was a banquet of melody and singing.

When Jahn retired, it was the end of an era; for Mahler, taking over the direction of the opera-house, introduced a new concept, that of complete musical drama – the final stage in the progress from 'only singers' to 'singing actors'. That is to say, the logical course of events dramatically, as created by a producer of great mental ability, was given the same importance as the musical development. Dramatic singing and the whole action had to be psychologically convincing; the almost infinite possibilities of light, now in the form of electricity, were effectively built into the production plans. The basic unity of the whole, in fact, was given priority over any individual performance. To realise this fully, it was essential to have a regular company, as homogeneous as possible, which could be directed towards common objectives and welded into a real team by patient, often tedious work on both drama and music. The concept of complete musical drama also depended, and still depends, on the principle that after a fine première created by hard teamwork the level should not be allowed to sink in later performances.

Of course there were already touring singers in Mahler's time. As we have seen, the top artists had fully discovered America; and there were famous guest stars visiting London's Covent Garden, the Monnaie at Brussels, the two opera-houses in Paris, Italy's opera-houses rich in tradition and sometimes the Russian stages. The best of the German-speaking opera-houses – Vienna, Berlin, Dresden, Munich, Hamburg – periodically exchanged their members. Hundreds of theatres in provincial towns were proud to have a guest star now and then from one of the court opera-houses. Even so, a director in Mahler's time found it comparatively easy to keep together his troupe of singers. Their conditions of engagement were fantastically rigid by present standards. In many of the contracts of the day the singer had to put himself at the disposal of his establishment for a continuous period of six, seven or eight months, with no paid holiday at all, and no time off for other engagements except during the summer months when the theatre was closed.

Mahler brought to the Vienna Opera two tenors who soon became as great favourites of the audiences as Gustav Walter, van Dyck and Winkelmann had been in their generations; Erik Schmedes from Denmark and Leo Slezak from near Brno in Moravia. Neither was a bel canto singer, for this was not required in the works on which Mahler chiefly concentrated. Hardly anyone before him had done so much for Mozart, it is true, but Mahler saw Mozart as composer of musical drama, not creator of bel canto. Richter and Jahn had both championed Wagner; Mahler fixed him in the repertoire for good, and also without the cuts often made in Wagner operas until then. Schmedes was Tristan, a blonde Nordic hero, partnered by the noble and passionate Anna Bahr-Mildenburg (she married Hermann Bahr, a well-known writer), who for a long time played a leading part in Viennese musical life. Mahler 'made' her, not only in her career, but in a far deeper sense – in her style, her dramatic approach; and it was she who passed on his legacy to the next generation.

Marie Gutheil-Schoder was also Mahler's creation. She did not have an especially fine voice, but she was a person through whom Mahler could realise completely his artistic principles; giving 'soul' to song, presenting true-to-life character studies which had a shattering impact on audiences. She came to Vienna in 1900, and the following year sang the three very different rôles in Offenbach's posthumous *Tales of Hoffmann* – one of the first to try this bold experiment, dramatically justifiable but vocally hard to carry off. In 1909 she was Vienna's first Elektra, in 1911 Vienna's first Rosenkavalier. She had a strong and deep feeling for the music of her time, and in 1914 was already singing Schönberg. After the end of her operatic career she worked successfully as a producer in Vienna and at the Salzburg Festivals. With her psychological insight and experience of the theatre she too was a great personality in Vienna's artistic life. She died in 1935 in Thüringen.

Richard Mayr, a bass from Salzburg, joined Mahler's company and became one of its brightest stars. His King Mark in *Tristan* was as moving as his Osmin in *Die Entführung aus dem Serail* was comic; while all later interpreters of the full-blooded rôle of Baron Ochs von Lerchenau, even today, model their performance on Mayr's subtle yet disarmingly natural character-study of a crafty, fascinating, *grand seigneur* who combines bluntness with his innate airs and graces. The sly whistle of relish when he recognises Mariandl as the Marschallin's alleged chambermaid, whom he finds highly delightful; and his resigned acceptance when the Marschallin finally tells him to 'put a good face on his defeat' and he has to decide whether or not to get his own back by spoiling the chances of others. All this originated from Richard Mayr and now, thanks to him, belongs to the rôle for good. As for when the great Lotte Lehmann played against him as the Marschallin – that great occasion comes into another chapter.

Leopold Demuth must have had a mellifluous, caressing baritone. Mahler made him a melancholy Wolfram in *Tannhäuser* and a darkly tragic Flying Dutchman. Friedrich Weidemann came from Riga in 1903 and was the first interpreter in Vienna of important Richard Strauss rôles, including John the Baptist in *Salome*. But this he had to sing at the Volksoper (People's Opera-house), since for a long time the 'immoral and blasphemous' work was banned at the Court Opera. In 1909 he was the first Orestes in *Elektra*, the following year he created Golaud in the first Vienna production of Debussy's *Pelléas et Mélisande* and in 1911 was the first Faninal in *Rosenkavalier*.

Mahler scored a great hit with the appointment of Selma Kurz, who developed from a mezzo-soprano to one of the most dazzling coloratura sopranos of all time. The length of her trill in the upper register became proverbial; she made it swell up and down at will, while the audience unconsciously held their breath as at a sensational trapeze act in the circus. She smiled too – part of the singing technique, anyhow, for coloratura singers in the upper register – and then 'landed' safely, with extreme elegance, on the ground of the final note supported by the orchestra. But she was more than a precious song-bird whose performances could be timed; she had a lyric register of great sensitivity, which made her outstanding as Vienna's first Mimì and first Madam Butterfly. Opera-lovers from all over the vast Austro-Hungarian Empire streamed into the capital to go to the Court Opera and see the wonderful Selma Kurz.

Mahler's greatest tenor discovery, besides Erik Schmedes, proved to be one of the finest singers of the century. It is hard to remain serious when recalling Leo Slezak, for he was blessed with an inexhaustible vein of imaginative humour, which he retained all his life. 'What time is the next swan?' he called into the wings on one occasion when he was the Knight of the Grail and the swan was pulled off the stage too early and therefore without him. In his hilarious film rôles he has been enjoyed by a fair number of our own generation. But anyone assessing him mainly as a 'comic' would be doing a great injustice to an artist of genius. His Tannhäuser was shattering; no one in the audience could remain unmoved by his 'Rome-narration', when, broken by the Pope's curse, he returns home to the autumnal woods round Wartburg, to seek once more, and irrevocably, the secret road to Venusberg. Very tall, Slezak was splendid in appearance and voice as Lohengrin, a messenger from the higher world such as Wagner might have dreamed of. Few opera-houses anywhere, let alone the German-speaking ones, could boast an Otello of Slezak's power, showing first the Moor's pride and happiness in victorious arms and love's fulfilment, then under Iago's spur his decline into jealous madness, despair and destruction, until for the last time he seeks the lips of the dying Desdemona, to the wonderful strains of the E-major love melody, one of the purest ever written. Slezak also made an imperious and passionate Radames in *Aida*, a fanatical prophet in Meyerbeer's *Le Prophète*, a fiery old-testament figure as Eléazar in Halévy's *La Juive*.

The Vienna Opera in Mahler's time possessed a company unmatched anywhere else. Berlin and, of course, New York had a collection of magnificent singers; only Vienna could present a group of complete artists welded together as a team by a unified conception of drama and singing. Moreover, although on its own strength the opera-house could offer near-perfect productions, Mahler believed that he owed it to his audiences and to the house's international reputation to invite world-famous guest artists. The cast on such occasions accompanied the guests in the original language of the work presented, whereas otherwise almost all operas were sung in the language of the country presenting them.

In 1900 Gemma Bellincioni came to Vienna (with Giordano's *Fedora*). Nellie Melba came too, and for her benefit the austere director, who strictly rejected the conventions of earlier opera production, returned to these conventions, by allowing the prima donna to rise again after her death from consumption as Violetta in *La Traviata*, so as to perform, as a marvellous bonus, the mad scene from Donizetti's *Lucia di Lammermoor*. Applause was not yet measured in decibels, as it can be today, but those who heard Caruso's guest performances in 1906/7 say that the tumultuous ovations surpassed in volume and frenzy anything known before!

Applause, of course, though it was spontaneous for Caruso, could sound rather artificial and obtrusive – often, for instance, at the Vienna Opera; not surprisingly since it was produced, or at least led, by the 'claques'. These were organised groups strategically placed all over the house. Perhaps genuine opera-lovers to start with, they had seen a way of exploiting their enthusiasm. First they merely collected small souvenirs of their favourite; autographs, a picture, a postcard from a holiday resort. But soon they were asking for, and eventually demanding, complimentary tickets – for secret financial rewards directly related to the amount of applause that would be received. So the original idealism turned finally into an ugly and dangerous instrument of calculated applause, decided no longer by the singer's ability but by his monthly payments. Not that the *claque* was a new phenomenon in show business; some form of it is almost as old as the theatre itself. Those involved have often had the idea that such cheerleaders might be useful or even necessary as a stimulus to a cool, dull or snobbish audience. But in the long run they obviously do more harm than a serious company can tolerate.

Mahler came out energetically against *claques*, as he fought other abuses and solecisms, like people arriving after the performance had started, or clapping directly after an aria, drowning the orchestral postlude, which is often so beautiful and leaves such a magical dying fall (*eg* the Flower Song in *Carmen*). The battles he fought against the Philistinism of ordinary mortals were often Pyrrhic Victories, which wearied his artistic soul. In 1907, embittered and hurt by the opposition he met, he left the Court Opera, to which he had given the ten best years of his life and the unique benefit of his creative genius.

Under his successor, Felix Weingartner, there were many difficulties to overcome, as there always are after the end of a strongly individual, almost dictatorial régime. The new director, himself a brilliant conductor, still accepted today as a fine interpreter of Beethoven, tried to keep the company's standards as high as ever. He brought in a young American girl called Lucille Marcel, to whom at the last moment he gave the title rôle in Vienna's first production of *Elektra*. She soon became a favourite of Viennese audiences, and had a magnificent success as Tosca, although strangely enough this did not carry over to the opera itself, which was first made into a big draw by Maria Jeritza. But Lucille soon had to give up the stage, because she married the director; and in the strict conventions of the time this meant she could never star again in his opera-house – although in other, less particular theatres, star parts often went to directors' wives. Lucy Weidt became the Opera's first dramatic singer, Hedwig Francillo-Kaufmann took over many of the coloratura rôles from Selma Kurz, who was being increasingly drawn into international opera and, as she had married a prominent Viennese gynaecologist called Halban, was now calling herself Selma Kurz-Halban.

During the Court Opera's peak years a rival had emerged. In the seventeenth and eighteenth centuries it had been normal in the Italian opera centres for a big city to have more than one opera-house. Opera-houses sprang up like cinemas in our century, and the comparison can be taken further. With all these premises, a proportionately large number of operas or films were needed, and an immense number of singers or actors to appear in them; while audience enthusiasm created focal points, like the prima donna in opera and the film-star in the cinema.

Since impresarios had taken opera from renaissance palaces into the arena of commercial business, opera too became a matter of profit and loss. How these impresarios managed to make a profit with all the expenses of chorus, orchestra, ballet, equipment and fees, not to mention maintenance of the building, is one of the most remarkable things in the history of opera. But they did. And the more expensive the singers they engaged, the better their business prospered. The public preferred, and still prefer, to pay a small fortune to hear a genuine prima donna instead of a modest sum for an average performance.

Nowadays it has become common for opera-houses to be run by local authorities or from other public funds, which may mean the theatre manager having struggles with bureaucrats, and losses have increased. Not because singers' salaries have gone up (it would be hard to say whether they are proportionately higher or lower than in the past), but administrative overheads, staff and pension rights, have mounted rapidly, to add to the financial burdens which opera-houses already bore. This has meant the end of private management of opera-houses. The New York Met is the only famous one still in private hands, and even the Met has to count the dollars very carefully.

At the beginning of the century there were still bold *entrepreneurs* who hoped to achieve both artistic and commercial success with a private opera-house. Such was Rainer Simons, who came from Germany to Vienna in 1904 and started the People's Opera in competition with the Court Opera. He knew that the only chance of drawing audiences away from the famous old opera-house was to make the tickets cheaper, which meant engaging cheaper singers. These would be either less distinguished in their profession, or undiscovered talent – which Rainer Simons looked for and found very successfully. One of those who started at the People's Opera 'out in the suburbs' and became world-famous, was Maria Jeritza. Simons also had a flair for discovering new works; *Salome*, banned in the Court Opera, became a sensational success in the People's Opera, where *Tosca* was also played three years before its first production in the older opera-house.

In his highly amusing *Collected Works*, Leo Slezak gives a programme offering the 'best ever' company:

The Magic Flute

Opera in 2 Acts by Em. Schikaneder.   Music by W. A. Mozart.

Producer: Max Grube (Berlin).   Conductor: W. A. Mozart
Chorus Master: Richard Wagner (Bayreuth)

Sarastro	Emil Scaria (Vienna)
Tamino	Francesco Tamagno (Milan)
Speaker	Theodor Reichmann (Vienna)
First Priest	Jean de Reszke (Paris)
Second Priest	Theodor Bertram (Munich)
Third Priest	Edouard de Reszke (Paris)
Queen of the Night	Adelina Patti (London)
Pamina, her Daughter	Jenny Lind (Stockholm)
First Lady	Christine Nilsson (Kristiania)
Second Lady	Lilian Nordica (New York)

Third Lady	Lilli Lehmann (Berlin)
First Boy	Pauline Lucca (Vienna)
Second Boy	Sigrid Arnoldson (Stockholm)
Third Boy	Rosa Sucher (Berlin)
Papageno	Francesco d'Andrade (Lisbon)
Papagena	Nellie Melba (Australia)
Monostatos	Albert Niemann (Berlin)

Ticket prices were given as 2 mark, 1 mark, 50 pfennigs – when in fact up to 600 dollars were paid for tickets to a Jenny Lind recital in the United States, 100 marks and more were often paid to hear Patti. Clearly no theatre in the world could possibly have paid for such a production (unless all the singers were performing for charity!), and few millionaires would have been able to afford tickets to go to it. Apart from that, however, although many of the greatest singers of two generations are assembled here, they would not have formed any sort of company in Mahler's sense – they would have had very different approaches and could scarcely have worked together. For the exponents of bel canto are mixed with the 'naturalists', beauty of tone on the one hand, dramatic expression on the other.

When Patti conquered Vienna at the age of twenty, the dreaded Wagner critic Eduard Hanslick of the mighty *Neuen Freien Presse* (New Free Press) became her most enthusiastic follower. He admired her sparkling coloratura runs, her staccati, her vocal virtuosity, her sweet melodiousness, even more her 'infinite charm'; he had seen and heard nothing to compare with that. This aesthete, whose most important book was *Vom musikalisch Schönen* (On Beauty in Music) then came down clearly on the side of Italian bel canto singing as against Wagner's dramatic approach: 'Her rôles, it is true, never lack dramatic life and characterisation; but she does not allow these to interfere for a moment with the beauty of sound. That is always more or less sacrificed where dramatic expression is in excess.'

The two extremes of opera-singing were at that time irreconcilably opposed to each other, whereas today for the most part we expect our opera-singers to master both. Although pure bel canto has long disappeared from our stages, dramatic expression is by no means all that is required in productions of masterpieces from past centuries, *eg* by Mozart, Rossini, Bellini and Donizetti. Even with Verdi and Puccini we should miss beautiful singing very much if it were not present in good measure. Weber and Wagner, on the other hand, also Bizet, Debussy and Richard Strauss, are unthinkable without strong dramatic expression. So singers today have to possess a

versatility of which their early predecessors would hardly have
dreamed.

It is perhaps worth putting in a few words more on the subject of
bel canto, since for decades music critics have repeatedly deplored its
loss, making this equivalent to a decline in the art of singing and of
opera altogether. They forget that the development has occurred
through a change in musical style, that today a pure bel canto singer
could interpret only that part of our present opera repertoire which
comes from the bel canto times. Out of the hundreds of books
that have been written on bel canto, I would like to quote a
short summary by a great modern singer, Franzisca Martienssen-
Lohmann:

'Stylistically, bel canto means giving decisive priority to beauty
and the singing line (cantabile) over intensity in language and
expression. Singing can be thought of in two ways; as pre-eminently
an art of instrumental sound or as pre-eminently declamation enhanced by the sound. There are born bel canto singers as there are
born declaimers. Since the maximum merging of beauty and
declamation is the artistic (and also the healthy) objective for any
voice, the singer inclined to declamation must logically work hardest
for beauty, the singing line and instrumental balance. So the expression bel canto is well justified in his case too.'

Bel canto singing and the Italian singing method or school are very
closely connected, indeed can be regarded as more or less identical.
This method and school are still important today; singing teachers in
many countries often advertise their lessons in these terms. But what
Franzisca Martienssen-Lohmann was saying is that such a school and
method do not exist, because bel canto is basically nothing but
'assured knowledge about the natural law of the voice, striking insight into the variety of conditions, profound wisdom about what is
real and essential in the phenomenon of the voice'. And, I would add,
firm faith in the essential magic of sound. A voice should have the
same beauty of sound as a Stradivari or Amati violin, the cantilena of
a noble cello, lightly and elegantly played, evenly produced without
audible pressure, with pure vibrations full of melodiousness and un-
strained power.

New Voices for the New Century

Several great female voices of the time are chiefly associated with
Verdi. There was Teresa Stolz – or Teresina, as the Maestro called
her – first Leonora in *Force of Destiny*, first soprano soloist in the

glorious *Requiem*; Romilda Pantaleoni, first Desdemona; above all Giuseppina Strepponi, as a girl the first Abigail in *Nabucco*. She made a crucial contribution to Verdi's breakthrough, and afterwards became his second wife, a loyal and understanding companion for the rest of his life.

The heroes and heroines of Verdi's operas had gradually changed, just as Wagner's had. It is true that some Donizetti rôles, several rôles in Rossini's *William Tell*, and Bellini's *Norma* all demanded a vocal power scarcely known before. But the orchestra accompanying them played at less than full volume, with the loudest instruments (like trumpets and trombones) coming in rather seldom, so that for much of the time singers could produce gentle cantilenas and brilliant pianissimo effects, as required by bel canto principles. In the course of a few decades, Verdi's orchestra became progressively stronger, more polyphonic and more important in itself. To sing over it, at least from the time of *Simon Boccanegra* and *Don Carlos* and certainly after *Aida*, bigger voices were needed than before. They had first to develop, to mould themselves for the tasks they were set, before they became normal and part of the tradition. Similarly with Wagner; his immense demands at first seemed impossible to fulfil (the first Tristan, Schnorr von Carolsfeld, died soon after the première, no doubt from overstrain, in the prime of his career), but eventually Wagnerian voices arose and could be trained.

At the beginning of the twentieth century, if voices could have been measured then in decibels, they would no doubt have been found much more powerful in volume than a century before. Indeed new types of voice emerged, like the Wagner tenor and the 'high dramatic' female voice. These are furthest from the bel canto ideal, being largely based on power and penetration, so that they can fill the wide expanse of the modern opera-house, over the blare of a large orchestra.

Gemma Bellincioni and Roberto Stagno (mentioned earlier as guest stars at the Court Opera) were two world-famous singers, each of whom could fill a theatre and the impresario's pockets. They sang together on 17th May 1890 at the opening of Mascagni's *Cavalleria Rusticana*, when Gemma (Santuzza) was twenty-six and Stagno (Turridu) was fifty-four. Eight years later, when she launched Giordano's opera *Fedora*, Stagno was already dead and her new co-star was Enrico Caruso. In 1911, at the age of forty-seven, Bellincioni went to Berlin and gave singing lessons to an immense number of pupils. She did the same afterwards in Rome and Vienna, and then in Naples from 1933 until her death in 1950.

Enthusiastic followers in both Europe and America travelled long distances to hear her contemporary, Luisa Tetrazzini, another singer of world class, who was born in Florence in 1871 and was still singing as late as 1934. Her light coloratura voice and superb technique, especially her pin-prick staccato notes, continually brought wild applause during acts and even in the middle of arias. But beside the peaks of glory, her long career contained dark and tragic hours. She was well over thirty before she finally overcame the poverty of her early struggles and poverty returned after the decades of triumph, when she was cheated of their fruits by a young lover – how often, incidentally, this almost pathological trait features in the lives of prima donnas. She attended spiritualist séances as an escape from the bitter realities of her existence. In April 1940 she died in Milan, a merciful release. Like Bellincioni, she wrote her memoirs; those of her great rival bear the title *Io ed il canto scenico* (I and Stage Singing); hers, more modestly, were called *La mia vita di canto* (My Life of Song). She also produced a manual in English, *How to Sing* – a question to which she certainly had the answer.

Two other remarkable coloratura singers belong here, Amelita Galli-Curci and Toti dal Monte. The former, born in Milan, was a partner of Caruso, Chaliapin and Gigli under Toscanini – Mahler's successor as the leading conductor of his generation – in the almost fabulous times of the New York Met. She had been a piano teacher before she was discovered. In 1909, almost self-taught, she appeared in Rome as Gilda in *Rigoletto*. That was the beginning of a rapid climb, which brought her the conquest of new opera-houses every year. During the First World War she sang in Chicago, then for a decade and a half at the Met, where Meyerbeer's *Dinorah*, today almost forgotten but then extremely popular, offered her a rôle which required hair-raising vocal acrobatics. She retired from the stage in 1936.

Her younger rival Toti dal Monte, born in Venice in 1898, was then still in her prime. She too was at first studying the piano, but owing to a hand injury she had to give it up, like Robert Schumann who turned to composition for this reason, and so took up singing. In 1916, when she made her début at La Scala, she did not achieve any great success. For six years after that she scraped a living in the opera-houses of smaller Italian towns, until Toscanini brought her back to Milan. Now as Gilda in *Rigoletto* she achieved a success which opened up the world for her. In 1924, for her first rôle at the New York Met, she sang Donizetti's Lucia di Lammermoor, and it is said that even then the interplay of her crystal-clear soprano with the solo flute was so wonderful that the audience listened as if spellbound. In the following years she aroused tumultuous enthusiasm in this and many other rôles, and that despite the fact that she had to fight against the first impression which her appearance on the stage always created, for she was short and extremely fat. But directly she opened her mouth, she had the fickle public – often quite cruel, especially in Italy – completely under her spell. All mockery died away to be replaced at the end by tremendous ovations which went on and on. One wonders whether the same thing could happen today. Certainly if Toti dal Monte were alive and given the opportunity, she could still fascinate any audience, even though our aesthetic ideals have changed so greatly. Probably, however, any responsible singing teacher would have dissuaded her from a stage career, nor would any director or manager have engaged her – except perhaps on condition she took a very severe slimming cure, which she could scarcely have done without serious or even fatal consequences for her voice. More on that subject later.

Now to two singers who although not Italians achieved fame with an Italian singing style and in Italian opera. Hariclée Darclée was born in 1862 in Bucharest, where she also died in 1939. She started her international operatic career at the age of twenty-six, when she sang Marguerite in Gounod's *Faust* in Paris. In 1891 she went to La Scala, and there a year later created the title rôle in Catalani's delightful opera *La Wally*; in 1898 she did the same for Mascagni's *Iris*, and on 14th January 1900 in Rome for Puccini's *Tosca*. With this role she then travelled round most of the world, winning new laurels everywhere from St Petersburg to Buenos Aires. Here, in the famous Teatro Colón, a magnificent building opened in 1908, she was a regular guest star, often even in Wagner rôles. She sang in Italian, however, as was then the custom, for it was decades before Latin countries took Wagner's works into the repertoire in German. Hariclée Darclée could not only produce the whole soprano range from 'high dramatic' to coloratura, but had such a strong lower register that she could also sing mezzo and contralto parts.

The name Salomea Kruszelnicka may also, unjustly, be forgotten by present-day opera-lovers. She was born in the Ukraine in 1872, started her career in Trieste as Leonora in Verdi's *Force of Destiny*, and after visits to Chile and then to smaller Italian towns she became first singer in the Warsaw Opera. While performing in Russia she came into conflict with the authorities as a Ukrainian patriot, and went to Italy. At La Scala in 1907 she sang the first Italian Salome, and two years later the first Elektra. She was also a dazzling (Italian) Isolde and Brünnhilde. Ildebrando Pizzetti gave her the title rôle in his *Fedra* in the original production of 1915. She died in Milan in 1946.

Claudia Muzio had a remarkably beautiful voice, like many of the other singers I have referred to, but something much more besides. She was justifiably called the Duse of opera, for like Eleonora Duse – with Sarah Bernhardt the greatest actress of her time – Muzio had an immense gift for portraying character, so that she produced performances of deep humanity which are among the most moving in operatic history. Her star rose when she was twenty-two, singing the title rôle in Puccini's *Manon Lescaut*. By 1913 she was already at La Scala, in 1916 at the Met. Here, on 14th December 1918, she created Giorgetta in Puccini's *Il Tabarro* (The Cloak). From 1922 to 1932 she divided her activity mainly between North and South America, winning rare affection and admiration. In Rome she sang a *Traviata* which sent shivers down the backs of the whole audience; the death-scene of the young Violetta Valery had seldom if ever been so authentically presented. It was her swan song, to which by premonition she had given the moving tones of her own fate. She died very soon afterwards, on 24th May 1936, at the age of forty-seven.

Nor did the stage career of her contemporary, Gilda dalla Rizza, last much longer. Born in 1892 at Verona, Gilda appeared on the stage for the first time in 1910. In 1917 at Monte Carlo she sang one of Puccini's lesser-known operas, *La Rondine*, originally destined for Vienna but cancelled there because of the war. In 1918 she was the first Lauretta in his *Gianni Schicchi* at the first Italian production. In 1921 she launched an opera by Mascagni, in 1933 she was the first Italian Salud in Manuel de Falla's *La vida breve*, finally in 1936 the first Italian Arabella in Richard Strauss's opera of that name.

Like Lucrezia Bori, three other fine singers of the time were born in Spain. Two of them are connected by a very strange coincidence; their births took place in the same house in Barcelona, with twelve years' gap between them. In 1895, when Mercedes Capsir was born, Maria Barrientos was receiving her diploma for piano, violin and composition at the Barcelona Conservatoire; and while still a little girl she conducted a symphony of her own. She began to study singing at the age of fourteen, and appeared on the stage the following year. She was sent to Italy to perfect her art, sang successfully in Rome in 1899, and in 1900, when only seventeen, went on a tour of the most important German cities. Then she became a member of the La Scala company, a coloratura singer of incredible accuracy but also surprising warmth of tone. Triumphs followed at the Teatro Colón and the Met, where she sang bel canto operas with Caruso, until 1939; then she stayed in Buenos Aires as a teacher. She died in 1946 in the South of France.

Mercedes Capsir made her début at nineteen at the huge Teatro Licco in Barcelona, and in 1924 was brought to La Scala by Toscanini in the same rôle, Gilda in *Rigoletto*. She visited South but never North America. From a pure coloratura singer she developed her powers to sing Elsa in *Lohengrin*. Like Maria Barrientos – a special property of that house where they both were born? – she wrote music herself, and in one of her peak rôles, Rosina in *The Barber of Seville*, she put into the piano lesson scene a piece of her own composition.

Conchita Supervia, a mezzo-soprano, made her first appearance on the stage at fifteen, in Buenos Aires, and in the following year played the first Italian Rosenkavalier. She then conquered almost all the great opera-houses in the world, and was one of the first to achieve prima donna status for the mezzo voice, winning back for it some of the chief rôles in Rossini's operas, which for decades had been usurped by sopranos. These rôles in *The Barber of Seville*, *Cenerentola* and *The Italian Girl in Algiers* were originally created for the composer's wife Isabella Colbran. Conchita died in London in 1936 at the age of forty-one while giving birth to a child.

Two further mezzo voices should be mentioned here. Gabriela Besanzoni was born in 1890 in Rome, where at twenty-three she sang Ulrica in Verdi's *Masked Ball*. In 1918 she went to the Teatro Colón, and there, like Conchita Supervia, she played an important part in the Rossini renaissance. The next year she survived the sudden explosion of a bomb in the auditorium when she was a guest artist with Caruso in Havana (as Amneris in *Aida*). She sang in Chicago, London, Berlin and Milan, returning to her native city in 1939 to make a farewell appearance as Carmen. Her successor, Ebe Stignani, had a full, flowing mezzo voice of glorious quality, which reached high notes and low with equal ease. The former, indeed, were equal to those of Callas on the memorable evenings when they were both in the cast of Bellini's *Norma*. For twenty-seven years she was a principal at La Scala, an Eboli in *Don Carlos* that few if any have matched.

North America, and to a lesser extent South America, now became increasingly a source of distinguished singers. After Minnie Hauck it was above all Rosa Ponselle and Dusolina Giannini – both of Italian parentage – who crossed the Atlantic to achieve fame in Europe. Rosa Ponzillo was born in 1897 in the state of Connecticut and began her musical career there, in a cabaret turn with her sister Carmela;

they called themselves the Ponzillo Sisters and there was no hint yet of her future glory. She was discovered, in characteristic American fashion, and taken to the Met. Completely unknown, she made her début there, partnering Caruso in *Force of Destiny*. For eighteen years she was a Met star and an honoured guest artist in countless opera-houses. Then she married a millionaire and retired. If in former centuries prima donnas could not continue their stage careers after marrying into the aristocracy, the rule was largely extended to cover the new dollar-aristocracy as well. In 1954 she came out of private life to make some records, but that was the only time.

Dusolina Giannini was also the child of immigrants. She was born in Philadelphia, where her father was a tenor, her mother a pianist. She became a pupil of Marcella Sembrich, gave concerts in New York's Carnegie Hall, in London and Berlin – until at twenty-three she made her first appearance on the stage as Aida. In 1936 she went to the Met, and after the war she again went on an extended European tour, one of the great lyric and dramatic soprano voices of her generation.

After José Oxilia, the heroic tenor from Uruguay mentioned earlier, Bidu Sayao became the first great singer of world repute from Latin America. She was born in 1902 in the Brazilian town of Niteroi (opposite Rio de Janeiro in the glorious bay), received her training in Paris, and soon achieved striking successes in France and Italy. In 1937 she started fifteen years as a principal at the Met, enchanting the audience from her first evening, as Massenet's Manon, not only with her singing but also her exotic beauty. From 1952 on she sang only in concerts, and eventually returned to her home town.

V

Caruso, Chaliapin and Their Successors

Caruso

Of all the 'greats' of the past, Caruso is probably the one name familiar even to those who know little or nothing about music. To sing like Caruso has become almost a proverbial phrase, and a vast amount has been written about him by both professionals and amateurs. But to sum up his greatness I think it would be hard to beat the remark made by my mother when I was a young music student in Vienna going to the opera every evening. 'What a pity you never heard Caruso,' she said, 'one sat there and prayed he would never stop.'

Yes, I am sad that I did not have the chance to hear him. After the most fabulous career that any singer can have had, he died on 2nd August 1921. He was born in Naples on 23rd February 1873. His father was a locksmith – not a baker, as you sometimes read – it was a poor family with many children. But there was enough money for Enrico to begin a modest study of singing at eighteen, and in November 1894 he made his first appearance on the stage with a company of strolling players. It ended in disaster; an undiscriminating audience took one unsuccessful high note as an occasion for cat-calls and whistles. Caruso never forgave them; among the hundreds of towns he delighted with his singing, Naples was studiously omitted.

Des Grieux in Puccini's *Manon Lescaut*, which he had sung on that evening, was to become one of his star rôles; but then that could be said of them all. Perhaps his greatest was Canio in *Pagliacci*, who murders his unfaithful beloved in mad grief at finding himself deceived. Caruso knew the emotions involved from bitter first-hand experience, because he had lived for years with a married woman older than himself, a soprano of no great ability, who bore him two children. He was passionately in love with her, but in 1907 she ran away with his chauffeur, and he brought a law-suit against her, with charges of slander, embezzlement and blackmail.

All his life he was a completely uncalculating and also unpredictable personality, spontaneous, naïve and a man of the senses; he acquired an inner calm, however, through his marriage in 1918 to Dorothy Benjamin, an American, who gave him a daughter he idolised. A working-class boy from the slums of Naples, he remained basically a simple soul, and on the stage this enabled him to give deep expression to the simplest human feelings. No other tenor can have sung so movingly the Flower Song in *Carmen* or 'Vesti la giubba' (On with the motley) in *Pagliacci*. Many of his successors have tried to imitate the sob in his voice, but with him it seemed to come straight from a weeping heart full of inexpressible suffering.

Leo Blech, for decades Berlin's famous musical director, who conducted countless Caruso evenings, said in the great singer's obituary: 'Caruso had the ability to make one forget he was singing. He had the secret of singing "dramatically" to the last degree of consistency. He portrayed human destinies by way of melodies, notes, sounds. His singing was more than singing, it was always dramatic expression ... it was beyond all technique, there was nothing left but the soul, revealing itself through unforgettable modulations and vocal colourings ... With this great creative artist all singing became dramatic expression, all dramatic expression singing.'

So, unlike his contemporary, Alessandro Bonci, who was still a pure bel canto singer, Caruso put in the foreground dramatic expression of human experience. But he could also sing bel canto where a delicate melodic line demanded it. His 'una furtiva lagrima' from Donizetti's *L'Elisir d'Amore* was a jewel in that field. Perhaps one could say that he had not only his own interpretation for each of his rôles (which today we may almost take for granted) but – something very rare – a special tonal colouring, indeed almost a special voice, for every rôle.

Part of that came out in his daily practice. In contrast to nearly all singers of his time, this was far from being always the same. He did not prepare his voice just for singing, but for a particular rôle. If that needed great vocal agility, in the morning he would practise not only scales, runs and soft singing, but also moving in the rhythm he would adopt that evening; and for a Radames, a Don José or a Canio he would prepare just as fully for the physical characterisation. Yet paradoxically he achieved this much more by intuition than by reasoning or deliberately working it out.

Probably everything he did in his life was largely instinctive. Emil Ledner, his German impresario for many years, who travelled a good deal with him, described him as 'not easy to handle', and said he combined generous and mean character traits: 'The unpredictable Neapolitan came out, very racy and often making an irritating and provocative impression. His education was scanty. Never in all the years have I seen a book in his hands; nor could I ever persuade him to visit a museum or picture gallery, very seldom even a theatre. Sights which brought tourists from all over the world had not the slightest interest for him, although he certainly possessed a sharp if one-sided intelligence. He had the polish and manners of a great, honoured, admired artist, without posing; he had considerable natural tact, good taste in questions of toilet and dress. Together with a certain worldly wisdom, there was something imperious and obstinate in him, which it was generally useless to oppose. He could be affectionate, kind, indulgent towards mistakes or failures, but he was also at times extremely unfair . . .'

Later accounts, testimony from his maturest period, read more favourably. He had grown into a great man for whom nothing human was alien or impossible to understand. Nor perhaps can we judge an artist like him by ordinary standards. Every outstanding artist lives in his own world, by his own laws, which he did not make and yet unconsciously follows, laws which are only considered valid for part of the time (for theatrical artists, say between eight and eleven), but which may be inextricably bound up with his inner life.

One thing about Caruso would surely be accounted a great virtue by any standards, especially for a *primo uomo* of such stature and fame; he was a model colleague, even for other tenors. If he was on the stage with young inexperienced singers, he helped them all he could. He was never the star, never tried to upstage the rest of the company. Nor did he ever refuse to work with conductors or producers, to try to assert his own views against these natural lords of opera. Yet how easily he could have done. Even in his own lifetime he had become an almost unreal figure, idolised everywhere and surrounded by legends. Theatrical directors and managers showed him unusual consideration and sensitivity. He had long lost interest in the press; the only thing a critic could do was to think up finer and more glowing words for his performances. A paper which attacked him would have not only been boycotted or exposed to a storm of popular indignation, it would have become a laughing-stock. The tumultuous joy which greeted him at every appearance was a strange product of mass suggestion, entranced enthusiasm and the admiration of real professionals.

There are different opinions about when his fantastic rise began. On 17th November 1898, when he was in the cast of the first production of Giordano's *Fedora* at the Teatro Lirico, Milan? Or, as others assert, with his engagements at La Scala or his first triumph at Covent Garden? Early in 1903 he appeared as the Duke in a production of *Rigoletto* in Berlin, and some consider this to have been his decisive break-through. Admittedly he had in his pocket at the time a contract with the New York Met – he joined them the same year – but he was then no longer simply a promising tenor; he was already the leading singer of his generation, and one who would never be overtaken by any rival.

How did Caruso sing? The question has been asked hundreds of times, and long dissertations have been written on the subject; but, like the theories of singing generally, they do not agree. He could never give any information about it himself. Basically he probably felt as if singing just came out of him, so unconscious was the process. This is not contradicted by the many special ways, indeed tricks, which helped him to master particularly difficult notes or phrases. His greatest contemporary, Adelina Patti, when asked about her singing, always said with a smile 'Je n'en sais rien'. And probably she *didn't* know how she projected the marvellous notes from her throat into the vast area of the theatre. Caruso too may have had no precise knowledge of the rules he applied to give his voice its maximum melodiousness and expressiveness. So neither was trying to keep a trade secret, as was sometimes thought; no generally valid rules could be derived from their exceptional gifts. Caruso had, incidentally, the ability to expand his chest in breathing by nearly ten inches; once in his river-side suite in London, he pushed a piano across the room with his bare chest.

By 1909 at the latest, Caruso had achieved the peak position acknowledged by all without envy. Throughout the world the public were eager to hear him. The books about his life refer to innumerable towns where he appeared; he must often have woken up in the morning wondering where he was. Cities, opera-houses, people crossed his path fleetingly, often more fleetingly, no doubt, than he would have wished. But the character he had to play the following evening soon dominated his thoughts, for he was just as totally immersed in his two hundredth Canio or hundredth Cavaradossi as he had been in the first.

The New York Met remained his special artistic home until his death. It was then the world's greatest opera-house both for singing and for social prestige; by belonging to it, he brought it unrivalled fame. His fees reached figures which until then would have been considered impossible even for very famous singers – 15,000 dollars an evening on a Mexican tour, 7,000 dollars for each concert on an extended tour of the United States, with posters saying: 'For once in your life you can hear the world's greatest singer in person'. It would be absurd to call such figures unjustified; with such a unique phenomenon there is no basis for evaluation.

Caruso's life, with its aura of fantastic splendour, has been dealt with over and over again, in biographies (including one by his wife), in *romans à clef*, in a film which made Mario Lanza's voice world-famous, in radio and television programmes. Perhaps the most important thing is that there are over 260 recordings of his voice. They give us a rough idea of what millions of his contemporaries must have experienced. Only those familiar with today's recording methods who know how a singer's every note is tested by the finely trained ears of technicians, passed back and filtered through the most delicate apparatus, given greater or reduced echo; those who have observed a single aria being sometimes synthesised from different component parts, so that performances can be simulated which never actually took place; only such people can fully appreciate Caruso's extraordinary powers. For in those days the singer placed himself in front of a mouthpiece – and sang. The pianist accompanying him would be sitting somewhere in the room. Recordings with orchestra were extremely difficult and very rarely made. The orchestral accompaniment of many Caruso recordings now available has been added afterwards. Antediluvian as we may find this recording technique, the processing of the sound afterwards was equally so. Nevertheless, even in his life-time millions of Caruso records were sold; today those early and extremely fragile discs, mostly sung on one side only, are the pride of every collector, and an inexpressible magic still radiates from them. For all the defectiveness of the recording, we are still profoundly moved by that voice, and have the sense of a unique artist at work.

You often think at first that you are listening to a baritone, for Caruso's voice rests on a depth of sound possessed by few tenors. ('Rests' is the *mot juste*, for you get the quite correct impression that it rests securely and firmly on a broad base which cannot be shaken.) From that depth the voice climbs to the heights, not even 'effortlessly', as you often read in discussions of tenor voices, but equally broad, wide-ranging, with the finest timbre, warm and with extreme expressiveness. Caruso had the high C by which audiences are foolishly inclined to judge a tenor's quality, and it sounded powerful, penetrating, stirring. But scarcely anyone guessed that the highest notes, so glorious and so triumphantly produced, had to be struggled for every evening through a wall of fear, over a barrier of agonising stage-fright.

Of course many, or most, great singers and actors have to fight against raging nerves in the minutes or hours before their appearance, perhaps before the first moments of danger, or even until the last moment of the evening. But Caruso's stage-fright is better known than any, because his whole life has been so thoroughly held up to the light. He tried to fight it with his own methods – not to be recommended to anyone – alcohol and smoking. It was worst of all, his closest friends said, before *Aida*. Understandably, because in that opera Radames, the Egyptian commander, has to sing his dreaded aria to the *Celeste Aida* almost directly after the curtain goes up, and this demands great breath control, very relaxed singing and a very exposed high final note. It may be the one moment when Verdi, otherwise rightly revered with gratitude by tenors everywhere, receives a good deal of mental abuse!

Caruso's voice, that compound of strength and beauty, expressing the strongest masculinity, served also to reveal the soul, reaching to the deepest level of the unconscious. It could reflect all human emotions and arouse in the hearts of his hearers a completely unwonted sensitivity. We might think a little further about 'strength' as applied to a voice; for few people who are not professionals would realise the demands made on a voice like Caruso's, heavy in itself and always used with intense dramatic expression. He appeared on the stage or concert platform several thousand times during the twenty-six years of his career, from 1894 to 1920. He interpreted the greatest rôles in his lyric and dramatic range, never spared himself and always brought into play the full volume of his voice. He probably spent at least as much time on practice, vocal exercises, and still more on studying rôles and in rehearsals. So what must his vocal cords have endured! The whole mechanism of voice production may well be considered a wonder of nature, especially in a case like his. Those cords, only a few millimetres in length, can be strained almost to breaking point for a hundred thousand hours, and yet remain elastic, reacting to the finest impulse from will and brain. They allow the triumphant projection of thousands of top notes, above the orchestral wall of musicians playing fortissimo, to thrill the hearts of audiences in their thousands.

By his contract Caruso had to sing on sixty, seventy or even eighty evenings in the 'Golden Horseshoe' (as the Met was often called), and for at least as many hours he was a guest artist elsewhere. The most remarkable thing about this high number of annual performances, however, is that he was continually increasing his repertoire, for he was always ready to learn something new and sing in contemporary operas. This may have been normal in his age, a tradition from earlier times, but it seems worth mentioning today when star singers are very rarely available for unknown works. True, he was not yet 'The Great Caruso' in 1897, when he was the original principal tenor in Francesco Cilea's L'Arlesiana (a very popular opera in its day) and in the same composer's Adriana Lecouvreur in 1902 (this has been triumphantly revived in our own day thanks to the lovely voice of Renata Tebaldi). But on the 10th December 1910, at the peak of his fame, he became the first Ramerrez in Puccini's first première in the United States, The Girl of the Golden West. These are only the important works which Caruso helped to launch; in the course of his life he sang a considerable number of others, modern at the time.

In the autumn of 1920, before a packed audience at the Met, he was once more tearing at the heart-strings as Canio, deceived by his beloved Nedda and forced by the villagers to play Pagliaccio for their amusement. Some of those on the stage with him, perhaps even a few people in the front rows of the stalls or in the boxes near the footlights, noticed drops of blood on his white clown's costume. It seemed to be just a small injury to the larynx. Caruso, a child of nature with a strong mistrust of doctors, thought he was quickly cured. Then a further haemorrhage took place. He studied a new rôle, which he sang soon afterwards with immense success; Eléazar in Halévy's deeply tragic opera La Juive. Then the blood came again, and the pain – a delayed pleurisy, so it seemed. On Christmas Eve he had sung Donizetti's L'Elisir d'Amore, and was getting ready for a happy supper with friends, when he had a new warning, and the doctors gave strict orders for rest and immediate relaxation.

It was too late. Seven operations followed, so that the great chest was 'completely covered with scars' (in the words of his valet, Mario Fantini). When he was eventually persuaded against his will to take a long rest, he had a longing to go home. Despite the decades in the

United States and his American wife, home for him still meant Southern Italy. He was given the prospect of an extended tour the following winter—whether this plan really existed or whether his friends were simply trying to keep up his spirits is open to conjecture. He travelled to Europe, and home to Italy. He looked emaciated, almost unrecognisable. Nevertheless, on the terrace of the Hotel Vittorio in Sorrento, to an audience which had gathered by chance and recognised him, he sang the aria 'Martha' (from Flotow's opera of that name) addressed to the girl who disappeared and took away all happiness with her. It was the last time he sang.

In July 1921 after a bathe in the Mediterranean, he had to be taken to Naples with a high fever. There he died from acute peritonitis at the age of forty-eight, leaving an estate of two million dollars, larger than any opera-singer before him, or since. The greatest of all tenors had departed, but he was the first to have made records which could preserve at least a glimmer of his extraordinary radiance.

Chaliapin

The lives of Caruso and Chaliapin, greatest tenor and bass respectively of their age, show certain similarities. Both came from very poor backgrounds, both sang as boys in church choirs, both started their careers in travelling companies, both had to survive severe setbacks before the road to fame opened out for them.

Although at several thousand miles' distance, they were also born within a fortnight of each other, Fedor Chaliapin in Kazan, an insignificant small town on the Volga, on 11th February 1873 (according to the Russian calendar). His father was a low-grade clerk in an office, and a heavy drinker. His mother took in laundry, worked as a 'char', and if there was still not enough to live on, went begging. Young Fedor escaped from these conditions at an early age, becoming apprentice to a shoemaker and then a book-binder, meanwhile singing in the local church choir. He later related how when only eight he had watched a clown at the fair and felt irresistibly drawn to such a career.

One day the choirboys were given tickets to Kazan's rather shabby theatre. From then on Fedor went there constantly, and one day became an extra on the stage. Nobody else cried 'hurrah' with such enthusiasm when Vasco da Gama in Meyerbeer's L'Africaine set foot on his distant Eden. At seventeen Fedor took the next step, getting an engagement with a travelling company, for a salary of twenty roubles a month.

A teacher in Tiflis, one Professor Usatov – we know little about him, but he was himself an operatic singer – seems to have spotted the young man's talent, or perhaps he only had to allow the talent to reveal itself. Of course the voice needed some polishing, but it was well served by nature. Apparently it was then a baritone, or anyhow at nineteen Chaliapin did not have the deep 'black' tone which was afterwards to become one of his special characteristics.

At twenty he moved from Tiflis to St Petersburg, then to a Moscow private theatre, and at twenty-one to Moscow's famous Imperial Opera. It is very striking that in 1901 he was already singing the title rôle in Boito's *Mefistofele* at La Scala, which had no open doors for unknown foreigners. A few years later he went to Paris, where another Russian genius, the ballet director Diaghilev, had aroused interest in Slav art-forms. So here Chaliapin introduced Moussorgsky's *Boris Godunov* to the West. He brought such uncanny conviction to the rôle of the mad usurper that right to the present day all its great interpreters are measured by him; Kipnis and Boris Christoff, Ghiaurov and Miro Changalovich, Petrov, Ernster, Lagger and many others. He gave a terrifying picture of the tyrant and murderer harassed by the Furies. The majesty of the coronation scene, the demoniac frenzy of his outbreak of madness, belong for all time to theatrical as well as operatic history.

With his amazing psychological insight, Chaliapin would indeed have been a great actor, even without that mighty singing voice which was capable of such a wide range of expression. In conjunction they made up a personality which became almost as unique and legendary as Caruso. Among the many rôles he played, two others besides Boris became particularly famous and special to him. One of them, Massenet's Don Quixote, which had its première at Monte Carlo in 1910, was composed for him. Like its hero, this romantic opera did not have much luck, and was soon almost forgotten after Chaliapin's death. Fortunately, however, his voice has been immortalised on record in some of its very beautiful passages; above all the moving death-scene.

The other rôle was Méphistophélès in Gounod's *Faust*, musically very different from the character in Boito's opera and also further from Goethe's conception. That conception is a little blurred in Gounod's rather superficial score, but Chaliapin managed to bring it out, clearly presenting a splendid, colourful figure, a thoroughly modern Devil, who breaks into human lives in ever changing forms, defies God although a part of Him, and in the end achieves only a new awareness in God's creatures of the real value of human life.

Chaliapin had never read a book on psychology, but he played all these rôles with overwhelming subtlety and conviction.

As with Caruso, he created them by instinct and intuition. But Caruso's favourite rôles, like the tenor's own character, were more straightforward, mainly dominated by the intensity of a single great emotion. Chaliapin's favourite rôles were complex and often tormented people, so that he could continually turn new light on the different facets of their many-sided characters. Some of them would have deserved the clinical description of schizophrenic, like his wonderful Don Quixote, dreamer, knight and fool in one person; lovable, absurd, unworldly and pathetic. Often brought on to the stage in adaptations of the book, he generally remains a cardboard figure; Chaliapin brought him completely to life. Yet the singer's own character, very down-to-earth, a completely unromantic realist, to judge by his everyday life, seemed to contain absolutely nothing of Don Quixote. How did he do it? That, no doubt, is one of the secrets of an artist's soul, in which all aspects of humanity can lie dormant together, till each part is awakened to find expression on the stage, in book, picture, stone or sound.

Chaliapin was adored by the public, even though they could often scarcely appreciate his fine nuances. Connoisseurs had the highest admiration for him. Directors, producers and, above all, conductors feared him. He was accustomed to having his own way in everything, including the tempi he took when singing. If the conductor was wise, he fell in with Chaliapin's wishes. When an incident occurred in a rehearsal, it could be kept to some extent *en famille*, although even here violent scenes might result when the conductor with a different opinion was as prominent or as stubborn as the singer. Once when Toscanini was rehearsing *Boris Godunov* with Chaliapin, the argument ended with the conductor breaking his baton into bits and leaving his stand with a classic oath. (Chaliapin too could swear, though from native politeness he usually swore in Russian, which was therefore not understood outside his own country!) A less famous and inferior conductor was brought in, and in future Toscanini always chose other basses for *Boris Godunov*. It was worse if the difference of opinion occurred during a performance, for even then Chaliapin was by no means inclined to abandon his own ideas. Once at the Vienna State Opera, in Gounod's *Faust*, he did not agree with the tempo set by conductor Carl Alwin for the Rondo of the Golden Calf. So he came forward to the footlights to enforce his own view by huge conducting arm-movements and even stamping his feet.

Despite, or because of, such quirks, his popularity and fame reached a pitch usually accessible only to a tenor. Nor were the quirks so strange at that time; it was not till after the First World War that the conductor's position became sacrosanct, his opinion incontestable. Before that he stood far beneath a prima donna, a primo uomo or any respected singer. Chaliapin still insisted on the feudal sovereignty of the singer. He also believed, probably with justice, that no one understood *Boris Godunov* better than he did, that no one penetrated more deeply into the figure of Méphistophélès. To give these rôles the fully rounded interpretation they required, even tiny shifts of tempo had their significance. The only pity was the autocratic way in which he made his wishes into orders. Toscanini did not take orders; Alwin had no choice.

This absolutist, feudal attitude was also expressed in his style of life and political views. He came from one of the lowest strata of the Tsarist empire, the class which could only gain from a revolution; but he did not become a revolutionary. In 1911 Moussorgsky's posthumous work *Khovantchina*, never produced until then, had its première at the Imperial Theatre in St Petersburg. Chaliapin, then a guest artist in Russia, made it a resounding success. After that he continued his journeys all over the world, until at the beginning of the war he felt impelled to return home, where he was the darling of the nobility and fêted by the middle class. In October 1917 he was appearing as King Philip of Spain in Verdi's *Don Carlos* in St Petersburg. He produced a shattering study of this gloomy figure too ('Ella giammai m'amo'), weighed down by the burden of an empire on which the sun never set. Suddenly the theatre shook, and King Philip's crown rolled to the floor. It was the bombardment of the rebel fleet against a strong-point of Tsardom. The revolution had begun, in which another monarch was soon to lose both crown and head.

Lenin's régime named Chaliapin a 'People's Artist'. But such an individualist could not feel happy in the completely changed conditions. He left his beloved Russia. From 1921 on we find him at the Met. He was very fond of Paris and in 1927 made his home there. Ten years later he gave a farewell performance in the little court theatre at Monte Carlo, one of the last of these to survive. A lean, grey-haired man, still tall and upright in his sixties, he looked very much a Don Quixote figure, with a dash of Mephistopheles in his sharp, somehow haunting features. He died in Paris on 12th April 1938.

A Brilliant Generation

The first third of our century produced a host of splendid singers, who may all merit the term 'great', even if they did not reach the supreme greatness of Caruso and Chaliapin, Patti and Melba. The highest mountains are often only the peaks of a massive range, and it is the same in human life and art. Great composers, painters or poets appear where the conditions of their appearance have been produced by a generally high level of artistic appreciation and creative culture. With singers too, the most important of them rise to fame where they have countless gifted and even remarkable colleagues. Some of the men we shall now be considering are still accessible today on record, offering us the most vivid impressions of the generation before ours, and for a long time setting our standards.

Adam Didur, a magnificent bass, was born in 1874 in Galicia, then part of Austria (later Poland and today Russia). He studied in Lemberg and Milan, and made his début in Rio de Janeiro. He went to La Scala in 1896, then to the Warsaw Opera; in 1907 he joined the Manhattan Opera, and in 1908 the Met, where he worked for twenty years. In 1910 he appeared with Caruso and Emmy Destinn in the première, mentioned earlier, of Puccini's *The Girl of the Golden West*. Three years later he became the first Boris Godunov in America, under the direction of Toscanini (after the latter's quarrel with Chaliapin). In 1930, after a glorious career, Didur settled down in his native country, became for a time director of the theatre in Cracow and died in 1946 at Kattowitz, where he had just been made a professor.

Ricardo Stracciari must have been another magnificent singer. He belonged to a generation of Italian baritones possessing powerful voices and dramatic intensity, which included Giuseppe de Luca, Antonio Scotti, Carlo Galeffi, Pasquale Amato, Titta Ruffo, the bass-baritone Mariano Stabile and the still deeper Ezio Pinza – a real race of singing giants! Stracciari was born in 1875 near Bologna, made his first public appearance at twenty-four in an oratorio by Perosi and his first stage performance in 1900 as Marcello in Puccini's *Bohème* (then only four years old). After many performances throughout the world as a guest artist, he landed where all the distinguished singers of his time hoped to crown their career, at the Met. After that La Scala, the Teatro Costanzi in Rome and the Teatro Colón in Buenos Aires became his most important centres. He was still singing at sixty-four, had eighty parts in his repertoire, and sang Figaro in Rossini's *Barber of Seville* over 900 times. He died in Rome in 1955.

Giuseppe de Luca, born in Rome, was a year younger. He appeared hundreds of times with Caruso and afterwards Gigli, joining to theirs his beautiful voice and convincing acting. He made his stage début as Valentin in Gounod's *Faust*, at Piacenza in 1897. Then he sang in Lisbon, but was asked to return to Italy, where he took part in various premières, the most important, no doubt, being that of *Madam Butterfly* on 17th February 1904 – which at the time seemed to be a 'flop'. His Consul Sharpless in that opera showed de Luca in his true field, an intelligent actor and a virtuoso bel canto singer with great breath control, who although he no longer seemed 'modern', was an object of wonder and admiration to audiences. He sang in Vienna, Italy, London, Paris, Brussels, then went to the Met in 1915. He stayed there for thirty years, taking part in important premières, such as *Goyescas* by the Spanish composer Granados, and Puccini's *Trittico* (just before the end of the war), in which he created the superb part of the mischievous Gianni Schicchi. He did not retire from the stage until 1946, and when over seventy was still giving very successful concerts of his finest arias. He was master of all the important Italian and French works and some of the German. Among his most interesting rôles, in his own estimation, were the reactionary Beckmesser in *Die Meistersinger* and Méphistophélès in Berlioz's *Damnation of Faust*. He was particularly fond of the latter rôle and interpreted it with great brilliance in both concert and stage version. He died in New York in 1950.

Titta Ruffo (originally Ruffo Caffiero Titta), born in 1876, is generally considered the greatest baritone of his era; he certainly had the most powerful voice. The son of a blacksmith, he was proud of never having had any real singing lessons. His pride was the subject of many anecdotes. He was to sing Rigoletto at Covent Garden with Nellie Melba as Gilda, but attracted so much admiration during rehearsals that she refused to appear with him, saying he was too young to play her father. Years later the two world-famous singers were again to appear together in *Rigoletto*, but now Ruffo refused, saying that Melba was unfortunately not young enough to play his daughter! He had started his career with Wagner, singing the Herald in *Lohengrin* at Rome in 1898, in Italian, of course. Afterwards he sang all the great baritone rôles in Wagner's works, which were by then enjoying great popularity. From 1920 to 1928 he was a member of the Met, and had triumphs in Chicago and Buenos Aires, Paris and

Barcelona, Vienna and Berlin. He retired from the stage when nearly sixty, became a singing teacher in Florence and died in 1953. Although most of his records were made when he was past his best, they still give an idea of his greatness. He had a glorious voice, with a dark quality in the lower register and a ringing tone in the higher, but without any noticeable transition between the two. This, combined with enormous creative power, made him one of the most remarkable singers of all time.

Now for three great tenors, McCormack, Martinelli and Pertile. John McCormack, born in 1884, was the first singer of world fame from Ireland. He became one of Caruso's foremost rivals – perhaps a little more lyrical than Caruso – and was considered ideal in Mozart rôles. Lilli Lehmann wanted to take him to Salzburg to sing Don Ottavio, but this was frustrated by the war. At eighteen he won a singing competition in Dublin; the runner-up was the writer James Joyce! At twenty McCormack was singing at the St Louis World Exhibition, and after that, with varying success in Italy, where, as his name was hard for the Italians to pronounce, he changed it to Giovanni Foli. From 1907 to 1914 he sang a great deal in London, where he was received with immense enthusiasm. From 1910 on he was also with the Met, becoming an American citizen in 1917; in 1924 he became Chevalier de la Légion d'Honneur and in 1928 he was raised to the papal peerage. After countless brilliant operatic performances, he began devoting himself increasingly to concert singing and especially to Irish folk-songs. He gave his farewell concert in Dublin's Theatre Royal in October 1938. He died in Dublin in 1943.

Giovanni Martinelli, born in 1885 in Montagnana (near Venice), began as a clarinettist in a military band. At twenty-six he made his stage début at Milan in the title rôle of Verdi's early work *Ernani*. In 1912 he became, under Toscanini, the first Dick Johnson or Ramerrez in *The Girl of the Golden West* at La Scala and so a direct rival of Caruso, who had created this rôle in New York. After Caruso's premature death, Martinelli took over a great many of his rôles at the Met. As Alex Nathan has written, 'Like the seven cities which fought for the honour of being Homer's birthplace, people have never stopped arguing about Caruso's chief successor: Gigli, Pertile, Lauri-Volpi, Schipa, Martinelli or McCormack? It is a special pleasure to persuade oneself through records that it was, after all, Giovanni Martinelli.' There can be different opinions on this, nor is there any need to make such an impossible decision; I do not myself think that anyone inherited all Caruso's qualities. But certainly

Martinelli's voice had much of that special, vibrant quality which made Caruso immortal.

He was more of a heroic tenor than his predecessor. For instance, he once (at the age of fifty-five!) sang Tristan in German with Kirsten Flagstad, which would have been unthinkable for Caruso. On the other hand, he never sang the Duke in *Rigoletto*, because he considered his voice too voluminous to present 'Questa o quella' and 'La donna è mobile' in the correct style. It is said that he sang sixty-one leading rôles and appeared in 4,500 operatic performances. He sang a thousand times in the 'Golden Horseshoe', an achievement few tenors can surpass. He was an imperious Otello, forerunner of del Monaco, Ramon Vinay and James McCracken; a frenzied Samson in *Samson and Delilah*, a fanatical Johann von Leyden in *Le Prophète*, a brilliant Radames in *Aida*. He was still singing as a very old man, and he died in New York in 1970.

Aureliano Pertile was born in the same place (Montagnana), and the same year. While Martinelli was achieving his greatest triumphs in America, Pertile became the tenor king of La Scala; 'Toscanini's tenor', as he was sometimes called. For while he was still relatively unknown, the Maestro appointed him to Italy's first Operatic Institute, took him personally in hand, in 1922 gave him Faust in Boito's *Mefistofele*, and afterwards leading parts in world premières, including Boito's *Nerone* and Wolf-Ferrari's *Sly*. He was often a guest artist in North and Central Europe, had great success as Manrico in *Trovatore*, winning tremendous applause for his three high Cs in succession. But he was also one of the few Italian tenors prepared to tackle Lohengrin, or Walther von Stolzing in *Die Meistersinger*. He retired in 1940 and died in Rome in 1953.

The Russian bass-baritone George Baklanoff had a voice of great brilliance and a histrionic talent which made him a worthy rival to Chaliapin. He was born at St Petersburg in 1882. When he started singing, he travelled from Kiev to Moscow, back to his home town, to Vienna – first at the Volksoper then the Court Opera – and finally he became a coveted guest artist all over the world. He portrayed characters with rare skill, presenting a Rigoletto, a Scarpia, above all a Boris Godunov scarcely surpassed even by Chaliapin in his very different interpretation. Baklanoff died in Basle in 1938.

In Toscanini's own company, during his remarkable twenty years at La Scala, the foremost baritone was Mariano Stabile. Born in Palermo in 1888, he appeared on the stage for the first time in 1911 in his home town, as Marcello in *Bohème*. From the time when he was at the peak of his career a poster has survived, reminiscent of Slezak's ideal *Magic Flute* cast, only this kind of 'super-cast' really did appear once during the twenties at a Covent Garden production of *Don Giovanni*:

Don Giovanni	Mariano Stabile
Donna Anna	Frida Leider
Donna Elvira	Lotte Lehmann
Zerlina	Elisabeth Schumann
Don Ottavio	Richard Tauber

Conductor: Bruno Walter

Don Giovanni was one of Stabile's most celebrated rôles, but reliable witnesses seem to have found him even more outstanding as Falstaff. Toscanini presented him in this part in a new production at La Scala in 1921, giving him the chance thereby to break through to world fame. Alex Nathan wrote: 'His conception of the aristocratic old rascal was an extremely original caricature, but one which never allowed you to forget the noble origins. Stabile was drunk, crafty, cynical, fearful, insatiable, swaggering – and yet remained the perfect gentleman.'

In the thirties Stabile became one of the singers most sought after at festivals. He sang in Verona's Arena, with its twenty thousand seats, at Florence's beautiful Maggio Musicale, he was Salzburg's Don Giovanni in 1934, its Falstaff in 1935. With age he may have lost some of the power of his voice but nothing of its finely modulated delivery, and his achievement in these later years sounds almost miraculous. In 1955 he partnered Callas in Rossini's comic opera *Il Turco in Italia*, and at Venice in 1958 – *ie* at the age of seventy – he made an ideal Gianni Schicchi in Puccini's enchanting comic opera. A Cologne paper wrote: 'An artist who can sing with the same perfection three such different rôles as Rigoletto, Scarpia and Falstaff, may expect to have earned the term "genius".'

Now we come to another set of tenors, though leaving aside for a separate section three of the greatest, Gigli, Melchior and Tauber. Even without these three, in my view the most important 'trend-setters' in the Caruso succession, it was surely a great age for singers, with such names as Schipa, Lazaro, Lauri-Volpi and Fleta, Pinza and Baccaloni.

Tito Schipa was born at Lecce in 1889. Gigli, a year younger, was modest enough to call him the best tenor of his time. He made his début at twenty-two as Alfredo in *Traviata* at the small theatre in Vercelli. Two years later (1913) he was already singing in Buenos

Aires; in 1914 he was in Rome, in 1915 at La Scala. In 1917 Puccini chose him for the original production of *La Rondine* at Monte Carlo. From 1929 to 1949 he was to be heard every year in the relatively short La Scala season, which left him time for extensive guest appearances in North and South America. In 1957, at the age of sixty-eight, he was enthusiastically received in Russian towns; at seventy he was still singing in concerts. His voice retained its melancholy beauty and could still climb easily and lightly to the very highest notes. And where others, to achieve delicacy here, often resorted to falsetto, Schipa was still singing a true pianissimo which carried to the furthest ears. Long after his face became worn with age, with the greying hair cleverly masked by a jet-black wig, his voice, a miracle of nature and technique, showed no conspicuous signs of aging and still produced a splendour of pure and noble bel canto. He died in New York in 1965.

Hippolito Lazaro was a Spaniard. Born at Barcelona in 1889 (the same year as Schipa), he studied there and in Madrid, made his first stage appearance at twenty-one and three years later sang at La Scala. He won his earliest success through the tremendous power of his top notes. In 1917 he went to the Met, and extensive tours took him to all the most important opera-houses in Europe and America. He retired rather early, gave a farewell concert in New York in 1940, and spent most of his retirement in Havana.

One of Caruso's successors, with an even more powerful voice than Lazaro's, was Giacomo Lauri-Volpi, born at Rome in 1892. He started by studying law, changed to singing and first appeared in an opera in Viterbo. After great successes in various towns in Italy and South America, he went to La Scala in 1922, then the following year to the Met, where a strong rivalry developed between him and Gigli. His violent temperament was feared, and sparks flew when it collided with another stubborn character (like Toscanini). On good evenings his voice had an almost unequalled brilliance, if lacking Gigli's perfect technique. He and Maria Jeritza probably made the most superb couple ever in Puccini's posthumous work, *Turandot*, although neither appeared in the première. His 'O Paradiso' in *L'Africaine* was memorable; his Otello, despite many perhaps exaggerated histrionic effects, represents one of the peaks of operatic history. In Manrico's aria 'Di quella pira' in *Trovatore* he showed in his face and voice the pride of reaching the high C with such transparent ease. Opera here became an orgy of sound, the audience a frenzied mob. But Lauri-Volpi was far more than just a big voice. He had a fine brain, and besides his musical achievements produced several books. He was still singing when well into his sixties, in a world where freak voices like his seemed to be dying out.

The tenor preferred by Toscanini to the great Lauri-Volpi for the première of *Turandot* was Michele Fleta – or Miguel Fleta, as he was christened in 1893 in a Spanish village near Huesca. He was a miner in Belgium before starting out as a singer. At twenty-six he appeared on the stage for the first time, at Trieste. After that engagements followed in quick succession; the Met, Colón, Covent Garden, Paris, Vienna, Budapest, Spain, Italy. Then in 1926 he reached the peak of his career with the *Turandot* première at La Scala, sung before the international press and an élite audience. Toscanini's choice of Fleta was a surprise, for despite his fame there were more prominent tenors, whose supporters threatened boycott and scandal. (It was much the same nearly forty years later, when Karajan chose the lesser-known Gianni Raimondi instead of the 'official' principal tenor di Stefano for his celebrated new production of *Bohème*.) At any rate on that evening in 1926 (25th April) Fleta sang himself into the front rank of world singers. But he did not keep this position. For reasons that are still rather obscure he broke with the Met, which even brought a successful lawsuit against him; and by the end of the twenties he was only singing in Spain, never a leading country for opera. We do not know whether he gave up his international career voluntarily, or found his singing powers or physical or mental faculties declining. He was certainly a great singer with an extremely fine voice and technique. He died after an operation in 1938.

Finally, we come to two splendid basses of the period. Ezio Pinza may still be vividly remembered by many present-day opera-lovers; especially in the rôle of Don Giovanni, which he sang hundreds of times all over the world. Perhaps he did not have quite the demonic force of many others who have taken this part, but he presented a real-life character, brilliant in appearance, with physical and mental qualities closely allied, a personality equally fascinating to the women on the stage and those in the audience. But besides all that he had a very mellow bass with a rare, haunting beauty of tone. He sang in operettas, musicals and films as well as opera. In concerts of popular works he did much to spread enthusiasm among the wider public who could be reached through the mass media. He was at La Scala from 1921, then one of the stars of the Met from 1926 to 1948. In the thirties, under Toscanini, he was a central figure in the Salzburg Festivals. He died in 1957 at the age of sixty-five in Stanford, Connecticut.

Salvatore Baccaloni, born in 1909, was a choirboy in the Sistine

Chapel. At twenty-two he sang Dr Bartolo in *The Barber of Seville* in Rome; very soon he was at La Scala, Covent Garden, the Colón, at the Salzburg Festival, Glyndebourne, where he was an early favourite, and from 1940 at the Met. He was primarily a comedian. Audiences smiled directly he appeared, and you could not help laughing out loud at his Osmin and his Gianni Schicchi. He had a superb technique and could juggle with the most difficult arias as if they were folk-songs. On retiring from the stage, he enjoyed a second career playing comic parts in films, where he once more brought great enjoyment to his fellow-men.

Gigli, Melchior, Tauber

They sound almost like the three Kings from the Orient, especially as one was called Melchior. Kings of song they were, and 'Magi' too, for all three exerted a magical power over those who heard them.

By an amazing coincidence, Gigli and Melchior were born on the same day of the same year, 20th March 1890. An astrologer who worked out their horoscopes would probably find many points of correspondence between them, and could establish some of the special aspects of a date on which two of the greatest singers of all time were born.

Beniamino Gigli, often called the second Caruso, used to say he would rather be known as the first Gigli. His father, a shoemaker, was sacristan of the cathedral in the small town of Recanati in the Apennines (south of Ancona, near the Adriatic coast). Like Caruso, Melchior and many others, Beniamino sang in the choir, in his case at the age of seven. Such early training, especially when more practical than theoretical, as it generally is in Italy, undoubtedly helps with two of the main factors in vocal production, breath control and learning to open the mouth. Without any idea that it might be useful for his future development, Gigli also joined the town band and played the saxophone, which increased both breath control and lung capacity and also his musical awareness. Anyone who ever heard his Dream Monologue in Massenet's *Manon*, that wonderful mezzavoce, with its perfect breath control and most delicate articulation of the vivid but lengthy phrases, can give some of the credit to his first ventures in music as a boy, singing in the choir and playing a wind instrument.

As a matter of fact, Gigli continued all his life to give generous support to this band – which adopted his name – and sometimes even returned to his old place on the bandstand. Knowing the homage paid in Italy to singers, especially tenors, we can imagine the fame he brought to little Recanati. He himself insisted it was famous because Pope Gregory XII had died there and the great poet Giacomo Leopardi had been born there; but of course neither can rival Gigli's popularity in modern times. Among the many Caruso successors he was most deeply rooted in the soul of the Italian nation; especially as he was quite unaffected, a true son of the people, warm-hearted and natural. He was as proud of Recanati as the town was of him. Yet the poor shoemaker's son, apprentice carpenter, journeyman tailor, chemist's assistant, had to travel a long way to become the most idolised singer of his time, landlord and symbol of his town, honoured almost like a king.

The way was not an easy one. At sixteen he failed to secure admission to the Scuola Cantorum of the Sistine Chapel. He stayed in Rome, leading a very bohemian existence and living with one of his brothers who wanted to become a sculptor. In the end he won a scholarship to the celebrated Conservatorio di Santa Cecilia, which he could not have afforded without a free place. To keep himself alive at the time he had to take a job, first at a chemist's, then in the civil service. The turn of the tide started at Parma in 1914, when he entered for a singing competition along with a great many others – there were three dozen tenors alone – and won the first prize. More than that, the judge was Alessandro Bonci, then at the height of his fame, who in giving his verdict said 'Abbiamo finalmente trovato il tenore!' (We have at last found the tenor.) *The* tenor, not *a* tenor; Bonci must have guessed that this young man was going to be his own heir, and of course Caruso's.

On 15th October 1914 Gigli appeared on an opera stage for the first time, singing Enzo in Ponchielli's *La Gioconda* at Rovigo near Venice. Then he toured the chief Italian cities and also sang in Paris, Berlin, Madrid and Barcelona. In 1920 Toscanini brought him to La Scala, and the following year he joined the Met – making his first appearance there quite soon after Caruso's last.

The careers of all great tenors are very similar; travelling all the time, having to be always in top form, always contending with hot, cold, wet or dry climates; always surrounded by reporters, photographers, people asking for favours, people wanting to see the great man himself; by women of all ages, by impresarios and their assistants, who after deducting fat commissions hand over huge cheques which go to the secretary to look after; by hotel staff, who expect princely tips (and have to be given them so as to maintain the tenor's reputation); by financiers wanting to propose business ventures, mostly unsound; by insurance agents, house agents, snobs who like being in such company, and genuinely admiring followers.

For Gigli's generation even the summer did not mean a break. For that was winter in the southern hemisphere, so the tenor sang, for instance, at the Teatro Colón in Buenos Aires, and while in South America he included other towns such as Rio de Janeiro, São Paulo, Montevideo, perhaps Santiago and Lima, with stops in smaller places whose names he hadn't even heard of before, but where surprisingly big and enthusiastic audiences awaited him. Only on the liners did he get a little rest; but soon the aeroplane was invented, and festivals in cities all over the world – and the last breathing-space in the famous singer's life was gone.

Gigli sang from 1914 to 1955. Any who heard him towards the end of his career were amazed at the freshness and mobility of his voice, which with time had become progressively more powerful and dramatic. For decades critics said he was not particularly creative; such a charge is hard to understand. As Andrea Chénier, for instance, a rôle of which he was particularly fond in his later years, he put such elemental force into the freedom songs, such passion into the love cantilenas, that one cannot imagine any more fervent presentation of character and emotion. His mezzavoce was still perfect, the broad flow of his melodies still had a melting beauty. He made them accessible to very wide circles by singing in several extremely successful films. He seemed to sing with special grace when partnered by his own daughter, Rina. While many other tenors might resent growing old and try to hide it, Gigli's close and very Italian family feeling helped him to take this, like everything else, as in the natural order of things.

It mattered little whether or not he was a good film-actor. He was just the singing star of his films, extremely attractive and with a quite unforced appeal for a vast public, who were after all chiefly interested in the musical numbers, waiting to hear that glorious voice once more. Gigli was perhaps the first singer of world fame for whom the mass media of films, radio and records could be extensively used. Whereas with Caruso's recordings, for all the powerful impression they leave, we cannot avoid a sense of 'past history', Gigli on records seems a living presence. Had he lived a few years longer, we should have seen and heard Gigli on television, with his voice full of true beauty of tone and his supreme artistry in every rôle. He died in Rome in 1957.

Far from Recanati and its sunny hills, Lauritz Melchior, his 'twin', was born in Copenhagen. Lebrecht Hommel was his original name,

and singing was a legacy of the Hommel family, to which his father
and blind sister owed as much as he did himself.

If Gigli was still at his peak as a tenor at sixty, this could be said of
Melchior at seventy, when he sang Otello for a recording. His
entrance song amidst popular tumult and the roar of the sea had such
a thunderous majesty that neither Mario del Monaco nor any other
famous interpreter of the part in our day could surpass its overwhelming force. His voice sounded as fresh as forty years before, and
its exuberant power was now directed by a sharp controlling intelligence.

Writers on music at the time of the First World War, including
George Bernard Shaw, were inclined to compare the rising Melchior
with the tenor king of the previous generation, Jean de Reszke. To
us that name means only a distant past, splendidly embellished in the
chronicles of the time; whereas Melchior with his achievements is
still a towering figure up to our own day. He won many of his most
brilliant successes in the age after the Second World War.

There is, however, an interesting parallel with Jean de Reszke.
Both sang for years as baritones, before being discovered as tenors or
before their voices had developed into tenors. As a mezzo-soprano
with increasing maturity often turns into a dramatic soprano – for
whom a good low and middle range are paramount – the heroic
tenor, especially the rare Wagnerian tenor, sometimes develops from
a baritone. In a fascinating radio interview Melchior once said 'Every
true heroic tenor is a man who starts as a baritone. There, if things go
well, you acquire the high notes and keep your strength in the low
ones.' He studied singing in his native Copenhagen, after being a
choirboy. There was a very celebrated singer of the time who used
her husband's name, calling herself Madame Charles Cahier. She had
important successes at the Met, and Mahler chose her for the contralto solo in the memorable Vienna première of his *Lied von der
Erde*. One day she 'discovered' the young Melchior, and took him
along with her on a tour to sing the difficult baritone part of Count
Luna in *Trovatore*. Finally the Danish government, on expert advice,
awarded him a one-year scholarship 'to study changing from baritone to tenor', after which for the first time he sang Tannhäuser in
Copenhagen's opera-house.

After the end of the First World War he went to London, where
a patron sent him to Anna Bahr-Mildenburg. Under her tuition he
developed so well and so fast that when he auditioned before Cosima
and Siegfried Wagner, he was immediately given Siegmund and
Parsifal in the 1924 Bayreuth Festival, the year it was first resumed

after the war. He became the prototype of the Wagnerian hero for the first half of the twentieth century, a blond Nordic giant, very warm-hearted, with an attractive open face. Wholly uncomplicated, he made an ideal Lohengrin, von Stolzing and Siegfried. He was a very methodical person, and kept a record of his opera evenings. In this we read with amazement that he sang in all but three of the 515 Wagner productions staged at the Met between 1926 and 1950, and that he only missed fourteen performances (three at the Met) in his whole career. 'A lot of people have wondered how I did it. Perhaps it's because I have the constitution of an ox. Perhaps it's because I don't fuss.' The latter reason seems to hit the nail on the head. People who are always worrying over their health, nervously taking precautions on every occasion, are usually the ones who become ill directly some gap appears in their protective system. Those who are prepared to stand up to all conditions, climatic and otherwise, without worrying too much, are likely to keep mentally and physically fit – and that goes for singers as much as any.

In 1926, when Melchior went to the Met, Gigli was the star of Italian opera; they reached their peak, then, at the same time, another astrological correspondence. They became good friends, felt a bond of destiny as 'twins', sang together in many glorious, exhilarating performances to win tremendous ovations, and could delight an audience in less serious vein as well. On one occasion, to help the Met out of economic difficulties, they both took part in an evening of burlesque. Gigli, dressed as a gypsy girl, sang Carmen's Habanera; Melchior appeared as Salome, padded with balloons in certain places (but not the stomach, for his own was pretty big, as befitted a singer – especially a tenor – at that time). The disembodied head, handed to him on a silver platter as the text demanded, bore clearly the features of a prominent New York critic. This was his own idea, and after tremendous cheers and laughter from the audience, four more silver platters were handed to Melchior, containing the heads of four equally dreaded critics.

In the most exalted moment of the Liebestod in *Tristan und Isolde*, he could also say to his partner Frida Leider: 'Frida, take that fly away', when a fly was tickling his nose – for as a corpse he could not very well shoo it off. Melchior–Leider were for a long time regarded as the ideal Wagner couple. When the soprano aged, Kirsten Flagstad took her place at the side of the indestructible Melchior. It was only very gradually and reluctantly that he gave up the rôles of Siegfried and Tristan. Younger singers sprang into the breach in the hope of becoming a worthy successor to him; in this, Windgassen was probably one of the most successful. Windgassen also sang with Flagstad, although in figure he was already part of the new image of a Wagner hero; and when the great Norwegian retired, he and the Swede, Birgit Nilsson, who was just as physically suitable, made a new ideal pair. Meanwhile, beaming and erect, Melchior sat in a box listening benevolently and giving his blessing.

He was considered the most German of all singers, although he was never a German. Born a Dane, he later became a United States citizen. But you do not have to be an Italian to sing a perfect Otello nor a German to portray a Siegfried authentically. Melchior managed both in unsurpassable fashion. He felt his deepest bond with German music, as can be seen from some sentences in the interview mentioned above; 'We were by chance a wonderful German company at the Metropolitan Opera when the second war broke out. There were Kirsten Flagstad and Friedrich Schorr, and afterwards we had the young Astrid Varnay as well. That was the time when I was Germany's musical ambassador in America. In all those years we preserved Germany's good name. And when Hitler ordered the burning of the books and banned Mendelssohn's music, we wanted to show that there was another Germany – a Germany which is always there.' Melchior was a Dane and an American, Flagstad a Norwegian, Schorr a Jew, Varnay a Hungarian. It is a wonderful thing that such genuine art exists, far from ephemeral politics and far above all hate.

Melchior made films, like Gigli and many other opera-singers of his time. He made wonderful records which still today set the heart of every music-lover beating faster. As a very old gentleman he appeared in charity concerts. 'My voice has not lost its power or its pitch. I think it will last as long as I live,' he used to say. He died in California in March 1973.

Richard Tauber, two years younger than Melchior and Gigli, was born in Linz. Besides being a dramatic artist and an extremely accomplished musician, he had a special quality to his genius as a singer. It was unusual enough to hear a tenor singing Mozart's Don Ottavio on one evening in perfect bel canto style, on the next day to attend an evening of Lieder showing his profound insight into Schubert and Schumann, on the third to listen to his delightful re-creation of a Lehár operetta, on the fourth perhaps to marvel at Viennese folk-songs which in his rendering might have been thought classical romantic masterpieces, and then on the next evening to see and hear him again in opera as a shattering Don José or Pedro (in D'Albert's *Tiefland*). But it was more remarkable still to watch him giving himself completely in each of these performances. For him, as for any true artist, there were no second-class presentations; he was entirely absorbed in each, and brought to them all a perfect technique and his full soul.

The timbre of his voice was unmistakable, it could be clearly recognised among hundreds. It was fantastic what he could do with every individual note in every position. Authorities were always discussing the production of his top notes in pianissimo or his unusual capacity for colouring within the longest of phrases. Perhaps there was a trace of falsetto mixed with his most ethereal high notes? It did not matter, they sounded so magically sweet, so utterly controlled, so remote from all material things, that any sensitive listener was bathed in a glow of extraordinary happiness.

The result of Tauber's friendship with Lehár is well-known, the last blossoming of operetta. Lehár designed the principal rôles in *Paganini*, *The Tsarevich*, *Frederika* and *Land of Smiles* to give genuine operatic opportunities to his star singer. The festive premières of these works turned into real Tauber concerts. He had to give half a dozen encores of 'You are my heart's delight'; each time he did it with fresh nuances, a different force, with continual unexpected effects.

If a hypercritical expert should turn up his nose at such tricks, Tauber could soon afterwards invite him to the opera, to hear an un-surpassable Belmonte or a Tamino with the full Mozartian flavour. But his talent was by no means confined to this kind of lyricism; his voice was capable of dramatic grandeur, his true-to-life acting could be thrilling to the highest degree. His Canio came near to Caruso's. Anyone who saw him on the stage would find it almost incredible that he had acute rheumatism which made every movement a torment.

In films too he covered his physical impediment with masterly skill. Here, thanks to his perfect technique, usually the best guarantee of ability at a microphone, his voice achieved a greater brilliance than that of many other singers; as every collector knows, he sang ideally for records. He was one of the many artists of Jewish birth expelled by the Nazis, first from Germany and then from his native Austria in 1938. He went to London, and in 1940 became a British subject. In England he gave many superb performances, despite in-creasingly agonising attacks of rheumatism. After the war the Vienna Opera wanted to make it up to him for what had happened, and invited him to join their company for a guest appearance at Covent Garden, singing any rôle of his choice. The late Bernard

Grun, distinguished music-writer, conductor and composer, who knew Lehár and Tauber very well, has described this vividly in his biography of Lehár *Gold and Silver – The Life and Times of Franz Lehár* (published by W. H. Allen):

'At the beginning of August (1947), Tauber received a letter from Vienna, saying that the entire ensemble of the Staatsoper had been invited over by the Covent Garden Opera, and would consider it an honour if he, as an honorary member of the famous old house, would appear with the company in any rôle of his choice. Immediately his mood changed. He was as gay and energetic as ever, tiredness and huskiness had vanished. Of course he was ready to sing, he told the Viennese. The rôle? There was only one worth considering, the one in which he believed he had always given of his best vocally and artistically – Don Ottavio in Mozart's *Don Giovanni*. A shock for Vienna; it had long ceased to be a secret that Tauber's voice had passed its peak. Don Ottavio is considered one of the most difficult tenor parts in all opera. But there was no going back.

'On 27th September 1947, when Tauber put on his old Ottavio costume in the star's dressing room at the Royal Opera House, he was dismayed to find how thin he had become. "Beads of sweat appeared on his brow," Diana (his wife) relates. "Anxiety and depression could be read in his eyes. He rallied all his powers, and with a pale smile walked towards the stage."

'What happened then can never be thought of by anyone in the audience that night as anything but a miracle. From the powerful "*Tutto il mio sangue*" to the "*Or che tutti*" at the end, the voice sounded as it had not done since its great opera days; sublimely beautiful, captivating and unmistakably Tauber. The jubilation of the crammed house knew no bounds, and Ottavio had to appear before the curtain about thirty times. "I made it! I made it!" he cried over and over again, back in the dressing-room with his wife. "And if I never sing another note, it was a glorious exit."

'An emergency operation a few days later showed that he had sung with one of his lungs almost completely decayed. His unshakable, dynamic nature kept him alive for another three months.'

There was no chance of the return Tauber planned to his beloved opera-house in Vienna. He died on 9th January 1948, only fifty-six years old.

VI

Opera in Germany and Austria Until the Second World War

Berlin

Berlin has an old tradition as an opera city. The foundation stone for the German Imperial Opera, later the State Opera, on the famous street Unter den Linden, was laid in 1741 and built by a great architect, Hans Georg Wenzelslaus. Frederick the Great, when Crown Prince, wished to adorn his future capital with distinctive buildings such as he had admired in Brunswick and Dresden. The first company of singers naturally came from Italy; the first ballet, just as naturally, from Paris. But the first musical director was a German, Carl Heinrich Graun. The building went up in an extremely short time and was opened in December 1742. There are two rather striking things we learn from publications of the time; attendants had strict orders not to go near the opera-house with lighted torches; and 'the magnificent palace has so much clear space all round it that a thousand coaches can easily be accommodated'. A parking problem solved in the eighteenth century!

According to a Berlin paper, '1850 people could comfortably stand and sit in the stalls and circle, 1950 in the boxes; when crammed tight the auditorium would hold about 5000 people'. This is considerably above the capacity of the present Berlin opera-house, and sheds a very favourable light on the musical enthusiasm of that time. Many present-day managers, who find their auditorium sometimes too big and sometimes too small, would be grateful for such an 'elastic' house where the audience could sit or stand in greater or less comfort. The newspaper article was written after a big fire in 1843 (despite the instruction to attendants!) in which the opera-house was burnt down. The king commissioned a well-known architect to restore it at once, 'without sacrificing the building's extremely beautiful and symmetrical forms' – and again with the classical opera colours, white and gold outside, red for the interior. From 1847 there was gas lighting, from 1887 electricity.

In the second half of the last century Berlin already had several other opera-houses, all of which had their great singers and played their part in the city's musical history. Henriette Sontag, who had become famous overnight from the first performance of Beethoven's Ninth Symphony, came to the Viktoriatheater and caused scenes of exultation which were repeated later with the Swedish Nightingale, Jenny Lind. Meyerbeer, in those days the most celebrated operatic composer in the world, brought the 'three-octave' prima donna, Pauline Viardot-Garcia. From Wilhelmine Schröder-Devrient, who won much of her fame here, there is a direct line to Lilli Lehmann. Patti went in 1861 when she was only eighteen but already admired all over Europe and America. Pauline Lucca and Désirée Artôt sang there. Albert Niemann, a heroic tenor of immense power, was probably the best Tristan of his day. Theodor Wachtel, another very good tenor, had his most successful rôle as Chapelou in *Postillon de Longjumeau*, a work popular at the time by Adam, composer of the ballet *Giselle*.

But the standard of an opera-house can never be judged by its principal singers, and there were many unsatisfactory things then about the opera in Berlin. The rest of the company was mediocre, the chorus weak, productions were badly adapted to the music, the management was extremely authoritarian, and seldom in the right hands; the manager could punish members of the company with arrest if he wished! The programme was uninteresting, with Verdi still almost unknown. *Die Meistersinger* was not produced in Berlin until 1870, and then only against strong resistance and with the press almost unanimous in 'slating' it. Ten years later Pauline Lucca crowned her career with a remarkable Carmen, which put the work firmly into the accepted repertoire for Germany. At the outbreak of the First World War it had the highest number of performances in Berlin (910), followed by *The Magic Flute* (905), *Der Freischütz* (875), *The Marriage of Figaro* and *Tannhäuser* (both 805), *Lohengrin* (775), *Fidelio* (770) and *Cavalleria Rusticana* (690).

Among the notable singers here towards the end of the century, Rosa Sucher must have been a very fine artist; and Berlin's rise to an outstanding city for opera seems to start with her. Another leading figure was Emmy Destinn, born in Prague (as Emmy Kittl) in 1878, who adopted the name of her revered teacher according to old custom. At twenty she made her début as Santuzza in *Cavalleria Rusticana*, and in 1901 she was already at Bayreuth as Senta in *The Flying Dutchman*. When only twenty-three she was appearing at the Met, and became world-famous in 1910 when she sang there with Caruso in the première of *The Girl of the Golden West*. On the outbreak of war she returned to Germany, but in 1919 went to America again and completed her stage career there. Four years later she died in her native country, now to her joy an independent state.

The beautiful Geraldine Farrar, a native of the United States, had studied with Lilli Lehmann and made her début at the Berlin Opera as Marguerite in Gounod's *Faust*. There she remained for six years, surrounded by admirers, her name coupled with various men, but always the *grande dame* in every gesture. In 1906 she went to the Met, where she launched Humperdinck's *Königskinder* and Puccini's *Suor Angelica* (from the *Trittico*). She was one of the first prominent theatrical artists to make a film, but of course it was then still silent. In her early forties she retired into private life and wrote her autobiography. She had one of the finest and most comprehensive voices of her age (from coloratura heights to contralto depths) and was a fascinating stage personality.

Frieda Hempel, a third prima donna of the time, was a native of Leipzig who studied in Berlin, received her initiation at Bayreuth when only twenty and in 1907 went to Berlin's Court Opera. In 1910 she was singing the Marschallin at the Met, in the first American production of *Rosenkavalier*, and had a clash with Richard Strauss which today sounds almost incredible; she seriously wanted to make him write some coloratura decorations for the rôle. Like the other two prima donnas, she often partnered Caruso, most notably in Donizetti's *Elisir d'Amore*. She was a guest artist at all the important opera-houses, but gave up the stage early and devoted herself to concert singing.

In this field she became involved in a strange and highly American venture. For the centenary of the birth of Jenny Lind, whose tour of America in 1850 had been such a sensation, an ingenious impresario suggested to Frieda Hempel that she should travel by exactly the same route with the same programme and in the costume of the Swedish Nightingale. With extensive publicity the new tour was extremely successful, proving that the curiosity of the American public had turned into a genuine interest in music; she was enthusiastically received even in the smallest towns. She too wrote an autobiography, called *My Life of Song*. She died in Berlin, scene of her first big successes, in 1955.

At the Berlin première of *Rosenkavalier* mentioned above, Sophie was sung by Claire Dux, who also achieved fame afterwards. She came from near Bromberg in Poland; at twelve she sang Gretel in a school production of Humperdinck's opera, then came training and the real début, at twenty-one, as Pamina at Cologne, where she later sang Mimì to Caruso's Rodolfo. In 1911 she joined the Berlin company. Then came the usual career; Covent Garden, Stockholm, half Europe, finally the United States – not at the Met, though, but at Chicago, which was periodically a strong rival. She too grew more and more involved in concert singing, and eventually left the theatre, to become an inspired interpreter of romantic songs on concert platforms.

Barbara Kemp went to the Berlin Opera in 1913. A year later she was singing Senta and then Kundry at Bayreuth. In Berlin's 'golden twenties', she was one of the city's favourite opera stars. She had meanwhile married Max von Schilling, a popular composer of the time, who was appointed manager of the opera-house. She was considered one of the best Carmens of the day, a fascinating Salome, a touching dyer's wife in *Frau ohne Schatten*, and an ideal Mona Lisa in her husband's opera of that name. After appearing as a guest artist in all the important opera-houses, she retired from the stage in 1932, and as a teacher passed on much of her fine technique to the next generation. She died in Berlin in 1959.

Frida Leider, already mentioned as Melchior's partner, was for a long time the most famous Wagnerian prima donna in the world. Born in 1888 in Berlin, she was for some years a bank clerk, before deciding to go in for an operatic career. She made her début at Halle in 1915 as Venus in *Tannhäuser*. In 1924 she went to Berlin, where her status rose swiftly. All opera-houses except the Italian vied with each other to obtain a dramatic soprano of such dynamic force and high musical quality. She was called to Bayreuth in 1928, and has ever since been rated the finest Isolde, Brünnhilde, Venus and Elisabeth of her generation. In Melchior she found the ideal partner in figure and voice. She was in trouble with the Nazis for refusing to divorce her non-Aryan husband, and finally this most German of singers left Germany. She returned after the war, produced at the Berlin Opera, directed a singing studio, was professor at the Academy of Music, and wrote her memoirs, *Das war mein Teil* (That was my Part).

The Berlin of that period had many fine contraltos as well. Emmi Leisner sang there from 1913 to 1921, with something solemn and almost mystical in her dark-toned voice. Her star rôle was Erda in *The Ring*; she also sang Orpheus in Gluck's opera, at Hellerau near Dresden, in a revolutionary production by Jacques-Dalcroze, and this was a memorable performance in operatic history. She was profoundly expressive, equally so in Lieder and oratorio – superficially the reverse, in fact, of what is called bel canto, although few sang so beautifully. She died in Flensburg, her home town, in 1958, at the age of seventy-three.

Karin Branzell, at first an organist in her home town, Stockholm, sang at the opera there from 1912 to 1918, when she went to the Berlin State Opera, of which she was a member until 1923. From 1924 to 1944 she was at the Met; in 1926 she won tremendous acclaim at the Teatro Colón and was repeatedly pressed to give guest performances there; she sang at Bayreuth and in all the great opera-houses of Europe and the United States. In 1946, after retiring for good, she taught for many years in New York's important Juillard School of Music.

The tenor Ernst Kraus was probably the member of this unusual company who stayed with it longest, from 1898 to 1924. He was primarily a Wagnerian singer, and for ten years at Bayreuth took the rôles of Erik, von Stolzing, Siegmund and Siegfried; but in Italian operas he was considered a serious rival of Caruso. His voice, which he kept until well into his sixties, must have been magnificent. He died in Bavaria in 1941 at the age of seventy-eight.

Hermann Jadlowker, another outstanding tenor of that brilliant Berlin era, was born in Riga (then German), the son of orthodox Jews; he began to learn singing in the synagogue choir, but he felt cramped by his environment, and his splendid voice showed him the way to opera. He went to Berlin, became a member of its Court Opera in 1909 and was very soon a great favourite of the public. At the Met, in 1910, he was with Geraldine Farrar in the première of Humperdinck's *Königskinder*, a work sadly neglected today. He was guest artist at the leading opera-houses, but in 1929 retired to Riga as precentor. In 1938 he settled in Tel Aviv and lived to see the state of Israel established. He died there in 1953.

East European Jewry, so rich in instrumental talents, endowed with a disproportionate number of notable conductors, has achieved little prominence in singing. Striving for worldly fame was alien to an orthodox Jew's deepest convictions, the possession of a fine voice merely imposed an obligation of more profound service to God. It was rare for those who sang in synagogues to find their way to limelight on the stage – in an activity always suspect to orthodox Jews.

(In our day Richard Tucker, the magnificent American tenor, has proved an exception to this rule.)

Joseph Mann, another tenor from the background of East European Jewry, had only a short career. Born at Lemberg, then part of Austria, he was a lawyer before deciding to go in for singing. He made his début in Lemberg at the age of thirty-one, was seven years at the Volksoper in Vienna and in 1918 went to the Berlin Opera, which had just changed its title from Court Opera to State Opera. There he had three splendid years which gave him an enthusiastic following. On 9th September 1921, at the age of forty-two, while singing Radames he collapsed on the stage and died instantly. Such a death in full song occurs less rarely than one might think – more of this in a later chapter.

The baritone Josef Schwarz was, like Jadlowker, from Riga, and like Mann he died tragically young. In 1900, at twenty, he made his début in Linz, then moved around with enterprising strolling players, was suddenly a guest artist in St Petersburg's Tsarist Opera and was invited to Vienna by Mahler. From 1915 on he sang at the Berlin Opera, a glorious lyric baritone and an impassioned actor. After the First World War a swift international career seemed in store for him, but he was struck down in 1924 by a serious illness, from which he died two years later.

Dresden

Dresden, the 'Florence of the Elbe', was musically of great importance before Berlin and Vienna; its operatic tradition goes back to the seventeenth century. But it had no regular home until 1841, when the first permanent opera-house was built, designed by the great architect Semper. Directly afterwards the Wagner premières of *Rienzi* and *The Flying Dutchman* took place there. In 1842 Wagner himself went to the city – where Hasse and Weber had been active before him – and met two remarkable singers, Wilhelmine Schröder-Devrient and the tenor Joseph Tichatschek who together helped to make *Rienzi* perhaps the decisive triumph of the composer's life. Schröder-Devrient sang also in *The Flying Dutchman*, but Tichatschek did not, either because he did not think the role of Erik important enough or because Wagner did not want to give it to him (Wagner had said to Liszt, 'His voice contains brilliance and tenderness, but lacks the accents of pain'). It is more surprising that the title rôle was not sung by Anton Mitterwurzer, one of the most dramatically expressive bass-baritones in German opera at the time.

Fedor Chaliapin the great Russian bass in his most famous role Boris Godunov

Paul Robeson, first in a long line of distinguished coloured American singers

Nellie Melba, for many years Queen of Covent Garden and a celebrated Mimì

Adelina Patti in a typical studio portrait of the period

Gemma Bellincioni, an early Santuzza

Maria Ivogün the German coloratura singer as Tatiana in Tchaikovsky's 'Eugene Onegin'

Enrico Caruso
(Jl Trovatore)

Enrico Caruso, the most famous of all Italian tenors, as Manrico in 'Il Trovatore'

The American tenor Jess Thomas in the title role of Wagner's 'Siegfried' at Salzburg

Graziella Sciutti and Luigi Alva in Cimarosa's 'Il Matrimonio Segreto'

A studio portrait of Elisabeth Schwarzkopf, distinguished operatic artist and great interpreter of lieder

Gwyneth Jones, one of the new generation of British singers who have forged an international career, as Aida at Covent Garden

The much-loved Renata Tebaldi in the Scala production of 'La Forza del Destino'

Erika Köth as Antonia in the Deutsche Oper Berlin production of 'The Tales of Hoffmann'

In 1845, when this trio of singers was wanted for the première of *Tannhäuser*, only Mitterwurzer seems to have been in full possession of his voice. In rehearsal Tichatschek, though only thirty-six, fell so short of requirements that his rôle and therefore the work had to be seriously cut down. Schröder was forty, and evidently did not really carry conviction as Venus, although audiences of the day were much less spoilt than ours in regard to optical illusions. The rôle of Elisabeth was given to Wagner's niece Johanna, who also bears some responsibility for the considerable cutting and simplification which was done. Two years later she sang the title rôle in Gluck's *Iphigénie en Aulide* with Schröder making her farewell appearance as Clytemnestra. Johanna Wagner gave up her operatic career when she was thirty-two to become a straight actress. Yet in 1876, amazingly enough, her uncle gave her two contralto rôles, a Valkyrie and a Norn, in his first Bayreuth Festival.

After Wagner's flight from Dresden in connection with the revolutionary events of 1849, the Court Theatre went into a serious decline; although in 1859, when Wagner as a political refugee was not allowed to enter Germany, Tichatschek sang the first Dresden Lohengrin (nine years after the original production at Weimar under Liszt). He had apparently recovered all his powers, and sang it so well that several years later Wagner wanted to secure his services for the Munich première. But King Ludwig would not have this; Lohengrin was his dream figure who had led him to his idol Wagner; so he wanted a younger Knight of the Grail.

Schnorr von Carolsfeld, born in Dresden, trained in Karlsruhe to become an ideal Wagnerian singer, a type which had only just come into being. He then sang in Dresden, but on 10th June 1865 suddenly stepped into world limelight at Munich, becoming the first Tristan. Six weeks afterwards he died, still very young, and for a long time there was a common idea that this rôle, which many considered unsingable, caused overstrain.

With the arrival of Ernst Schuch as artistic director of the Dresden Court Theatre, the opera-house started on a new period of prosperity which lasted for a long time. In 1878 the new building, again designed by Semper, was opened. Later, still under Schuch, it was to become renowned all over the world as the venue for Richard Strauss premières.

Schuch and Franz Wüllner, joint musical directors for many years, built up a remarkable company. Anton Erl, a lyric and above all a Mozartian tenor, was known as 'Germany's best coloratura'. Schuch's wife, Clementine, was an enchanting soubrette, but the most famous member of the company was probably Therese Malten, who alternated at Bayreuth with the great Amalie Materna as Kundry.

Enthusiasm for Wagner was mounting in Germany, and one of those who knew how to exploit it was the enterprising and brilliant impresario Angelo Neumann. In 1882 he took his 'Nibelungen Company' to Dresden, which included three outstanding singers, the tenor Scaria, and two sopranos, Reicher-Kindermann and Katharina Klafsky. Reicher-Kindermann, still in her twenties, died soon after this, probably as a result of singing Wagner almost every evening, a task to which the throats and bodies of that first generation were not yet adapted. Wagner singers were now urgently needed everywhere, and a fine stock of them grew in Dresden itself, including Heinrich Gudehus, who first sang the title rôle in Wagner's last work, *Parsifal*, when the legend of the Grail was first presented to a respectful world at Bayreuth in 1882.

In 1884 Gudehus and Therese Malten sang Tristan and Isolde at Dresden, a year later Siegmund and Brünnhilde in *Die Walküre* and Siegfried and Brünnhilde in *Siegfried* and *Götterdämmerung*. Schuch was directing, and Dresden had become a Wagner city of the first rank. Obviously Therese Malten was prominent in this. She was also a splendid Pamina in *The Magic Flute* and Agathe in *Der Freischütz*, became Dresden's first Mignon and a brilliant Marguerite in *Faust*, could sing Italian and was, in fact, the first Dresden Santuzza in *Cavalleria Rusticana*, but her highest achievements were in the great Wagner rôles. Born in 1855 in Austria, she was pre-eminent for nearly three decades among Dresden's dramatic singers, but despite the immense strain this entailed, she kept her voice till an advanced age. She died in 1930.

Clementine Schuch gradually developed into one of the best coloratura singers. For a short while she had, in Marcella Sembrich, a formidable rival, but Sembrich quickly outgrew Dresden and also Berlin, becoming a world star on the international circuit, winning immense acclaim. From 1898 she was a member of the Met, until she retired from the stage in 1909. She died in New York in 1935.

Karl Scheidemantel and Karl Perron were two heroic baritones, who far from being rivals were great friends, showing model team spirit. They alternated with each other in several rôles, were pleased when they could be in the same opera, and each respected the stage characters which the other had made more or less his own domain. Both sang Don Giovanni; Scheidemantel perhaps more seductively,

Perron with more demonic force. Scheidemantel was a cheerful Hans Sachs, and an ideal baritone in Puccini's operas. Perron specialised in lonely, suffering rôles with supernatural overtones, like the Dutchman and Amfortas. In 1905 he had the honour of becoming Richard Strauss's first John the Baptist, in 1909 the first Orestes and in 1911 the first Baron Ochs. Strauss did not want to give him this rôle, for he did not think this wild Dutchman, this impressive King Mark, would catch the craftiness of the boorish nobleman. He would have liked to engage Mayr from Vienna or Bender from Munich, but in the end Perron was chosen – and in fact *Rosenkavalier* achieved a more rapid success than any other Strauss work.

Around the turn of the century a new generation of singers came into view. Marie Wittich gradually took over several of Therese Malten's rôles, then sang Brünnhilde and Kundry at Bayreuth and in 1905 crowned her career as the first Salome in Strauss's new opera. That she did not herself carry out the Dance of the Seven Veils seemed natural enough at the time, as the figures of most dramatic singers would have made such a thing impossible! Dancing and singing were two disciplines completely separate from each other. Today, when a high degree of suppleness and extensive physical expression are regarded as almost indispensable qualifications for a career in singing, these ideas have changed, and what was then an exception is today the rule. The rôle of Salome must have done a great deal to make the *physique du rôl* one of the prerequisites for singers. The new generation of sopranos became more and more eager to take into account both sides of the composer's wishes, the dancing as well as the singing. If a soubrette could have sung Salome, the problem would have been a good deal less, for soubrettes had always been expected to be mobile. But Salome is a dramatic soprano rôle, and those who sang it were almost all rather stout, to ensure the power and endurance of the voice. Still, the task was set, and as early as 1906, *ie* the year after the première, the Croatian soprano Fanchette Verhunc, the first singer capable of both requirements, sang Salome and also performed the Dance of the Seven Veils. Today both types of Salome can be found; those who perform it themselves and those who get it done by a double, as skilfully disguised as possible by the producer—mostly out of concern for the great singing scene which comes directly after the dance and brings the work to its lyrical climax, for this demands special breath control, which is a difficult matter after several minutes of strenuous dancing.

Minnie Nast created Sophie in *Rosenkavalier*, when after *Salome* and *Elektra* this Strauss opera had its first production in Dresden.

Every time the curtain went up for the second act, showing the mansion of the newly-rich Herr von Faninal, audiences applauded loudly, a tribute both to the magnificent set by Alfred Rollers, who was Mahler's colleague in his great Viennese productions, and to the charming appearance of Minnie Nast. She shared the coloratura soubrette field with Erika Wedekind, the poet's sister.

The chief Dresden tenors at this time were Georg Anthes, Alfred von Bary – who sang the great heroic parts at Bayreuth for ten years, but at the end of the First World War resumed his original profession of doctor – and Karl Burrian, who created the rôle of Herod in *Salome* and was called 'the best Tristan' by Toscanini. In 1900 Schuch discovered in his chorus a powerful bass-baritone, Friedrich Plaschke, who came from Prague and married the outstanding soprano Eva von der Osten. For decades they were the leading operatic couple in Dresden, indeed one of the most brilliant in German-language opera of the time. Plaschke made a haunting Dutchman, an engaging Sachs, a sombre Wotan and also, like Karl Perron, took a big part in three Richard Strauss premières, as the first Altair (*Ägyptischer Helena*), the first Waldner (*Arabella*) and the first Sir Morosus (*Schweigsame Frau*). His wife Eva could claim the glory of singing the first Oktavian in *Rosenkavalier*.

Specialisation in voices had not gone so far as it has today and the same soprano, Annie Krull, could therefore sing Pamina, Elisabeth in *Tannhäuser* and Elektra at the world première in 1909. Today it would rarely happen in a big opera-house that the same singer should have such different rôles as the Marschallin and Zerbinetta in *Ariadne auf Naxos*, but this was the case with Margarethe Siems, who also sang Chrysothemis in the original production of *Elektra*. So she, too, was in three Richard Strauss premières. Born in Breslau in 1879, she was with the Dresden Opera almost continuously and died in that city in 1952.

Toscanini said of Elisabeth Rethberg (originally Lisbeth Sättler), 'The most beautiful soprano voice I have ever heard.' Born in 1894, she made a successful début in Dresden as Agathe in *Freischütz*, before starting on her world career. Called to the Met in 1922, she also sang at Covent Garden and La Scala, in Rome, at the Salzburg Festivals and, in 1928, back in Dresden, she created the title rôle in Strauss's *Ägyptischer Helena*.

For several decades Dresden remained an important centre for Strauss operas, and special efforts were made to give them worthy casts. Sopranos were always fighting for the rôle of Salome which, as the composer wrote before the première, 'demands a singer of very great style, accustomed to Isolde and such rôles'. Consequently, it was taken from the coloratura singers and given to the dramatic, first Marie Wittich, then Annie Krull, then a guest artist from Finland, Aino Ackté, who could dance as well as sing. So could Gerta Barby, who gained a firm place in the Dresden company with a performance which the critics praised for its sensuous beauty. Eva von der Osten took over the rôle in 1916. In 1930 it was sung for the first time by a lighter coloratura voice, Maria Rajdl. Fritz Busch conducted and Strauss retouched the orchestral score so that smaller voices would come through. Barbara Kemp, mentioned in the last section, sang it in Dresden as a guest artist and also won special success as the Marschallin. The last Salomes at Dresden, before the city was tragically destroyed near the end of the Second World War, were Elisa Stünzner, the magnificent Margarethe Teschemacher (who was at Dresden from 1934 on and in 1938 sang the title rôle in the world première of Strauss's *Daphne*), and finally Christl Goltz, who started an international career there as a specialist in Strauss and other very dramatic operas; her first rôle at the Met in 1954 was Salome. For this rôle, the one most coveted by every soprano with the human and vocal maturity for it, Dresden has always had a specially large number of brilliant voices to offer; Martha Fuchs, Tiana Lemnitz, Margarethe Teschemacher, Elisa Stünzner, Martha Rohs, Elisabeth Höngen, Elsa Cavelti, Meta Seinemeyer, Claire Born, Maria Rajdl, Erna Berger and Maria Cebotari. Of course, most of them also sang at other leading opera-houses, for the age of hectic world tours had started and companies had begun to fall apart.

Fritz Busch was the musical director at Dresden from 1922 to 1933. The beautiful opera-house was once more in its full glory, and in the Italian repertory, which had an old tradition there, could be heard the splendid voices of Meta Seinemeyer and Tino Pattiera. Why this tenor did not reach the highest level internationally is hard to understand, as it was with Alfred Piccaver from Vienna. Pattiera was born in 1892 in Ragusa, today Dubrovnik. Trained in Vienna, he made his début in 1915 at Dresden where he remained until 1941, though also appearing as a guest artist – with very great success – in Vienna, London, Paris, Brussels and Chicago. He belonged, too, for several years to the Berlin State Opera, but his real artistic home was Dresden, where his radiant and inspiring voice won tremendous popularity. In 1948 he was still giving concerts, after that he went to Vienna as a teacher.

Meta Seinemeyer, born in Berlin in 1895, made her début at the Berlin State Opera at twenty-three and, in 1925, after an American tour, went to Dresden. There, with Pattiera and the powerful bass Ivar Andresen, she launched a Verdi renaissance which spread across Europe, partly in the new German libretti by Franz Werfel. But with her voice still in full bloom, she was struck down by an incurable blood disease and in 1929 died tragically young.

So did Andresen, who can be claimed for Dresden despite his Norwegian origins and world career. He was born in Oslo in 1896, started as the Landgrave (*Tannhäuser*) at Stockholm in 1919, was at Dresden from 1925 to 1934, and during this period was also at Bayreuth, a guest artist in London, Barcelona, Vienna, Hamburg, Munich and often in Berlin. He joined the Met in 1936, but died in Stockholm in 1940.

The name inseparably associated with the Busch era at Dresden is that of Erna Berger, one of the most astonishing soprano voices in the coloratura range and also a very sensitive Lieder-singer. Born near Dresden in 1900, she was forced to emigrate to South America while still in her teens, first to the Paraguayan bush, then to Montevideo as a governess. In 1923 she was able to return to Germany and devote herself to singing. In 1925 she began her career in Dresden; from 1934 until old age she was a member of the Berlin State Opera where now, after Busch, Furtwängler had a special esteem for her, calling her 'a classical singer with a very romantic soul'. From 1929 she also appeared regularly at Bayreuth. Once in a delightful broadcast interview she sketched her whole life, bringing out the true artist's infinite and obsessive love of singing, which could triumph over the disadvantages of extreme shortness in height and a voice that was weak, even though naturally endowed for the highest of high notes. From that broadcast I remember particularly her saying that one had to put as much creative intensity into a little three-minute Lied as into an entire three-hour operatic rôle.

The tenor Max Hirzel made his mark in his native Zürich, but developed in Dresden under Busch's direction to become an outstanding Tamino and Lohengrin, and was also highly acclaimed in Vienna, London and other leading opera centres. His colleague Curt Taucher became in 1928 the first Menelaus in *Ägyptische Helena*, and his Wagner interpretations opened doors for him at the Met, Covent Garden and the Teatro Liceo in Barcelona. In 1925, while singing the young Siegfried at the Met, he fell through a trap-door on the stage, but despite considerable injuries carried on to the end of the performance. The baritone Robert Burg, member of the Dresden company from 1916 to 1944, was in 1926 the first Cardillac in Hindemith's opera of that name, and from 1933 to 1942 a towering

Alberich in *The Ring* at Bayreuth. He had a fatal heart attack during a concert in 1946 when he was fifty-five.

There are many other singers of international fame who were associated with Dresden. Paul Schöffler went there as a young man under Busch and remained until 1937. Max Lorenz sang there from 1926 to 1931 and made himself into one of the most superb heroic tenors of the century. Martha Fuchs was for years a concert singer, but after a début at Aachen went in 1930 to the Dresden Opera, where she developed into a dramatic soprano and then gave memorable performances at Bayreuth in the rôles of Isolde, Kundry and Brünnhilde. In 1936 she came with the Dresden Company to Covent Garden, where she won great acclaim as Donna Anna, the Marschallin and Ariadne. Maria Cebotari was discovered by Busch and sang in Dresden for twelve years. Dresden was also important in Viorica Ursuleac's career, for in 1933 she created the title rôle in Strauss's *Arabella*.

Munich

Munich's opera-house, the 'National Theatre', was destroyed by fire in 1823. Restored two years later, it remained for over a century one of the finest opera-houses in Europe and indeed in the world. In Germany only Berlin and Dresden could compete with its building, and few other cities on an artistic level.

There was also at Munich the splendid Cuvilliés-Theater, a rococo opera-house of incomparable grace, opened as early as 1753. Mozart conducted there, and it was an ideal place for operatic works of that age.

Who was Munich's first great singer? Does anyone from the time of Mozart's *Finta Giardiniera* (1775) deserve that title? No one can say. At the première of *Idomeneo*, six years later, the cast included 'very experienced singers'. Anton Raaff was in the title rôle, the two Wendling ladies were Ilia and Elektra, Idamante was sung by the young *castrato* Vincenzo dal Prato, one of the last examples of the use of *castrati*. He is hardly heard of afterwards.

Half a century later there are reports of Georg Mittermayr, Munich's first Pizarro in *Fidelio* and Ottokar in *Freischütz*, who appeared in both bass and tenor roles – something which would scarcely happen today! Schröder-Devrient also went there as guest artist and sang Leonore in *Fidelio* among other rôles.

Then there was a period of decadence. In 1836, when the composer Franz Lachner was appointed opera director, the opera-house could not find a cast from its own company for more than sixteen out of its sixty-five productions a year. Lachner set about restoring the company with great energy. One of those who joined it was a fine baritone called August Kindermann, the first Wotan in *Rheingold* and *Walküre*. His daughter Hedwig was an outstanding contralto, and several descendants with his name became well-known, including Lydia Kindermann in our own time. The soprano Sophie Stehle was engaged in her teens in 1860, just at the right time to fulfil important functions in the Wagner era then starting; singing the first Freia in *Rheingold* and the first Brünnhilde in *Walküre*. On 10th June 1865, a date mentioned earlier as an exceptional landmark in musical history, the von Carolsfelds sang Tristan and Isolde. King Mark was 'Herr Zottmayer', Kurwenal 'Herr Mitterwurzer', as they are called in the programme (which incidentally does not mention the conductor, Hans von Bülow). That was the custom of court theatres at the time; there were no first names, only Herr and Frau, the latter even for the unmarried. Another curiosity is that after von Carolsfeld's early death, *Tristan* could not be played for years, because there was no tenor who would have dared tackle the part.

On the occasion of the second historical event of Munich's Wagner years, the première of *Die Meistersinger* on 21st June 1868, the following artists were in the main rôles: Franz Betz (Hans Sachs), Kaspar Bausewein (Pogner), Gustav Hölzl (Beckmesser), Franz Nachbaur (Stolzing), Max Schlosser (David), Mathilde Mallinger (Eva), Sophie Diez (Magdalena). Two years after the first Bayreuth Festival, Munich took over *Siegfried* and put in the married couple Heinrich and Therese Vogl for the two leads. The distinguished bass Eugen Gura was in the company, and the versatile Lilli Dressler, Munich's first Nedda in *Pagliacci*. Verdi was also performed, though no more intensively than could be expected of a Wagner city. In 1877 Mathilde Weckerlin, Franz Nachbaur, Josefine Schefzky and Theodor Reichmann sang, respectively, the rôles of Aida, Radames, Amneris and Amonasro.

In 1904, when the great conductor Felix Mottl became Munich's general musical director, Heinrich Knote was the leading tenor, acclaimed as Lohengrin, Tannhäuser, Stolzing, Siegfried and Parsifal, probably one of the most accomplished singers of his age. Georg Stieglitz sang Leporello, Falstaff and Daland (*Flying Dutchman*), Friedrich Brodersen the Count in *Figaro*, Kurwenal and Sachs, to the full satisfaction of audiences and leading critics. Berta Morena, though she had a notable international career, always remained a member of the Munich Opera, where she won resounding successes. For almost thirty years the opera-house had the services of the coloratura soprano Hermine Bosetti, Munich's first Zerbinetta and first Butterfly. Other notable singers like Maud Fay, Charlotte Kuhn-Brunner, Josef Geis and Fritz Feinhals completed a company which could be matched by few cities in Europe.

There was one towering figure, Paul Bender, for several decades among the most famous of German opera-singers. The son of a pastor, born in the island of Sylt, he went via Breslau to Munich, where he quickly became the leading bass, above all the best of comic basses. He was Munich's equivalent to Vienna's Richard Mayr, but also an impeccable Lieder-singer who gave delightful renderings of Loewe's ballads. The power of his humour on the stage was overwhelming, although, like so many comedians, he was a man with great depths to his character, as can be seen from his striking self-portrait which stands out among the pictures of past great artists in the foyer of the Munich Opera.

Felix Mottl's régime came to a moving end on 21st June 1911 when he collapsed from a heart attack while conducting a performance of *Tristan*. On his deathbed he married the soprano Zdenka Fassbender, one of the best Isoldes in history. He died on 2nd July, and his widow sang Wagner rôles in memorable fashion for a further fifteen years.

It was also *Tristan* with which the new musical director, Bruno Walter, opened in 1913. He brought a number of brilliant singers to the opera-house, and in such a galaxy it is hard to know where to start. Perhaps with Maria Ivogün, born in Budapest. She made her début at Munich in 1913 as Mimì, and four years later created Ighino here in Pfitzner's masterpiece *Palestrina*. From 1925 she was a guest artist at all the world's great opera-houses, but in 1932 she retired from the stage, far too early not only for her loyal followers but for her completely intact vocal and artistic excellence. She had once said early on, 'I'll give myself twenty years', and perhaps was simply keeping to this intention. But there may have been some truth in the story that when attacked by an eye disease she vowed to give up her stage career if she did not go blind. A legendary figure in her lifetime, in 1948 she became a teacher at Vienna's Academy of Music and in 1950 at the Berlin Academy. Her pupils included Elisabeth Schwarzkopf and Rita Streich among many others. An extremely modest, simple person, she gave whole-hearted service to both her art and humanity.

Her first husband was Karl Erb, who also bears the stamp of a rare artist. Born in Ravensburg in 1877 (where he also died, in 1958), he has gone down in history above all for his Evangelist in the Bach oratorios, creating a style which has become an essential part of these works. Many who hear him today on records may be surprised to learn he was not only a singer of oratorios and Lieder but had a successful operatic career, for his Evangelists seem to be sung with a completely 'spiritual' quality, with nothing theatrical in his amazingly sweet, supple, very high and ethereal tenor. But in his younger years he sang lyrical rôles in opera, even the first Palestrina in Pfitzner's work, which seemed just made for his personality and type of voice. It seems almost like a stroke of destiny that after an accident in 1930 he was obliged to devote his future completely to concert singing.

Walter brought a married couple with him, Delia Reinhardt and Gustav Schützendorf (from a family in which several brothers were distinguished opera-singers) and discovered the very fine contralto, Sigrid Onegin. Of German parentage, born at Stockholm in 1891, she was in the première of the first version of *Ariadne auf Naxos* at Stuttgart, went to Munich in 1919 and from there began the conquest of all the great opera-houses. She was Fricka and Waltraute at Bayreuth, a notable Orpheus in Gluck's opera at the Salzburg Festivals. After 1931 she lived mainly in Switzerland, where she died in 1943. Her second husband, the doctor Fritz Pentzold, gave her a worthy memorial in his book *Alt-Rhapsodie* (Contralto Rhapsody).

Walter, indeed, very much a pupil of Mahler's in this, showed how an understanding musical director can build up young artists, develop their talent and guide them to full maturity. When he resigned his post in 1922, the same tradition was carried on by his successor, Munich's great favourite for over a decade, Hans Knappertsbusch, and after him – in hard times as well – by Clemens Krauss. One of Walter's company, discovered in the chorus, was Luise Willer. Born in Munich in 1888, she was still singing a splendid Erda in *The Ring* as late as 1955. The two main heroic tenors were Heinrich Knote, a wonderful Tannhäuser, and Otto Wolf, who as Tristan gave his utmost in soul as well as voice. Paul Kuhn made a brilliant David in *Meistersinger*, while Fritz Feinhals grew into a Wotan of mythical grandeur. Friedrich Brodersen, endowed with an unusually fine voice, often appeared five times a week, without ever sparing himself or showing signs of debility and overstrain. The baritone Emil Schipper and his equally outstanding wife, the mezzo-soprano Maria Olczewska, who reached their peak in Vienna, were for several years singing very successfully at Munich. With Felicie

Hüni-Mihaczek it was the other way round; she came from Vienna and was for twenty years a favourite of Munich audiences, developing from a coloratura singer (Queen of the Night) to a dramatic soprano who could portray the Marschallin and Arabella. Zdenka Fassbender is still remembered as one of the greatest Elektras (together with the superb Rose Pauly, a later singer of the rôle); her scenes with Anna Bahr-Mildenburg's Clytemnestra belong to operatic history. Alfred Bauberger and Josef Geis were two good baritones, and time and again there was Paul Bender, captivating and unsurpassable whether in serious parts like Sarastro and King Mark or comic ones like Osmin and the Barber of Baghdad, in the opera of that name by Peter Cornelius, another work which is seldom performed these days.

The prominent names in the next generation come almost down to our own day. Julius Patzak, born at Vienna in 1898, became one of the leading tenors of the age. He was a very thoroughly trained and extremely cultivated musician, who like Tauber and Duhan, could conduct – as he did until 1923, when he decided on a singing career. By way of the provinces (Reichenberg and Brno) he moved to Munich in 1928, and remained there until 1945. In some fields he followed in Erb's footsteps, wonderful as Palestrina and the Evangelist and, also like Erb, an accomplished Lieder-singer. He was also a full-blooded actor, who often gave his audiences powerful experience of his art. In several ways, not least vocally and to a certain extent in technique, he was similar to Tauber. In the Salzburg Festivals and at the Vienna Opera he was still singing many rôles, notably Mozart, until well into his fifties.

Julius Pölzer was his colleague in the Knappertsbusch company as heroic tenor. Like Lorenz and later Windgassen he looked the part of Siegfried besides having the right radiance of voice. There were several outstanding baritones in the company, Wilhelm Rode, Heinrich Rehkemper and Georg Hann. Rode, who joined it in 1920 at the age of thirty-three, was a guest artist in Milan, Paris, Prague and Amsterdam, and often too in Vienna, where he was at his most successful. His unusual versatility, his sombre heroic voice, combined with psychological flexibility, enabled him to create convincing character studies in rôles ranging from Scarpia to the Dutchman, from Telramund (in *Lohengrin*) to Sachs, from Wotan to Iago and Amonasro. Rehkemper, a magnificent lyric baritone, besides being a haunting Lieder-singer, specialised in elegant Italian opera and in Mozart. A critic noted that he 'spiced Papageno's dialogue with improvised additions, so that one felt transported back to the days of

Schikaneder'. Hann, also a notable Lieder-singer, sang bass as well as baritone rôles on the stage. At the Salzburg Festivals he sang Pizarro, Sarastro, Leporello and Faninal. Berthold Sterneck offered Munich audiences many beautiful performances as Kecal (*Bartered Bride*) and Baron Ochs, and an extremely amusing Zsupan in *The Gypsy Baron*. Ludwig Weber, a bass from Vienna, spent twelve important years at Munich on his way to a busy international career.

So Clemens Krauss, succeeding Knappertsbusch, found very good material in such singers as Felicie Hüni-Mihacsek, Luise Willer, Patzak, Pölzer and Hann; also in the Czechoslovakian Hildegard Ranczak, a member of the Munich company for sixteen years, who sang Salome in London, Oktavian in Paris and in 1942 the first Clairon in Strauss's last work *Capriccio*; and Hans Hermann Nissen, who developed into one of Europe's best baritones. He sang Sachs at Bayreuth, was very successful at the Met, a much sought-after guest artist in Milan, London, Paris, Stockholm, Antwerp, Brussels and Barcelona, and also appeared regularly in Vienna.

One of the most notable artists that Krauss brought in was Viorica Ursuleac, who after Dresden and Vienna achieved in Munich the climax of her career. A critic called her 'a dramatic singer with the attitude of a *grande dame*'. She was outstanding in all rôles of the lyric and dramatic range, almost unsurpassed in Strauss rôles, and triumphed as the Countess in the première of *Capriccio*, despite the sombre wartime atmosphere. She had a gloriously warm voice reminiscent of Lotte Lehmann, noble expressiveness and a flawless technique. Gertrud Rünger, after several years in Vienna and Berlin, built up a big reputation in Munich as a superb dramatic soprano. She too was a Strauss specialist, a truly demoniac Amme (*Frau ohne Schatten*), a hideously ravaged Klytämnestra in *Elektra*, but also a *Fidelio* Leonore of profound feeling. London, Amsterdam and New York were almost as strongly stirred by her tremendous dramatic power as were audiences in German-speaking countries. For many Wagner rôles such as Venus, Isolde, Brünnhilde and even Brangäne, she was considered a model of her time.

Two of her colleagues were Helena Braun, a much lighter dramatic soprano, and for younger rôles Trude Eipperle. Adele Kern, who was singing in Munich in her late teens from 1924–1926, grew into the enchanting soubrette we shall meet again shortly in Vienna. In 1938 she returned to Munich, now a glorious Zerlina, Susanna, Despina and a captivating Sophie in *Rosenkavalier*; in 1942 she handed over this rôle to Hilde Güden, whom we shall also meet again at the height of her career. Georgine von Milinkovic, a mezzo-soprano from Zürich, also set out from Munich on her path to international fame.

The tenors included Peter Anders, Horst Taubmann – the first Flamand in *Capriccio*, but obliged to give up a very promising career prematurely owing to loss of voice – and Günther Treptow, who specialised in Wagner parts, sang Siegmund at Bayreuth and later went to Berlin. Among the baritones, Krauss discovered the young Hans Hotter, made him the Commander in Strauss's *Friedenstag* in 1938 and Olivier in *Capriccio* in 1942; this was before he became world-famous and one of the leading artistic personalities of our time. The Hungarian Alexander Sved, after decisive development under the guidance of Weingartner in Vienna, sang in a great many Munich performances. For ten years this rich, lyrical baritone, flowing in purest beauty of tone, delighted the Met and was sought after by the greatest opera-houses in rôles such as Hans Sachs, but also for Verdi. It was a voice slightly reminiscent of Leonard Warren, his great American colleague. Among other fine singers of the thirties at Munich, I would mention Karl Kronenberg, Walter Höfermeyer and Hermann Uhde, the last-named destined for a hard-working career all over the world after the war.

The opera-house was destroyed in an air-raid at the beginning of October 1943. It took twenty years before it was restored in its old splendour.

Vienna

Hans Gregor was much criticised as an opera director in his day. Successor of Mahler and Weingartner, he had the difficult task of bringing the opera-house through the First World War and the end of the monarchy into the new era. The magnificent theatre seemed almost outsize for 1919, now that it was in the capital of a small state suffering from grim poverty. But Gregor can be remembered with gratitude for three artists in his company whose names were enough to keep Vienna's reputation as a leading operatic city for a further two decades; Maria Jeritza, Lotte Lehmann and Alfred Piccaver.

Maria Jeritza was the last *prima donna assoluta* before Callas. A working-class girl from Brno, her mother-tongue Czech, she made her stage début under her real name, and the Viennese form of her Christian name, as Mizzi Jedlitschka. With her natural talent – or genius – she won sensational triumphs when still very young in both opera and operetta. Max Reinhardt brought her in to sing the first Ariadne in his production of Richard Strauss's opera of that name at

Stuttgart, on 24th October 1912. She was then twenty-five, and
dazzlingly beautiful. Rainer Simon, with his keen eye and ear, took
her to Vienna's Volksoper, where she sang Elsa in *Lohengrin*, Elisabeth in *Tannhäuser* and Agathe in *Freischütz*. An inspiring quality
radiated from her, which was more than the effect of her golden
hair, her open Bohemian face with the broad cheek-bones, sensual
lips and gleaming white teeth. She was a strange mixture of 'sweet
Viennese girl' (in Schnitzler's phrase) and vamp – a word then unknown in this sense. Nature had given her unlimited ability for
transforming herself, she could present innocence and sincerity as
perfectly as extreme sexiness and wild passion. Twenty years later
she might perhaps have become a Mae West or a Marilyn Monroe in
Hollywood, neglecting some of her stronger talents. As things were,
however, she luckily became an opera singer and, thanks to her
genuine radiance, a true prima donna. This term fitted her as it fits
only the really great women singers; not because there were scandals
about her, or because she kindled the fantasies of the public, but because on stage she was a dominating figure who exercised immense
fascination far beyond the mere effect of her singing.

In 1913 she sang in the Viennese première of *The Girl of the Golden
West* – for which she was brought from the Volksoper to the Court
Opera – and Puccini, who was present, called her with conviction his
'best Minnie'. But that was a rôle made to measure – plucky, smart
(in the American sense), as good as the men at all the accomplish-
ments of the Wild West, but also the girl of all their dreams, strongly
feminine and touchingly affectionate. Jeritza was perhaps also Puccini's best Tosca, for she had all the qualities the composer could
have desired for this picture of a radiant diva and a self-sacrificing
love. She sang the great aria at the end of the second act, 'Vissi d'arte',
crouching low, in fact almost lying down; and as Santuzza in
Cavalleria Rusticana she fell headlong from a high step. These were
not movements and poses subtly thought out, but the spontaneous
action of a born stage artist. Her creative power was crowned by her
luminous, sensual, stirring voice, which was capable of the whole
range of dramatic expression.

The Met, of course, were soon bidding for such a star, and in her
prime Jeritza, like many other great singers, belonged more to the
New World than the Old. But she repeatedly gave the Viennese
public the joy of having her back. Many years after the Second
World War, still majestic and even beautiful despite her age, she
made a farewell appearance in Vienna, still possessing the radiance
with which she had held people spell-bound for over half a century.

With Alfred Piccaver too, Gregor gave the Viennese public – who called him 'Pikki' – a favourite for many years. He was born in England in 1883, of Spanish parentage. It is strange that his world reputation did not approach Caruso's, for there can scarcely have been such a soft, beautiful, noble, yet very masculine and expressive tenor. He went to Vienna with an Italian seasonal company, and was at once engaged. For his unique popularity with the opera-fanatics, which in Vienna meant most of the population, he could have been called the uncrowned king of the Opera. Tall and burly, he dominated the stage, although he was never a powerful actor. He looked more like a 'père noble', not the passionate lover his rôle demanded. But his voice had just that quality and, when he began to sing, it was clear (as required by the plot) no soprano could resist him. There was such a seductive sweetness in that voice, a tear, a dark melancholy, an innate nobility, so that to hear it was an unforgettable experience.

It was also extremely sensitive, and he refused to sing more often than was usual with principals; the remark 'have you fixed your indispositions for next season yet?' was much quoted in connection with Pikki. He also had mediocre evenings when, although he was still very good, one had the feeling that he was not giving his utmost. But when he did give it, perhaps swept along by a great partner like Lotte Lehmann, he could rarely be surpassed by any other tenor of his time. He was then an ideal Cavaradossi, whose love scenes were as convincing as his song of defiance hurled into the face of the detested tyrant, and whose dying aria, 'E lucevan le stelle', touched every heart. His duet with Butterfly caught so fully the magic of the Japanese night, with all its fragrance of flowers, that one felt really transported into a distant land. For pure singing, even Caruso could not give a more perfect rendering of 'On with the Motley', though he was, of course, superior to Piccaver as an actor. And as for Des Grieux's dream in Manon, probably only Gigli could have sung it with such ethereal, other-worldly, truly dreamlike beauty.

Alfred Piccaver, darling of the public and teenagers' idol through the hardest times – war, revolution, hunger, inflation, crises, unemployment, political hatred, rebellion – quietly left Vienna in 1938 when Austria ceased to exist. Retired except for periodic successful concerts, he lived in London, and in 1955 went back to Vienna as a grey-haired guest of honour at the opening of the restored opera-house. More or less unrecognised among all the new stars, he sat modestly in the background of a box. Three years later he died in Vienna, again 'his' city where an immense procession escorted him to his last rest.

The third bright star of Viennese opera at that time was from Prussia, but became grafted to Vienna and its opera even more firmly than Piccaver, her partner on so many memorable evenings – Lotte Lehmann. She began her career in 1910, at the age of twenty-two, in Hamburg, as Elsa in *Lohengrin*. Four years later Gregor brought her to Vienna, where she remained for almost twenty-five years, supremely honoured, admired and loved. For everything about her was lovable; the pervasive warmth and sincerity of a balanced, flowing soprano voice which could radiate joy and suffering alike, her fine personality, to which all meanness was completely alien, and which in 1938 impelled her to the most painful of renunciations, to leave Vienna of her own free will. She felt nothing would be the same there, and she did not want to condone even implicitly by her presence the persecution of her friends and colleagues on political or racial grounds.

To return to her earlier career; on 4th October 1916, in the middle of the war, Vienna's Court Opera experienced an evening of incomparable brilliance. It was the première of the second and now definitive version of *Ariadne auf Naxos*, with the three women's rôles sung by unsurpassable artists: Ariadne by Maria Jeritza, the Composer by Lotte Lehmann, Zerbinetta by Selma Kurz. Three years later, when Lotte Lehmann sang the Empress in the Vienna Opera's next Strauss première, *Frau ohne Schatten*, Austria no longer had an emperor. But the opera-house was still standing, and on its façade the plaque inscribed in gold ('Kaiser Franz Joseph I – 1869') was not removed; indeed it was carefully and lovingly restored in 1955 after Austria had been a republic for nearly forty years.

Gregor was succeeded by the conductor Franz Schalk, who for a time was joint director of the State Opera, as it was now called, with Richard Strauss. So under the composer's direction his works were given magnificent productions. Jeritza made a primitive Salome; Rose Pauly, with immense dramatic power and conviction, an outstanding Elektra; and Lotte Lehmann took possession of the Marschallin, a rôle which seemed made for her and with which she is still identified by opera connoisseurs today, however brilliant her successors. She was every inch the Viennese aristocratic lady, but also a woman *entre deux ages*, disappointed though never embittered by life, who kept her full power of profound love and displayed it in a moving blend of melancholy, superiority, worldly wisdom and resignation. Two unforgettable moments in Lotte Lehmann's performance were the Marschallin's monologue and aria as she looks in the mirror and recognises the inexorable march of time, and the cadences in her voice when she tells Oktavian how she sometimes gets up in the middle of the night and stops all the clocks in the house.

Schalk and Strauss as directors were followed by other big names; Krauss, Weingartner again, and then, though without the title of director, Bruno Walter. The company contained Lehmann, Jeritza, the magnificent Selma Kurz; two new tenors besides Piccaver, the Norwegian Karl Oestvig and the Hungarian Koloman von Pataky. Oestvig was a good Wagner singer with a heroic voice, Pataky a highly trained bel canto artist at the beginning of a world career, splendid in Mozart operas and very good in works of the old Italian opera which needed extreme delicacy of melodic line.

Mozart was a speciality, too, of a young singer also destined for world fame, Elisabeth Schumann. Richard Strauss often accompanied her in Lieder evenings, and she was as brilliant an interpreter of his songs as she was of Schubert's. She was guest artist at all the great opera-houses, for eighteen years a member of the Met, accepted as supreme portrayer of classic Mozart characters such as Zerlina, Blondchen, Susanna and Despina. She was also part of the almost 'dream' cast of *Rosenkavalier*, singing Sophie to Lotte Lehmann's Marschallin, Richard Mayr's Baron Ochs and Maria Olczewska's Oktavian.

The company had its fine women's voices for the most dramatic rôles as well. In 1919 Helena Wildbrunn returned to her native Vienna, after making a name as a contralto in Dortmund, then in Stuttgart and Berlin. She was Kundry at La Scala, a Wagner heroine in many other cities too, and also in the Vienna Opera's sensational guest tour of South America just after the First World War, the first visit to this sub-continent by a high-ranking company. She remained a member of the Opera till 1932 and then taught for many years at the Viennese Academy of Music. Meanwhile a worthy successor had emerged in Maria Nemeth, who had been brought to Vienna from the Budapest Opera. She had one of the most powerful women's voices ever heard, her high notes rang out over chorus and orchestra. Two special events are associated with her, one happy and one sad. Shortly after the world première of Puccini's posthumous *Turandot* at La Scala, Vienna had its first performances of the opera. Schalk had arranged two festive evenings for this; on the first the voices of Lotte Lehmann and Leo Slezak showed the art of singing in full maturity, but on the second, they were outdone, at least vocally, by Maria Nemeth and the young Pole Jan Kiepura, who lacked their artistic mastery but whose sensational power produced tumultuous applause.

On that evening Kiepura laid the basis for his world career. He had no finesse as a singer, but a voice of rare penetration, and his shattering high B, B flat and C could have brought down the walls of Jericho. He was very much a child of nature, natural in his acting and his singing, unconcerned with conventions of speech or traditions. If the audience demanded it, he would sing a few Lieder long after the final curtain; or, when forbidden to do this, on the roof of his car outside the stage door. In Vienna and many other cities there was a real Kiepura craze. He sang as guest artist in most of the important opera-houses, became a celebrated film-star, married his screen partner, the delightful Martha Eggert, and sang every evening for three years at a theatre on New York's Broadway in Lehár's *Merry Widow*.

The second incident involving Maria Nemeth was in 1934, when she was chosen to sing the soprano solo in the solemn Requiem for Dollfuss, the murdered Austrian Chancellor. Toscanini was conducting, and in the final rehearsal he was dissatisfied with something in her singing and worked himself up into one of his legendary outbursts of rage, the full force of which can be imagined only by those who had first-hand experience of them. It lasted for several minutes, the wretched singer fainted and for quite a while no one dared to rush to her help. Then another soprano was needed, and the Requiem had to be postponed.

Vienna found some notable new baritones. Hans Duhan made an enchanting Papageno, one of the most engaging in a long line of superb Viennese Papagenos which stretches to our own day, a brilliant Count Almaviva and an artistically first-class Don Giovanni; Duhan was also a fine Lieder-singer. He stayed a member of the Vienna Opera from 1914 to 1940, and afterwards as conductor and teacher kept the closest of associations with the city. The extent of its attachment to him came out in the honours he received on his eightieth birthday. His colleague or rival, Alfred Jerger – from Brno like Slezak and Jeritza – was no less versatile, singing, acting and conducting. He was a splendid character actor, completely in his part as John the Baptist or Scarpia, as Don Giovanni or as Nigger Jonny (in Krenek's *Jonny spielt auf*), as Sachs or as Beckmesser – seldom within the range of the same artist. Not having a specially strong voice, he made a virtue out of necessity by beautiful diction and an unmistakably individual style.

Franz Höbling, a prominent actor, also made periodical excursions into opera, where he sang the Dutchman remarkably well. Emil Schipper, the darkest and probably the most powerful of Vienna's baritone voices at the time, was a doctor of law when he began to have his voice trained in Milan. By way of Prague, Linz, the Vienna Volksoper and Munich, he moved to the State Opera in 1922, just in time to go on the South American tour mentioned earlier. He made an impressive Sachs and Rigoletto, his Carlos de Vargas in *The Force of Destiny* was as haunting as his Orestes in *Elektra*; 'Ich muss hier warten' carries a special echo in the memory as sung by that towering figure standing near the palace and foreshadowing vengeance on Klytämnestra. Josef von Manowarda was also extremely fine in this rôle, in fact his very dark bass in that short scene sent shudders down the back, whereas other interpreters of Orestes had a concept of the part which at least momentarily kept the brighter emotion of a brother's love for his sister. Manowarda took part in several important new works; in 1919, in the world première of *Frau ohne Schatten*, he was a magnificent Barak both for singing and acting, and in the Austrian première of Berg's *Wozzeck* he gave a deeply felt performance in the title rôle.

Among low female voices, I have already spoken of Gertrud Rünger from Munich, who often sang in Vienna, and have mentioned Maria Olczewska as a member of the *Rosenkavalier* super-cast with Lehmann, Schumann and Mayr. For his first contralto, Schalk engaged the beautiful Hungarian, Rosette Anday – a Carmen 'fatale' and also a seductive Delilah – who remained loyal to the house for forty years. How strange that seems today, when famous singers seldom have an artistic home and dash from one place to another as guest artists.

Although theatre managers had headaches over the shortage of good tenors, a leading opera-house still managed to collect a number of strong names. Piccaver was there, the indestructible Slezak, a wonderful voice until well into the nineteen-thirties, and there were glorious evenings with Tauber. Trajan Grosavescu moved over in 1925 from the Volksoper to the State Opera, sang himself into the front rank of tenors, but two years later was shot dead by a jealous wife. When Oestvig, married to the soprano Maria Rajdl, went to Munich about this time, his heroic tenor rôles were taken over by Richard Schubert, a fine musician with a glorious voice, and Gunnar Graarud, who was Bayreuth's Tristan, Siegmund, Siegfried and Parsifal. William Wernigk, one of the opera-house's most valued and loyal mainstays, was an outstanding character tenor, a singer and actor of great artistry, excellent in a great many rôles from Monostatos (*Magic Flute*) to Mime (*Rheingold* and *Siegfried*).

Although for a long time the house had no women singers in the same class as Lotte Lehmann and Jeritza, there were a whole lot of admirable voices in the between-war years, the sisters Konetzni among the foremost. Anni sang high-drama rôles with a powerful voice and was one of the important Wagner singers of her time. Hilde was more lyrical, though her warm and beautiful voice was capable of dramatic expression as well. She sang many Lehmann rôles, and only the unfairness of comparing her with the incomparable Lotte slightly reduced her well-earned fame, which, like her sister's, led to many international tours as guest artist. Vera Schwarz was an artist of first-class ability, whether she sang lyrico-dramatic rôles in opera, or with Tauber as partner brought unusual vocal splendour to Lehár operetta. She was Oktavian at a Salzburg Festival, Lady Macbeth at Glyndebourne, and later went to live in the United States, where she appeared in various opera-houses. Finally she returned to Vienna, and died there in 1964. Margit Schenker-Angerer, a 'lady of the company', became overnight a surprisingly accomplished opera-singer, who brought great charm to her singing and playing of lyrical soprano parts; she remains in the memory as Dorota in Weinberger's delightful *Schwanda*. Luise Helletsgruber and Aenne Michalsky completed one of the most notable companies in the world of that period.

The curtain fell on this act of Viennese opera in gloom and violence. After the Nazi occupation and the Second World War it went up again, with many things destroyed and many changes; but still the same love of music, opera and singing.

Berlin's Golden Twenties

Few cities at any time can have had so varied and exciting a musical life as Berlin in its 'Golden Twenties'. It was gripped by an opera fever which can scarcely have been known since the earliest days of the *genre* in the Italian cities of the late Renaissance; while operetta, too, reached a peak unknown since the founding era of Johann Strauss, the Waltz King. Fritzi Massary was the brightest star shining exclusively in operetta, which also had the service of great operatic artists like Tauber, Vera Schwarz, Gitta Alpar and many others. As for opera, there were performances nightly at three splendid theatres, with leading impresarios such as Tietjen, Schillings, Ebert, Reinhardt and Piscator, and under the greatest of conductors – Leo Blech, Erich Kleiber, Bruno Walter, Richard Strauss, Otto Klemperer, Fritz Stiedry and Paul Breisach. Premières took place of pioneering works like *Wozzeck*, *Dreigroschenoper* (Threepenny Opera), *Die*

Bürgschaft, Christoph Colomb and equally pioneering productions, especially by Klemperer. The singers of the time were no less notable.

One outstanding personality, Michael Bohnen, left for New York in 1922, but he returned very often as a guest artist and the Berlin public always regarded him as 'their' Bohnen. Excellent both as bass and baritone, he had deep psychological insight, so that the press had long called him the 'German Chaliapin', and he was their realised ideal of the singing actor. A Berlin paper of those days said, 'Before Bohnen has even appeared on the stage, you can feel that he is near, some secret fluid radiates from the darkness.' It was the inexplicable magic of a tremendous stage personality, which did not depend on the quality of his singing; the magic was working before you heard the first note. He reigned for years in Berlin's operatic world. When he and Tauber sang the duet from *The Bartered Bride*, the audience applauded tumultuously until it gained the encore desired – and with the bonus of a splendid surprise, for the two artists, obviously carried away by sheer delight in singing and acting, gave an improvised rendering with completely different nuances. Born at Cologne in 1887, Bohnen became director of the Berlin State Opera in the very difficult period of reconstruction after the Second World War.

Helge Roswaenge, born at Copenhagen in 1895, unlike the Met star Melchior, his countryman, achieved most of his successes in German theatres; in his best days he was a member of five German-speaking opera-houses at once, Berlin, Vienna, Munich, Hamburg and Dresden. Member, not guest artist! That meant about two hundred performances a year, a figure which sounds terrifying for any ordinary tenor. But he had wonderful vocal facility, and could sing Mozart with as much stylistic purity as Verdi, besides possessing a freely vibrating, effortless high D. He kept his voice until he was quite an old man, then made his comprehensive knowledge accessible to singing devotees through lessons, and also by writing a manual.

Marcel Wittrisch was another favourite of Berlin, and far beyond, thanks to his extremely popular recordings, for which his tenor seemed particularly adapted. Born at Antwerp in 1901 of German parents, he went to Berlin via Halle and Brunswick. His range extended from Mozart to Wagner, and in 1937 he sang Lohengrin at Bayreuth. He gave up opera fairly early, and was very successful in operettas, films and concerts.

Among the artists who appeared regularly at Berlin, I have already mentioned Tauber and Slezak, Joseph Mann, Hermann Jadlowker and Karl Erb, and Maria Ivogün, for decades Germany's leading coloratura singer, whom we have already met in Munich. Towards the end of her career she was drawn quite often to lyric rôles in which the human message takes a more important place than coloratura virtuosity. Her voice too, as almost always happens, had become bigger and more expressive especially in the lower register. So Berlin audiences experienced an almost new sort of Ivogün evening, in which the famous artist sang Mignon, for instance, a rôle with strong inner feeling especially in the middle range; while the fantastic coloratura of the merry Philine went to a young Greek girl called Margherita Perras, a star just beginning to rise in the operatic firmament. Combining a sweet and high soprano, brilliantly trained, with an enchanting appearance and natural, attractive acting, she soon found the world's opera-houses opening for her, from Vienna to Buenos Aires, from Covent Garden to Glyndebourne and Salzburg. Among her memorable parts were Constanze, Rosina, Zerbinetta and Violetta (*Traviata*).

Two other favourites of Berlin audiences were the lyric soprano Maria Müller and Jarmila Novotna. The former, a native of Bohemia, a superb Elsa in *Lohengrin* and Elisabeth in *Tannhäuser*, had a warmth of voice reminiscent of Lotte Lehmann and the radiance of an artist who was deeply inside her rôle. Why she was completely forgotten after the Second World War is hard to understand. Novotna was also a Czech, of great physical beauty, who with extreme simplicity sang an ideal Marenka in *The Bartered Bride*, a notable Gilda, a touching Mimì, and a very pure Eurydice in Gluck's opera. Lehár had her services as his first Giuditta. She later completed her world career, which also included films, in the United States.

Leo Schützendorf, from a family of good singers mentioned earlier, sang the first *Wozzeck* on 14th December 1925, in a highly controversial première which ended in triumph. He was a baritone who came from operetta and returned to it. Willi Domgraf-Fassbänder, another celebrated baritone, again thanks especially to records, who was at Berlin from 1923 to 1925 and from 1930 to 1946, was wonderful in Mozart parts from Don Giovanni to Papageno, which he sang at Glyndebourne and Salzburg, and also an extremely mellifluous and noble baritone in Italian rôles, with a legato few can match in our times.

Theodor Scheidl, a heroic baritone, made his début in 1911 when he was twenty-one, and by 1914 was already at Bayreuth, where in the course of many years he sang Kurwenal, Donner (*Rheingold*) and both Amfortas and Klingsor in *Parsifal*. From 1921 to 1932 he was a member of the Berlin State Opera. In 1931 this company gained another fine baritone in Jaro Prohaska, born in Vienna in 1891. He was a soloist in the Vienna Boys' Choir, but was called up and then spent four years as a prisoner of war, before finally starting his singing career in Lübeck. His rôles at Bayreuth included the Dutchman, Telramund, Wotan and Wanderer in *The Ring* and a touching Hans Sachs, beautifully sung, which was one of the most polished performances of his or any generation.

Heinrich Schlusnus, who in 1915 made his first stage appearance as the Herald in *Lohengrin,* only a few months after being wounded in the War, had his début at Berlin two years later as Wolfram. He was there for nearly thirty years, became one of the city's greatest favourites and one of the most mature artists of his time. With his wide range of sensitivity, he had an immense repertoire in opera, and was also a masterly Lieder-singer, especially Schubert and Hugo Wolf. He sang Rigoletto several times, but gave over 2,000 Lieder recitals. The Americans called him the German Battistini, the highest possible tribute to the perfection of his art. But he had a great gift for characterisation as well and a clarity of diction which rarely fits in with the bel canto principle. He died in June 1952, the day after singing one of his favourite songs, 'Im Abendroth', in a concert at Frankfurt: 'O wie schön ist deine Welt, Vater . . .' (how lovely is your world, Father).

The Hungarian soprano Gitta Alpar started in Budapest, where she sang a brilliant Gilda in 1925. Two years later she made a hit in Berlin as Rosina and the Queen of the Night, but in 1930 she went over to operetta. She was well suited to it in figure and temperament, and became an operetta star in Vienna and later in the United States.

The Wagner baritone Friedrich Schorr was also from Hungary. From 1923 to 1933 he made many appearances every year in Berlin opera-houses. He was a majestic Wotan; a mighty ruler in Valhalla, he was often a head taller than his partner and with his dark, noble voice brought the sense of a higher world. His Wotan became a universal figure of all religions rather than a purely Germanic one. Like Hotter after him, he radiated the deepest of tragic feelings, and few have given such an awe-inspiring presentation of the end of the world. He was also a splendid Hans Sachs, made a stirring figure of Günther, often dismissed as a weakling, and as the Dutchman brought out the infinite drama of homelessness and eternal searching. In 1933 Schorr had to leave Germany, but Vienna enjoyed his accomplished performances for five years, and he then settled down in New York, where he had been a member of the Met since 1924. He died in 1953 on his estate in Farmington, Connecticut.

Many would say that the finest bass of his generation was Alexander Kipnis, a Russian. Born in the Ukraine in 1891, he began his career in Hamburg and in 1919 went to Berlin, where he remained until 1935. There is scarcely any important opera-house where Kipnis did not sing, throughout Europe, in North and South America, in Australia and New Zealand, and from 1940 he was a member of the Met. A bel canto singer even in the lowest register, he had a beauty of tone which cannot be described in words. The melancholy of his native steppes and the heroism of forgotten times vibrated in his voice. His Boris Godunov, though different from Chaliapin's, was a worthy successor, and he sang Sarastro with a rare beauty, nobility and solemnity.

Among the fine female voices, we have already met Helene Wildbrunn in Vienna, which shared possession of her with Berlin. Another was Lotte Schöne, also from Vienna, with her extremely sweet lyric soprano, which sounded enchanting in Mozart rôles. She became London's first Liù in *Turandot*, and was strikingly successful in France as Debussy's Mélisande, a rôle in which few foreigners shine. Maria Hussa, yet another of Viennese origin, had two highlights to her career; in 1920 she was the first Marietta in the première of Korngold's *Toten Stadt* in Hamburg, and in the same city seven years later the first Rautendelein in Respighi's poetic setting of Gerhard Hauptmann's fairy opera *Die versunkene Glocke*. In the years between she was at Berlin, where her lyric and dramatic soprano voice was very highly regarded.

The singers mentioned in this section are only a few of the important names closely connected with Berlin during those Golden Twenties, and almost every illustrious singer of the time went to that city. I cannot go into the deeper reasons why there should have been such an immense concentration of talent and achievement in that particular place, manifesting decisively the spirit of the age, but certainly it was an example of brief glory before decline, before the barbarities of the Nazi régime, which were followed by the war and general destruction.

Opera becomes International

Idealists tried to keep opera going, while it was still materially possible; to drown the noise of war with beautiful voices and to soothe shattered nerves and broken hearts with glorious music. But when the war became total, air-raids completed the work of physical destruction, so that by the end – except in Switzerland, that island of peace – all the finest opera-houses in Central Europe lay in ruins, Vienna and Berlin, Hamburg and Munich, Cologne and Frankfurt, Dresden, Leipzig and Warsaw, Genoa and Milan.

Even with their shrines destroyed, devotees of opera kept their cult alive, to make possible the tremendous revival after the war which would have been beyond the most sanguine hopes. This was partly due to the unprecedented technical discoveries, no longer devoted to destructive processes, which now opened up equally unprecedented new perspectives. The mass media, already increasing in importance between the wars, made an enormous advance, which was perhaps of special benefit to music. Recording made a decisive break-through as a valid element in musical artistry. Slowing down the rate of revolutions stopped the distracting needle noise, new horizons of high fidelity appeared in both reception and reproduction, and the possibilities of stereo were revealed, with a two-channel reproduction through separate speakers giving a far more life-like effect. Listening to records became a real aesthetic pleasure, which cannot of course replace the direct experience of hearing the sound as played or sung, but has enough intrinsic merits and advantages to contribute a good deal to modern musical life. There is also the tape-recorder with its potential for perfect reproduction of music; today's radio and television would be unthinkable without it, and through it the private music-lover too can provide himself with hours of pure joy.

Finally, we had television, the most powerful of all the mass media, which some authorities have called the most decisive discovery for civilisation since printing. This is no place to consider its general importance, we need only look at its consequences for music. A singer in 1900 during a long and intensive professional career could be seen and heard on average by a million people, assuming that he sang a thousand times before a thousand people each time. By 1935 he would reach ten or a hundred times that number, though only with the sound of his voice, not with the other components such as his acting and his whole artistic personality; neither the radio, which brought about this miracle, nor records could transmit those elements, at best it could offer some intimations of them. But in our age visual experience is predominating more and more over what is heard or read.

The singer of today has no limits to his audience; television can transmit him to countless millions, can allow them to hear him singing but also watch him acting, as if they were actually in the best seats of an opera-house. Or even better in some respects, for the television camera can see events on the stage in close-ups and even double images, both of which are impossible for the eye of the opera-goer. It is futile to ask whether opera, for instance, can be transposed for such a mass audience without damage to its inherent values. We cannot put back the clock; this is the way things have developed, and the only positive attitude is to make the best of it. The art of singing has suddenly become a commodity delivered to the houses of the most untrained and, perhaps for the time being, the most insensitive, for the sound of it is very often quite strange to them. The names of singers which formerly meant something only to the initiated have often now become household words. Without any doubt a new age has begun for singing as well.

The nations have also come closer to each other, which has had its obvious effects on the musical life of our time. Opera has always been an international art-form, where national and linguistic barriers are easier to break down than elsewhere, and the famous prima donnas and *primi uomini* have always been welcome in other countries. That was mainly due to the predominance of the Italian language and style, which opened up the way to a real internationalism. The young singer of today sings in several languages almost as if he had been brought up to be multi-lingual, whereas two generations ago it was an accomplishment which had to be laboriously acquired. This cannot and should not wipe out local and national individuality, but it can help to bring a sense of world-wide solidarity and belonging together.

In the first centuries of opera everything was sung in Italian. One of the important things about *Die Entführung aus dem Serail* was that Mozart composed it for a German text.* Indeed national barriers began to go up from the rise of German Opera with *Entführung* and then *Fidelio*, with Weber, Marschner, Lortzing and finally Wagner; from the rise of French Opera with Berlioz, Cherubini, Méhul, Gounod, Halévy, Thomas, Bizet and Meyerbeer; from the founding of 'National' operas in Russia and in Polish and Czech opera-houses. All this certainly provided big new possibilities for the singers of these countries, previously at a serious disadvantage compared to the Italians, but it also set up a new obstacle, the obstacle of language.

Today the great opera-houses of the world are going over more and more to having works sung in their original language. This had always been a basic principle in both North and South America, at the Met, for instance, and at the Teatro Colón; but that was easy enough for them, because they simply drew their singers for Italian

* *Translator's note:* In England it is still referred to more commonly by its Italian name, *Il Seraglio*.

operas from Italy, for German operas from German-speaking countries, for French operas from France and so on. But today, what was an exception is now the rule; young opera-singers in all countries are trained to master the standard repertoire in the original languages. Even in the past great stars had to be skilled linguists unless they came from Italy – the Italians had so long regarded opera as their domain that they scarcely sang rôles in other languages. The stars of the last century spoke their mother tongue and Italian, and sang in both, but the most important rôles in French opera did get established in their original language. *Carmen*, for instance, became sung in French more and more frequently, except in Italy, where the idea still obstinately persisted that Italian was the only language in the world for singing.

Caruso, however, conditioned by living for a long time in New York, was more 'international', as can be seen from an identification form in his own hand-writing, dated 27th September 1912:

(Name)	Enrico Caruso
(Place of Birth)	Naples
(Date of Birth)	25 Fevrier 1873
(Country of Birth)	Italy
(Profession)	Artiste Lyrique
	K.K. oestr. Kammersänger★
	K. Preussischer Kammersänger†

So he was mixing three languages, indeed four, considering his very Italian name. 'Artiste Lyrique', which he put for his profession, was the same term of course, with slightly different forms, as was used for opera-singers in all Latin languages, as opera was a lyric art and an opera-house was a Théâtre Lyrique, teatro lirico and so on.

To sing works in the original language, once the initial language barrier has been overcome, has two advantages for the singer; even the best translation of an opera (and most are not really that well translated!) cannot reach the unity of words and music which exists in the original, and it is also easier with this practice to be a guest artist in other countries. The German tenor, for instance, who is used to singing Alfredo in Italian in German cities, can now step into the rôle at short notice in London, Paris or Barcelona, which he could not have done if he always sang in his own language.

Having the repertoire so international makes things difficult for

* *Translator's note:* Kaiserlicher-Königlicher (Imperal-Royal) Austrian Court Singer. Austro-Hungary was both an Empire and a Monarchy.

† *Translator's note:* Kaiserliche (Imperial Prussian) Court Singer.

audiences, however. The average member of the audience, unless well prepared beforehand, loses much of the opera's plot and meaning, and in comic operas like Mozart's *Figaro* and *Così*, Rossini's *Barber of Seville*, Verdi's *Falstaff* or Puccini's *Gianni Schicchi*, verbal jokes and puns miss their effect. A few years ago Rolf Liebermann, manager of the Hamburg State Opera, sent a questionnaire to the subscribing members of his opera-house, to find out whether they preferred to hear foreign works in the original or in German. There was a very good response and, interestingly enough, a clear though not overwhelming majority voted for the original language.

In our time the desired internationalism of opera has received a further considerable impulse – from the composers. As early as the nineteen-twenties Stravinsky wrote his *Oedipus Rex* to a Latin libretto, on which a narrator comments in the language of the country where it is being performed; so only the narrator has to be changed when the work is being transplanted to a different country. About ten years afterwards Orff composed his *Carmina Burana* in a mixture of vulgar Latin and mediaeval German. Werner Henze composed for Italian texts as well as German, in the tradition of Mozart, who wrote fluently in both languages and in the last year of his life was working simultaneously on the Italian *La Clemenza di Tito* and the German *Zauberflöte*.

A third factor in the development of internationalism in singing today, which puts the other two in the shade and also anything from former times, is the composition of opera companies. Nationals from a dozen different countries are often working harmoniously together not only in the great opera-houses but in medium-sized and quite small ones. The Tower-of-Babel atmosphere which prevails nowadays in an opera-house gives place in the evening to a unified performance. Here, in fact, the highest degree of world-wide cooperation has been attained.

The speed of travel, of course, has also contributed to the same development. Actors and singers were always in a profession which did a lot of travelling; but actors were usually stopped at the frontier of their own language, whereas for singers their audiences were the whole world. Geographically, of course, this is a big exaggeration, but it reaches the nub of the matter, the internationalism of music. Today, with airlines making thousands of flights to all corners of the earth, the singer's mobility has attained a new peak and, as mentioned earlier, he is often chasing almost continuously from city to city, even from continent to continent. As Oscar Melba wrote in a satirical article in *Oper 1967*, 'Met a splendid opera company at

Frankfurt Airport. Leopold Ludwig was flying to Rome, Hillebrecht to Berlin, Miss Jones to Vienna, Zeffirelli to Milan, Windgassen to Paris, del Monaco to Stuttgart, Kuchta to San Francisco, Fischer-Dieskau to Amsterdam, Talvela to Naples, Sutherland to Sidney . . .' This is the picture of the decades after the Second World War, which I shall try to describe in detail in the next chapter.

However, despite this round-the-world chase, the greater part of a musician's life is probably concerned with records, radio, films and television, which often make travel unnecessary. And even then opera-house and concert-hall remain, or have so far remained, the singer's true artistic home. This may be attributed partly to the custom or tradition of centuries, but partly to his need – which is unlikely to change – to maintain personal contact with his audience as the one constant in the flux of circumstance.

VII

Opera All Over the World

New Opera-Houses

Opera occupies a very large part of this book, because most of the great singers have been chiefly connected with it. Many of them, of course, have also been fine artists in the concert-hall, and today the singer is often working in broadcasting, recording and television studios. But the opera-house is still very often his main scene of action, and to start with I will deal with the buildings.

The massive new interest in opera after the Second World War, during which so many fine opera-houses had been destroyed, led to problems which had never before arisen, at least in so intense a form. It is remarkable how often opera-houses have burnt down, even in peace time. Most of the fires, luckily, have been by night, so that there was no threat to human life, although one gruesome exception was the fire at the Ringtheater in Vienna in December 1888, with its thousands of fatal casualties. But when fire destroyed an opera-house, it was usually rebuilt without much debate, and in the style of the old building. It would not only be serving the same purpose but the same more or less feudal society, symbolised by the boxes in which the higher social strata could keep their distance from the lower. These opera-houses were the show-pieces of a society based on the luxury and comfort of its ruling classes. Merely to go through the portals gave the feeling of leaving ordinary life behind; the feeling increased with climbing the wide marble steps, and reached its climax in the foyer, furnished in the style of the most elegant *salon*, and the auditorium. This was generally in rich colours, especially gold and red, often with ivory tints in between. Chandeliers of the finest glass enhanced the impression of being in a different world. There was a festive atmosphere, which not only gave the audience a sense of great well-being but prepared them for the pleasures in store, raising their minds from the plains of the humdrum to the high peaks of culture and art.

Even after the First World War, when the opera-houses began opening their doors increasingly to wider strata, there was a discrepancy between the splendour of the buildings and the social condition of many of the new audiences. Indeed the contrast went deeper than that, extending to the art-form itself, suddenly confronted with people outside the tradition and culture and perhaps without the psychological capacity for appreciating its conventions.

Before 1914, indeed, there were pioneers experimenting in theatrical design, notably Mahler's colleague, Alfred Roller, and above all Max Reinhardt, who started a modern form of 'theatre in the round' and an extensive use of the apron stage, eliminating the proscenium arch, so that a soliloquy from an actor or an aria from a singer would have more direct impact on the audience. Reinhardt produced his Salzburg *Everyman* after the fashion of the old Mystery Plays, outside the grandiose façade of the cathedral, and the first part of *Faust* (at Hofmannsthal's suggestion) in the grounds of a well-known riding-school, with an almost natural setting. In 1934 John Christie founded the Glyndebourne Festival, performing Mozart operas in the theatre he had built adjoining his house, with Carl Ebert as producer and Fritz Busch as conductor. More and more experiments were made with open-air productions, different types of stage and any new forms which could overcome the rigid separation between stage and audience.

The destruction left by the Second World War at least gave architects a chance to redesign and rebuild from scratch, and in the theatrical and operatic world this brought some bold and even revolutionary solutions to the problems facing them. But here they met an unexpected obstacle, for the public was attached to the old-fashioned forms of theatre and was scared of the audience participation demanded by playwrights like Brecht. While dramatists and producers aspired to a new and revolutionary style, the public – and quite often the singers and actors too – still looked to the theatre and the opera-house for 'uplift', passive entertainment or festive occasion.

In every city where the opera-house was being rebuilt, there were violent arguments in which large sections of the population became passionately involved. In many cases the new, forward-looking plans were frustrated. In Munich, for instance, there was no modernisation, except for the stage devices – revolving stage and backcloth, easily assembled sets, internal television apparatus, light fittings and so on. In Vienna, after years of vigorous debate, the compromise was reached of restoring the exterior of the old Court Opera and updating the interior, at least to the extent of dispensing with boxes and bright colours. This modernisation was taken further in Hamburg and Cologne, where changes were also made to improve acoustics and visibility for all the seats.

We have so far been considering mainly the audience, but what about the singer? He wants the opera-house to have the right atmosphere which will help him to give his best performance, but of course his primary concern is with its acoustics, which should be as uniform as possible, without an echo and not too dry. The problems of acoustics have by no means been fully solved in practice, and there are often unpleasant surprises after a hall, theatre or opera-house has been built. Generally concrete is used, lined with wood instead of material, though this may often lead to a rather spread, even dull sound, in place of the rich and noble sonority of the old opera-houses, where voices and orchestra merged perfectly.

In general the question of old or modern opera-houses cannot be answered. If nothing but contemporary operas were being staged, all the red-and-gold opera-houses with baroque decorations would be hopelessly outdated. If nothing but works of past ages were being staged, contemporary buildings would be equally incongruous as a setting for them. As our opera-houses are both a platform for present-day works and 'museums of sound', institutions which try to keep alive the masterpieces of over three centuries, no single opera-house could be appropriately designed for such a wide variety of contrasting operas. Perhaps the auditorium should be altered and re-decorated for each work, as is done for the stage and the singers by scenery and costume!

Germany*

For the organisation of opera, Germany, Austria and German-speaking Switzerland are probably well ahead of most other countries. They have the largest number of opera-houses continually in action, with long seasons, often as much as ten months, whereas in Italy the seasons are a good deal shorter.

* *Translator's note:* This section has been condensed, as some of the details would be of little interest to English-speaking readers.

As in the twenties, Berlin now possesses three first-class opera-houses, but now they do not even belong to the same state. The German State Opera suffered its first war damage in April 1941, after which it was used as an ordinary theatre until December 1942, when it resumed its old status. At the end of August 1944 it gave its last performance, Mozart's *Figaro*. Then its members were drafted into arms factories, and in the last days of the old Berlin the building was destroyed by fire and bombs.

On 1st June 1945, only three weeks after Germany's collapse and the end of the war, the reappointed manager Heinz Tietjen handed to the occupation powers a memorandum which seems worth quoting, because it helps one to appreciate fully the revival of German opera in the following years: 'Berlin opera is in a hopeless position. Only a few of the members of the former companies, who have not lost their lives in the chaos of the last months, are available for rebuilding . . . The properties which are the condition and basis for any operatic production, such as decor, lighting, instruments and costumes, have been almost completely destroyed or are in distant warehouses. For the present no performances can be given anywhere.' Yet a fortnight later a first 'operatic concert' was given, at which Erna Berger, Margarete Klose, Peter Anders and Ludwig Suthaus were among the singers.

On 8th September an opera, Gluck's *Orpheus and Eurydice*, was staged for the first time in the Admiral's Palace, which began to be used as a temporary opera-house, as it had been during the war. In 1951 the architect Richard Paulick began rebuilding the old Court Opera, and the ceremonial opening took place in September 1955. But although this was now in East Berlin, *ie* under Russian control, there were no great Communist innovations. Like the old opera-house, it was a public building of great dignity and beauty and it opened with *Die Meistersinger*, most bourgeois of all bourgeois operas, with quite a dash of nationalism as well. In the first years the division of the city was not so complete as it became afterwards, and the same distinguished singers could appear in both sectors. Jaro Prohaska was a glorious Hans Sachs, alternating with Josef Hermann and Rudolf Gonszar, Peter Anders a Belmonte with great beauty of tone, Karl Schmitt-Walter a superb Beckmesser and Papageno, Gottlob Frick a fine Sarastro, Erna Berger an ideal Queen of the Night. Tiana Lemnitz made a lovable Marschallin, the admirable Gerhard Unger was both character tenor, as David in *Meistersinger*, and Italian bel canto singer as Nemorino in *Elisir d'Amore*. Willi Domgraf-Fassbänder repeated his impressive rôles from the golden days of opera; his Scarpia, with Hilde Scheppans as Tosca, is a treasured memory for those who heard them. Hans Reinmar sang Boris Godunov, Christl Goltz sang Janacek's Jenufa, Martha Mödl Verdi's Lady Macbeth; great operas with outstanding singers, but very few experiments.

They were to be found, however, in East Berlin's second opera-house, Walter Felsenstein's Comic Opera. Here each work, before it is declared ready for public performance, is rehearsed for ten or even twelve months, allowing ensemble productions which would have been thought no longer possible. The opera-house is even closed for several days before a première, so that all preparations on the stage can take place in complete calm. 'To make singing a con-vincing, authentic and indispensable expression of humanity' (as Felsenstein put it), a high point of realistic opera has been achieved, far removed from commercial theatre, the star system and routine repertory. Unfair as it may seem to pick out individuals in a real 'collective' like this company, I would mention Hanns Nocker's Otello, Anny Schlemm in many full-blooded character parts and Rudolf Asmus's skilful interpretations of baritone roles.

West Berlin's German Opera stands on the site of the old Char-lottenburg opera-house. That was an impressive building with 2300 seats, which opened in 1912 with *Fidelio*. It was destroyed by bombs in November 1943 and for a year the company moved into the Admiral's Palace. Michael Bohnen, Rudolf Schock, Karl Schmitt-Walter, Hans Heimar, Josef Hermann, Irma Beilke tried to present worthy classical opera amidst daily air-raids and news of defeats and disasters. Three months after the end of the war rehearsals were taking place again, and soon afterwards performances: of *Fidelio*, as in 1912. Tietjen, Ebert and, finally, Sellner were the managers. The company included Karina Kutz, Irma Beilke, Emmi Hagemann, Elisabeth Grümmer, Günther Treptow, Hans Beirer, Josef Metter-nich, Karl Schmitt-Walter and Hans-Hermann Nissen. In September 1961 the new opera-house was opened. No more red and gold, no boxes or foyers gleaming with mirrors; everything was contem-porary and in sober colours, with quiet anterooms of exquisite taste designed more for relaxation than exhibition. The whole building was designed by Fritz Bornemann in the modern style of architecture, the former Greek pillars of the façade transformed into a huge ex-panse of bare wall, and in sum an opera-house technically equipped to cope with the highest demands, with seats for 1900 people.

The opening performance, conducted by Ferenc Fricsay, who died tragically young, was of *Don Giovanni* and on the second night

Klebe's *Alkmene*, a contemporary work, was performed. From then on the opera-house succeeded in assembling once more a company of unusually fine singers, of which I shall have more to say later on.

Munich's rebuilt National Theatre, as already mentioned, has remained a real Court Opera-House indeed, something of an anachronism with all the elements of its former glory, the statues in gold, the court boxes, the three-branched chandelier and the reliefs on the flat triangle above the Corinthian columns at the entrance. It seats 2100, but still looks rather intimate, perhaps because of its spherical vault shape, which increases the contact between stage and audience all over the house. Destroyed by bombs in October 1943, it was not re-opened until December 1963, under the sign of the two Richards who had determined the city's operatic history in the last hundred years, Wagner and Strauss: *Die Meistersinger* and *Die Frau ohne Schatten* were the first two operas performed in the new building. It is a stage, too, for contemporary composers like Carl Orff and Werner Egk, who have been closely associated with it; and, as with West Berlin's opera-house, there will be more to say later of Munich's company of brilliant singers, unmatched today anywhere in the world.

Hamburg was Germany's first operatic city. The 'Goose-market Opera' was started in 1677, and Handel's first stage productions were performed there, before it closed its doors in 1738; a new opera-house was not opened until 1827. This also was damaged by bombs in 1943, but three years later performances were possible in the ruins. Then followed the new building, designed by Gerhard Weber, containing 1700 seats, using the old form of the stage but with a completely transformed auditorium. Hamburg became one of the first 'modern' opera-houses in the world, with the special feature of separate balconies containing small units of seats which project into the theatre. In keeping with this modernity, Hamburg has a policy of putting on many contemporary works, which gives its manager a challenge in establishing and maintaining his company. He needs not only big, fine voices for the usual repertoire consisting of a large amount of Verdi, Puccini, Rossini and Mozart, but actors with the psychological range of present-day operas, and singers who can cope with the unprecedented musical difficulties which these often involve.

Jacques Offenbach was brought up in Cologne, and the city's new opera-house, opened in 1957, is in the spacious square which now bears his name. A panoramic view of the reconstructed city centre presents an amazing contrast between the famous old Gothic cathedral and the cubist-expressionist lines of the opera-house, which is an impressive example of contemporary architecture. Its interior is also very unusual, for it takes to an extreme Hamburg's concept of separate units, having tiers of balcony seats with a toboggan-like appearance. The idea is to bring all members of the audience nearer the stage and the singers and, compared with the horseshoe shape, the distance is indeed greatly reduced. (Perhaps an attempt is unconsciously being made to match the projection of film and television screens and the possibilities of close-ups which they offer.)

Most of the world's important opera-houses are surrounded by the rush of traffic and the noise of any big town. Stuttgart's opera-house is a fortunate exception in its wonderful setting, overlooking a beautiful park with a pond and coloured fountains. Built in 1912, it was one of the few spared in the Second World War, and the long, happy régime of Walter Erich Schaefer has made Stuttgart a stronghold of fine singing. Despite a relatively small subsidy it has a company scarcely attained by much bigger opera-houses, and has been on numerous world tours. For many years it provided the basic stock of singers for the Bayreuth Festival, including such names as Martha Mödl, Astrid Varnay, Anja Silja, Grace Hoffmann, Wolfgang Windgassen, Gerhard Stolze, Gustav Neidlinger and Otto von Rohr.

When the prosperous citizens of Frankfurt built their opera-house in the 1870s, they adopted the slogan *Das Wahre, Schöne, Gute* (the true, beautiful and good). These words in gold letters could still be read for a long time on the black ruin which it became in 1944. After the war there were only temporary buildings, until all three opera-houses were united in a single imposing new structure of glass and concrete. The showpiece in its interior is a Chagall mural (as in Paris and Tel-Aviv). Düsseldorf and Duisberg have joined forces to form the 'German Opera on the Rhine' which, under the management of Hermann Juch, has assembled an excellent company of singers from many different countries.

In East Germany, the most notable operatic cities are Dresden and Leipzig. All Dresden's theatres, including its opera-house, one of the most beautiful in the world ,were destroyed in the terrible air-raid of February 1945. Opera was already being performed, however, by August that year, but although a new State Theatre was opened in 1948, Dresden is still waiting for its own opera-house to carry on an honourable tradition. In Leipzig, too, no theatre survived the Second World War, but a new opera-house with 1700 seats was opened in 1960, and includes in its programme many Slav operas little-known or seldom performed in the West.

These are only the most important opera-houses in Germany. There are a great many others, both in the West and the East, some of which have played a big part in the careers of famous singers.

Austria

Austria has always had a great singing tradition, to which Hungary and Bohemia, once part of the Hapsburg monarchy, contributed their full share. The capital itself is noted, of course, for Lieder, operetta and opera, and the great evenings in Vienna's opera-houses are part of musical history. In 1814, at the Kärtnerthortheater, Beethoven conducted his *Fidelio* in its third and final version, and in 1825 he 'took part' in the direction of his Ninth Symphony (the posters said 'took part' in an attempt to persuade the Master that no one thought him deaf). In 1869 music-lovers from all over Europe attended a performance of *Don Giovanni* which inaugurated a magnificent new building, the Court Opera Theatre. Eleven months later the Kärtnerthortheater, next door to it, was demolished and the Hotel Sacher arose in its grounds, offering a natural continuation of operatic life. Guest artists stayed there, presents and flowers poured in for them, intimate suppers took place and banquets after a success, conversations were started which led to important engagements, and there was always the famous *Sachertorte* with whipped cream, the delicacy to which Richard Strauss even dedicated a ballet.

The last performance in the Court Opera was on 30th June 1944, and the opera, suitable enough, was *Götterdämmerung*. Two notices in the programme were signs of the times: 'The audience are requested to rise from their seats when our wounded soldiers from the front appear in the centre box before the beginning of the performance' and, 'In case of an air-raid warning maintain calm'. The celebrated opera-house was destroyed by bombs in March 1945. After the war, amidst hunger and foreign occupation, nothing was so passionately discussed in the new Republic as how it was to be rebuilt.

Meanwhile business began in two other houses, the Theater an der Wien and the Volksoper. There were fine singers still in Vienna, and others came there. Few casts even in peace time could have surpassed that of the post-war *Don Giovanni* with Paul Schöffler in the title rôle, Ljuba Welitsch, Hilde Konetzni and Irmgard Seefried in the three women's rôles, and Anton Dermota, a glorious bel canto tenor. Music-lovers came to the two temporary theatres and applauded rapturously. A Mozart Renaissance had started, leading to outstanding ensemble performances. But as soon as free travel was possible again, combined with the increasing opportunities from recording, radio and eventually television, great singers were always off on the international circuit, and the days of company ensemble achievement were over.

Ten years after the war's end, at the same time as the peace treaty was signed restoring Austria's independence, the new opera-house was finished. It represents a typical Austrian compromise. The exterior was just as it had been before the destruction; the interior gleamed with the basic colours of the old opera-house, red, gold and ivory, and there were still boxes, but much of the former rococo ornament and stucco had been replaced by modern straight-line design. The capacity of the auditorium was slightly reduced by the elimination of seats with bad visibility, but even so it could take up to 2000. An audience of people from all over the world went to admire the magnificent theatre at the official opening.

Since then much water has flowed under the Danube bridges. The routine of repertory, against which Mahler had fought so bitterly, inevitably set in. 'Gäste kamen und Gäste gingen' (guests came and went), to quote *Die Walküre*. Touring stars stayed in Vienna as much as ever, but opera there was more and more being sung in the original language, instead of in two or even three languages, as used to happen in many earlier productions. Now German singers could no longer sing great Italian opera in their own tongue, and 'Che gelida manina' could be heard from Anton Dermota, 'Di quella pira' from Rudolf Schock and 'Recondita armonia' from Karl Friedrich.

There were often glorious evenings, especially when Karajan was conducting. Milan sent not only its star solo singers but complete operas to Vienna. There were as many crises and dramas as ever. It is still one of the great opera-houses, and its great singers share it, as today is customary and inevitable, with all the great opera-houses in the world, Munich and Hamburg, London, New York and Buenos Aires. But it has one unique possession in the magnificent Vienna Philharmonic, one of the most perfect of modern orchestras. Under a conductor worthy of them, their full sound carries the singer as a gentle yet mighty sea carries the good swimmer.

Although Vienna is the centre of Austrian opera, there are many other places of considerable interest to opera-lovers, such as Graz, Linz, Innsbruck, Bad Ischl, Baden, Bregenz on Lake Constance – with its festival, now twenty-five years old, where performances are given against the beautiful back-cloth of the lake – and of course Salzburg. The Salzburg Festival started off as an offshoot of the Vienna Opera, and though it is now quite independent, they still have cultural and musical connections, clearly to their mutual advantage. There will be more about the Salzburg Festival later in this chapter.

Switzerland

Peace and prosperity for many decades, a central position in Europe strongly accentuated by the territorial changes after the Second World War, a quiet but open-minded cultural attitude combining tradition with progress – all this has given Switzerland an importance quite disproportionate to its size and population in many spheres – very much including music. The country has a surprising number of theatres, several of which stage extremely good operatic productions. Many distinguished singers have started from Switzerland on their road to international fame: Max Hirzel, Charles Panzéra, Ernst Haefliger, Maria Stader, Else Scherz-Meister, Lisa della Casa, Peter Lagger and Ursula Buckel, to name only a few, and Swiss folk-song choirs and singing groups of all kinds offer a living proof of the country's deeply rooted love of music.

After various attempts in the operatic field, Zürich, which today is Switzerland's leading city for opera, set about building a permanent opera-house in 1830. This was given the rather prosaic name of *Aktientheater* ('shares' theatre), because it belonged to the middle-class subscribers and not to any prince as elsewhere. Schröder-Devrient was a guest artist here in 1843. In 1850 Wagner was conducting, having found political asylum in Zürich, and in 1854 he nearly became director of the Zürich opera. In January 1890 the Aktientheater was burned down. A start was immediately made on a new building and two Viennese architects, Hellmer and Fellner, then 'wholesale' opera-house suppliers for half the world, put up the impressive Haus am See (House on the Lake), which opened in 1890 with a performance of *Lohengrin*. D'Andrade came here as guest artist in 1894, and in 1913 there was a production of *Parsifal*, one of the first to be given outside Bayreuth, with Willy Ulmer in the title rôle, Karl Gritzbach as Gurnemanz and Emmy Krüger as Kundry. A wonderful artist who also sang Zürich's first Rosenkavalier, Emmy Kruger was remembered long after her retirement from the stage as a living part of operatic history. In 1917 the Darmstadt Opera performed here under Felix Weingartner, who twenty years later, after countless journeys all over the world, was to return to Switzerland as director of the Basle opera-house and conservatoire. The same year, Nikisch was conducting Wagner works, Richard Strauss twice directed Mozart and his own *Elektra*, and Pfitzner staged his *Palestrina* with Bruno Walter as musical director. The opera-house is a pleasant size, with very good acoustics, and the most celebrated singers have performed here for shorter or longer periods. As was to happen repeatedly in later years, crises and conflicts in the world outside bounced off the borders of Switzerland almost without impact, indeed contributed to the country's cultural advance.

It was in Zürich at that time that Busoni staged premières of his operas *Turandot* and *Arlecchino*, with Alexander Moissi singing the title rôle in the latter. And in 1918, when French and Germans were facing each other on the battlefields with desperate bitterness, a French company playing *Werther* and *Pelléas*, and a German company under Richard Strauss, were giving guest performances in Zürich almost simultaneously.

The same sort of thing happened again in the thirties. As the world darkened, the exodus of artists from Germany and later Austria on racial or political grounds brought precious talent to the Swiss theatre and opera and gave it a leading position recognised all over the world in German-speaking cultural and musical life. The programme of the Zürich June Festival in 1937 contained the world première of Alban Berg's posthumous opera *Lulu*, with Nuri Hadzic in the title rôle, and others in the cast were Maria Bernhard, Paul Feher, Asger Stig, Peter Baxevanos, Albert Emmerich and Fritz Honisch. A year later Hindemith's *Mathis der Maler*, probably his most important work, was heard for the first time with a cast including Asger Stig, Judith Hellwig, Leni Funk, Peter Baxevanos, Fritz Honisch, Simons Bermanis, Albert Emmerich, Ernst Mosbacher and Marko Rothmüller. To underline Zürich's international status in opera, there were also the guest performances of artists like Dusolina Giannini (as Tosca and Butterfly), Franz Völker (Lohengrin), Martha Roh and Alfred Jerger (*Rosenkavalier*), Erna Sack (*Fledermaus*), Aureliano Pertile under Mascagni's baton (*Nero*), Toti dal Monte (*Lucia di Lammermoor* and *Sonnambula*). There was a complete *Ring* cycle with Max Lorenz, Erich Zimmermann, Max Hirzel, Kurt Böhme, and Zürich also had *Fidelio* under Furtwängler with Hilde Konetzni. Maria Caniglia, Gina Cigna and Ebe Stignani also sang in Zürich.

In the following years Richard Strauss's bond with Swiss musical life was strengthened. Zürich can boast of having presented his works with the finest singers and in productions of rare brilliance; *Capriccio* as a guest performance by the Vienna Opera as early as 1944, *Die Liebe der Danae* with a company from Munich in 1953. June 1942 had seen the first production of *Johanna auf dem Scheiterhafen* (Joan at the Stake) by the Zürich composer Arthur Honegger, with Maria Becker and Heinrich Gretler in the (spoken) principal rôles. In 1945 Gershwin's *Porgy and Bess* was heard there in German for the first time, and in 1951 Stravinsky's *Rake's Progress*. In 1957 Zürich's City Theatre (its name was not changed to opera-house till later, although it had long been devoted exclusively to opera) was again in the centre of world musical interest, when Schönberg's posthumous and in-complete opera *Moses and Aaron* was staged for the first time under Hans Rosbaud's direction.

The Zürich Festivals in June brought stars of world singing, including Gigli and Mario del Monaco, Kirsten Flagstad and Maria Cebotari, Margarete Teschemacher, the sisters Konetzni, Peter Pears and Birgit Nilsson. But the opera-house's own singers also reached a high standard and the resident company often gave remarkable per-formances. It had Judith Hellwig with her clear, warm and beautiful soprano, the lyric tenors Simons Bermanis and Libero de Luca, Max Lichtegg, a well-known favourite of operetta, who tackled the lead in *Rake's Progress* with outstanding success, the baritone Andreas Böhm, who seemed to be heading for the heights until his tragic accidental death, Willy Ferenz, a singer of great interpretative depths, still remembered today for his masterly performance as Wozzeck, the mighty bass Ralph Telaskos, a highly intelligent portrayer of Kur-wenal, Pizarro and the animal trainer in *Lulu*, with which he made successful guest appearances in the greatest opera-houses, Ira Mala-niuk, a mezzo voice of rare timbre, and many other splendid singers, like Charles Gillig, Willi Heyer, Julia Moor, Margrit von Syben, Leni Funk, Alois Pernerstorfer, Eva-Maria Duske and Heinz Borst.

Basle, too, has a strong musical tradition and the standard of per-formances in the nineteenth-century Stadt-theater is often very high. Singers of international fame such as Grace Bumbry and the English mezzo-soprano Patricia Johnson have in the past been members of the ensemble there. A new, extremely modern-style opera-house is at present being erected next door to the existing building, and this may well increase Basle's prestige and its importance as an operatic centre, and also stir up some of the age-old traditional rivalry between that city and Zürich.

Italy

Liszt relates how in the home country of opera he was at once recognised as a foreigner, when on arrival in Milan he asked friends whether they were going to La Scala that evening. For going to the opera, at least in the circles he frequented, was something taken for granted.

In its history of several hundred years La Scala has twice been destroyed by fire, in 1708 and 1776, and once by bombs in 1943. Each time it rose as beautiful as before, or even more so. In 1770, a few years before the second fire, there was an evening on which a four-teen-year-old boy from Salzburg, with an orchestra of seventy musicians, conducted his own opera, *Mitridates, König von Pontos*, a work underrated today, for all our veneration of Mozart. A year later the young composer returned to direct his *Ascanio in Alba*, and in 1772 *Lucio Silla*. In retrospect that seems enough to make an opera-house famous, for La Scala it was only a few pages in a long and glorious history.

In the same year as the second fire, the Empress Maria Theresia in Vienna (for Milan was then Austrian) approved the plans for a new building, presented the site plus a half-derelict church, so that a really magnificent opera-house could be built. The church, officially called Santa Maria in Porta Nova, but commonly known as Santa Maria alla Scala, gave its name to the new building, which was the creation of an outstanding architect, Giuseppe Piermarini. With an area of 4300 square yards, it was probably the largest opera-house in the world at the time, as also in its capacity of 2600 seats with standing room for a further 400 (more, that is, than the later opera-houses at Vienna and Paris, although both were larger than La Scala).

On 15th August 1943, the opera-house was severely damaged by bombs, but reconstruction went ahead fast. A year after the end of the war, La Scala was re-opened in its old form and traditional splendour, including the restoration of even the massive chandelier of Bohemian glass with its 365 lamps. But the greatest splendour came from the conductor's desk; there stood Toscanini, as in the glorious days before his emigration twenty years earlier, surrounded with legends, stern as ever, loved and feared. With the old maestro there, great singers began to return to the house.

What La Scala has meant for singing emerges from many pages of this book. There is scarcely any great singer who has not performed there. It could almost be said that since the beginning of our century the operatic world is a triangle based on the three points of La Scala, the Met and the Teatro Colón in Buenos Aires. As far back as the eighteen-twenties and thirties La Scala had an unequalled gathering of singers; the Grisi sisters, Pasta, Carolina Ungher, Tadolini,

Candori, Malibran, and among the men Battista, Rubini, Lablache and Tamburini.

So it remained for many decades. Great singers made their reputations here or came with reputations already made, to have them either confirmed or sometimes diminished. Could such glory return after the Second World War? Any who doubted this must soon have been converted by the list of names in the company; Tebaldi, Callas, Fedora Barbieri, Ebe Stignani (still going strong), Antonietta Stella, Giulietta Simionato, di Stefano, del Monaco, Tagliavini, Gobbi, Siepi, Rossi-Lemeni, plus hundreds of famous guest artists including Kirsten Flagstad, Birgit Nilsson, Leontyne Price, Elisabeth Schwarzkopf, Hilde Güden, Joan Sutherland, Hans Hotter, Boris Christoff and Sandor Konya. The opera-lover is inclined to believe that with the passing of 'his' generation of singers the great days are irrevocably over, but in fact there is a continual re-birth. A new generation steps into their shoes with surprising rapidity. Of course not all the gaps are completely filled, singers like Caruso, Tauber, Lehmann and Callas are unique. But then some of the new generation may be unique too. At La Scala it was represented by such singers as Mirella Freni, Ilva Ligabue, Renata Scotto, Graziella Sciutti, Fiorenza Cossotto, Anna Moffo, Maria Chiara, Bergonzi, Raimondi, Corelli, Taddei, Cappuccilli, Panerai, Pavarotti and Prevedi, plus a list of guest artists longer than Leporello's catalogue of Don Giovanni's conquests.

The Scala season opens traditionally on 7th December every year. To sing on that evening is evidence of the highest distinction; the flower-decked horseshoe in red, ivory and gold makes a fantastic spectacle scarcely conceivable anywhere else in Europe. The show has already started beforehand, with a solid wall of people flanking the entrance to the opera-house, enjoying the parade of luxury and ostentation in the parties arriving. But in recent times the radiant picture of this 7th December has been somewhat marred. The ordinary citizens of Milan, for years dumb spectators, indeed admirers of the upper strata, gathered here in an assembly rarely found elsewhere, no longer accept this passive and uncritical rôle. The result has been outbreaks of hatred and class-consciousness, riots and demonstrations. Again, as so often in history, art has become mixed with politics. It does not, however, affect the opera itself, only the social forms connected with it. In their enthusiasm for opera as such. all classes in Italy are united. That is just why the manifestations on 7th December may even herald justified claims by the poor to enjoy opera themselves.

For the rich and the very rich, who make their self-conscious and now often disturbed entrance, the show starts a little later than for the 'spectator' public, but still before the curtain goes up. After being solemnly shown to their seats by ushers, who resemble senators of the old Italian republics, they take a look round the magnificent auditorium, which admittedly has nothing to do with art, but still prepares the spirit in a special way for the operatic feast of sound to come.

La Scala has a short season, like all the Italian opera-houses. This is based on the *stagione* system. A number of works, usually twelve to fifteen (correspondingly fewer with smaller opera-houses), are rehearsed during a season and then performed as often as there is a public demand. The most suitable singers for every rôle can be engaged from the whole Italian and even the world market, and not just from the members of a permanent company as with the repertory opera-houses; consequently there is generally a very high standard, and this remains more or less intact throughout the short period, during which works are repeated only a few times. I shall be returning later to the two basic principles of opera production - *stagione* or repertory - when discussing the fundamental problems of the musical theatre today.

On 20th December 1955, La Scala incorporated in their 'big house' a small one in the same building, the 'Piccola Scala'. This is a pleasant modern auditorium with about 600 seats, an excellent venue especially for the chamber operas which are again attracting large audiences. I should mention, too, that the Scala's orchestra is one of the best in the world, and the value of this to the singer on the stage scarcely needs reiterating.

Venice's Teatro Fenice, also rich in history, ranks high among Italian and indeed international opera-houses. In 1613, twenty years after the new art-form of opera had first been presented on the stage in the palaces of Florence, the first modern musical dramatist, Claudio Monteverdi, went to Venice. A musical life began there which we can scarcely imagine today. In 1637 the first opera theatre opened its doors to 'the public' (a novel term), and ever since then wide circles were gripped by a wave of enthusiasm for the 'melodrama'. Up to a dozen theatres at the same time catered for the new genre in what was probably still the richest, most powerful, most highly populated and most enterprising city in the world. On 16th May 1792, after a building period of only two years, the Teatro Fenice, designed by Giannantonio Selva, was in operation. It burned down in 1836, but was rebuilt within seven months by the brothers

Tommaso and Gianbattista Meduna – a lovely theatre in light blue and silver, as Venetian (writes Giovanna Kessler), 'as if the two architects were trying to catch the dancing sun-shapes on the rippling waters of the lagoons'.

The artistic history of the opera-house is almost as distinguished as that of La Scala. Here too the prima donnas and *primi uomini* of the great bel canto days sang; here Rossini worked with his star singer and later wife, Isabella Colbran; here Verdi staged the premières of his early work *Ernani* and later of his 'break-through' operas *Rigoletto* and *Traviata*, finally in 1857 *Simon Boccanegra*. In our time important works like Britten's *Turn of the Screw*, Stravinsky's *Rake's Progress* and Prokofiev's *The Fiery Angel* were presented here, and the Wagner grandsons Wieland and Wolfgang brought the Bayreuth productions with their top singers on to the stage of the Teatro Fenice.

It is a relatively small theatre, seating only 1,200, but the greatest voices have sung in it, and some, like Callas, Tebaldi and Simoniato, first achieved fame there rather than at La Scala. The season, previously always a short one, has been lengthened in recent years, because there is a good permanent company which plays for several months, as well as the high season with the international names. This is a very good arrangement, rarely carried out elsewhere in Italy.

The country has several hundred opera-houses, but few cities can boast more than periodic guest performances. Of these the next to be mentioned should probably be those in the capital. Rome's Teatro Apollo was opened in 1671, burnt down in 1781, re-opened fifteen years later. In 1853 *Il Trovatore* had its première there, in 1859 *Un ballo in maschera*; the building disappeared for good in 1889. A second opera-house, the Teatro Argentino, was established in 1732, and on 20th February 1816 the world première of *The Barber of Seville* took place there with Manuel Garcia in the lead. Here too there were Verdi premières. A third opera-house was built in 1880 and was originally called Costanzi after its first impresario. After extensive alterations its name was changed in 1928 to the Teatro Reale dell'Opera (the Royal Opera-House). Here *Cavalleria Rusticana* was heard for the first time (1890) with Gemma Bellincioni and Roberto Stagno in the leading parts, afterwards *Tosca* (1900) with Hariclée Darclée, Emilio de Marchi and Eugenio Giraldoni. When Italy was proclaimed a republic, the theatre changed its name to Teatro dell'Opera. Callas gave many sensational performances there.

As the Apollo and the Argentino are no more, Rome has since 1936 confined its winter opera to the official institute, the Teatro

Reale – but there is an interesting summer addition – the open-air
stage in the fifth-century ruins of the Emperor Caracalla's Baths, the
Terme di Caracalla, a magnificent setting with a huge seating area
and surprisingly good acoustics.

Naples and Genoa have famous old opera-houses. The one at
Naples is called San Carlo, after the patron saint of its builder, King
Charles de Bourbon. He opened it in 1737 to replace another which
had been used since 1654. It was a splendid building, a match for La
Scala. It burnt down in 1816, but was quickly rebuilt, thereby
allowing the continuation of a long series of premières of works by
Rossini, who was specially attached to it. There were also two Verdi
premières (*Alzira* and *Luisa Miller*), and many of the greatest singers
appeared there; Giuditta Pasta, Malibran, Giacomo Davide. Fanny
Tacchinardi sang the first Lucia di Lammermoor there in 1835, and
towards the end of the century the superb voices of Patti, Gayarre,
Stagno and Tamagno, today almost legendary, were heard there. A
glorious and imposing theatre, with a great deal of gold in its interior,
it has 184 boxes and a vast painted ceiling.

Genoa's opera-house is called Carlo Felice, after the Sardinian king
who opened it in 1828. Like most of Italy's important opera-houses,
this also has no less than six rows of boxes. In the Second World War
it too was severely damaged, but was re-opened in August 1948
although, in contrast to La Scala, Genoa decided on a relative
modernisation.

Florence, the birthplace of opera, naturally has one of the oldest
opera-houses, the Teatro della Pergola. Its construction began in
1652, and it was opened four years later. Though numerous changes
have been made on many occasions, its interior still breathes the
atmosphere of an ancient operatic festival. In its history we meet the
name of Galli Bibiena, the family of brilliant architects, painters and
creators of baroque scenery who played a considerable part in the
history of opera north of the Alps as well. In 1847 Verdi's *Macbeth*
had its première there, and nearly a century later, in 1940, Dallapiccola presented his *Volo di Notte*. Since 1925 the opera-house has
been designated a national monument.

In 1862 another opera-house had been built in Florence, at first
named after King Vittorio Emmanuele II. It was originally designed
for open-air performances and so had no roof, but could seat 5000.
A year later it was burnt out during a ball. Afterwards it was made
into an ordinary opera-house, which in 1933, with further alterations,
became the Teatro Communale. It is best known internationally for
staging the splendid May Festival, the Maggio Musicale Fiorentino.

Mention of open-air performances leads us directly to Verona's vast Arena, most impressive of open-air theatres, once built for animal-baiting and other barbarous 'entertainments'. For several weeks every summer, opera is performed to over 20,000 spectators, who often follow score and text by the light of candles which they bring in with them. The stage is equally huge, allowing impressive sets to be used. Understandably, monumental and spectacular operas have the greatest impact; *Aida* holds the record for audiences and performances, but a lot of other works presented here are tremendously effective, especially as many of the world's finest voices are to be heard in them.

The largest Italian opera-house, about 6500 square yards in area (over double the size of La Scala) and the most grandiose building, is the aptly named Teatro Massimo at Palermo in Sicily. It opened in 1897 with a performance of Verdi's *Falstaff*, composed four years earlier. Bologna has an old operatic history. When the Teatro Malvezzi, which had been in use for a long time, was burnt down in 1745, Antonio Galli Bibiena built a new opera-house. This opened in 1763 with a new Gluck work (now virtually forgotten) and was notable in the next century as well for its special attention to German opera; the Italian premières of *Lohengrin*, *Tannhäuser* and *Tristan* took place here. Despite later destruction (in 1931 by fire, in the war by bombs) it still shows traces of its former glory. Other cities worth mentioning are Parma and Turin, Trieste and Busseto (Verdi's real home), Pisa and Salerno. Pesaro naturally called its opera-house after Rossini, Bergamo after Donizetti, Catania after Bellini. There are also Cremona, Mantua, Reggio Emilia, Novara, Belluno, Pavia, Lucca, Rimini and scores of others, which may be unimportant from the viewpoint of international singing, but have more than once discovered voices which later achieved world fame. And it sometimes happened, as with Caruso at Naples, that artists who had great renown in store for them were booed off the stage by a provincial audience!

Britain

For over two hundred years London has been one of the most important cities in the world for music generally, and for opera in particular. Covent Garden, the famous theatre which is now the Royal Opera House, was first built in 1732 by the actor Rich, who had produced Gay's *Beggar's Opera* four years earlier ('making Gay rich and Rich gay'). Handel was one of the first great names associated with the theatre, and in the miraculously short time between 22nd August and 14th September 1741 he had composed *Messiah* (thirteen years later than the other early masterpiece of oratorio, Bach's *St Matthew Passion*). It was performed for the first time on 13th April 1742 in Dublin at a charity concert; the first London performance took place at Covent Garden on 23rd March 1743, in the presence of King George II, who led the audience in standing for the Hallelujah Chorus, establishing a tradition which is still maintained. Handel conducted the work each year until his death, for the benefit of the Foundling Hospital in Coram Fields, to which he also gave his original manuscript.

Extensive alterations in 1792 turned Covent Garden into what amounted to a new theatre. It was burnt down in 1806 and rebuilt by Smirke. On 12th April 1826 Weber conducted his *Oberon* here for the first time, a few days before he died. Some years later Maria Malibran came to Covent Garden and conquered London in Bellini's *Sonnambula*. Soon afterwards she sang Marzelline in *Fidelio* (today not regarded as a star part) and left the title rôle to Schröder-Devrient; an attractive and, by today's standards, remarkable example of modesty in a prima donna. It had been an ordinary theatre as well (by 1803 John Kemble was part-proprietor and stage-manager, with his sister Mrs Siddons as leading actress), but after financial difficulties and further changes of management it opened in 1848 as the Royal Italian Opera House; the interior, which seats 2200, is in red and gold and has the classic opera-house splendour. In 1888 Nellie Melba came to London, and from then on, until her retirement from the stage nearly four decades later, she was one of the dominating figures here.

It was generally a 'star theatre', like the Met, and for a long time so completely geared to Italian singers that even works from the German repertory were sung here in Italian, hence the name of the house, but in the 1890s the word 'Italian' was dropped and it acquired its present name of Royal Opera House. Before 1914 Hans Richter conducted two cycles of *The Ring* in English, but singing in English was extremely rare until after the Second World War, when Covent Garden became a really national opera-house, with works by British composers being commissioned and sponsored; in the early post-war period, indeed, most of the normal repertoire was sung in English, so that on one occasion Flagstad and Hotter had to learn an English version of their *Walküre* rôles.

This practice, however, was gradually suspended, and in 1958, for instance, there was a memorable Visconti production of *Don Carlos* in Italian with Carlo Maria Giulini as musical director and a cast led by Gré Brouwenstijn, Fedora Barbieri, Jon Vickers, Tito Gobbi and Boris Christoff. Covent Garden now has a permanent repertoire, mostly sung in the language in which the original operas were written, and mainly performed by its own company; many members have meanwhile advanced into the world class. There are also famous guest artists appearing every year; to take at random the 1964/5 season, it saw Maria Callas, Joan Sutherland, Lisa della Casa, Renata Scotto, Mirella Freni, Windgassen, Wunderlich, Fischer-Dieskau, Gobbi and Frick. *Arabella* with Lisa della Casa and Fischer-Dieskau drew all the critics' superlatives, and there can seldom have been a *Tosca* like the Zeffirelli production with Callas and Gobbi in the leads.

A second London opera company was established in 1931, after complete rebuilding of an old theatre in Islington, Sadler's Wells (named after a surveyor called Sadler who discovered chalybeate wells there). This was part of the 'Vic-Wells' combination inspired by Lilian Baylis. From 1931 to 1934 the drama and opera companies interchanged between Sadler's Wells and the Old Vic, but after that the Old Vic returned to its full-time drama programme, while the opera company worked solely at Sadler's Wells, together with the Sadler's Wells Ballet. During the pre-war years the company mounted over fifty productions of opera. The theatre was closed during the war, reopening in 1945 with the première of Britten's *Peter Grimes*. In 1959, to meet the resurgence of interest in opera all over the country, the Arts Council asked Sadler's Wells Opera to take the main responsibility for touring opera in the United Kingdom. Two equally strong companies were created, one for London and one for touring, but for practical, artistic and financial reasons this system was suspended in July 1970. One large company was formed with a London season from August till March, touring extensively from April until the end of May. Meanwhile, in 1968, Sadler's Wells Opera had moved to the vast Coliseum Theatre, which holds 2350, and opened there with a performance of *Don Giovanni*. The company is still looking for a new name, to avoid confusion with the theatre in Islington, which is now used as a home for touring opera and ballet companies.

A word should be said about the Savoy Theatre, traditional home of that amazing partnership, Gilbert, Sullivan and D'Oyly Carte, and the D'Oyly Carte Company, which for nearly a century now has produced these enchanting comic operas to packed houses both at the Savoy and all over the English-speaking world. Since Gilbert's copyright expired in 1955, other professional companies have achieved equal success with 'G and S', which remains really popular opera, much loved by a large section of the British public, constantly performed by amateurs, and a favourite programme for thousands at the Promenade Concerts. (Lortzing operas present a similar equivalent in the German-speaking world, where they enjoy great popularity, but are rarely performed outside it.) Clarity of diction is essential for Gilbert's brilliant lyrics, unsurpassed in their kind, supremely well set in Sullivan's sparkling melodies, and G and S may have helped to discover many fine voices. It does not require great singing, of course, but notable British singers – like Heddle Nash, Owen Brannigan, Geraint Evans and Richard Lewis – have often appeared, to their and the audience's delight, in G and S performances and concerts.

The Royal Festival Hall on the South Bank of the Thames, opened in 1951 (year of the 'Festival of Britain'), though mainly for concerts, is also used sometimes for opera and ballet, but it is largely thanks to the Covent Garden and Sadler's Wells Opera companies that London has remained a centre of opera, giving opportunities for British composers such as Britten, Walton, Tippett, Searle and Maxwell-Davies, and also for a phalanx of magnificent singers. A list of these is bound to be subjective, but should include Peter Pears, Geraint Evans, David Ward, Jon Vickers (a Canadian by birth but launched on a world career by Covent Garden), Stuart Burrows, Benjamin Luxon, Peter Glossop, Richard Lewis; Heather Harper, Gwyneth Jones, Josephine Veasey, Janet Baker; and the 'Antipodeans' Joan Sutherland, Yvonne Minton and Donald McIntyre. Most of these are still in their thirties or forties, and should still have a long career ahead of them. The unique Kathleen Ferrier, who died of cancer in her early forties after so many lovely performances in oratorio and song recitals, appeared in only two operatic rôles, both wonderful performances, as Gluck's Orpheus and Britten's Lucretia.

The British have not, as in Europe, had a long tradition of arts subsidy from public funds. It is only since the war that this has been established and is carried on by the Arts Council of Great Britain, which supports both Covent Garden and Sadler's Wells; at present operatic productions are considered too expensive to have a larger share of the limited funds available. Partly as a result, though public taste of course is also involved, England has only one other permanent opera company, the English Opera Group. This was founded in 1946, launched the Aldeburgh Festival in 1949, and is responsible for the Festival's artistic direction. The Group devotes its energies mostly to the works of Britten and Purcell, and in 1961 was brought under the aegis of Covent Garden. It has a high reputation, goes on many tours, and is the first British opera company to have visited the USSR.

But in the last few years opera has been making considerable headway in Britain. Philip Hope-Wallace, *Guardian* critic, wrote early in 1973, 'It must have been much simpler to sum up a year's opera and ballet activities when events were largely limited to one season at Covent Garden and one visit by Les Ballets Russes. But now the picture is so wide it eludes sharp focus, and this without the fact that most people's operatic listening and some people's dance viewing is enriched by broadcasting and television. For instance, the BBC has just poured the whole of this year's Bayreuth Wagner Festival into our homes. How do you relate that to visits to Cardiff for the Welsh National Opera, which climbs to new heights, or the expansion and blossoming this year of Scottish Opera which fairly deserves the adjective "glorious"? Glyndebourne (at home and touring), Aldeburgh; new television fodder?

'It would also be wrong to exclude such things as the one-night "star" concert opera performances such as those of *Mefistofele* or *Ernani*, to say nothing of the enterprise of Guildhall School, Hammersmith Municipal Opera, the London Opera Centre, revivals of curiosities such as *La Navarraise* and exotic visitors such as those wonderful Kabuki players from Japan at Sadler's Wells (host this year to a whole raft-load of singers and dancers) . . . At the Coliseum they (the Sadler's Wells Opera) have gone on with their magnificent *Ring* in English . . . mounted with the Brünnhilde of that enterprising soprano (Rita Hunter), a *Trovatore* under Charles Mackerras which packed a terrific punch, and have kept a wide repertory going. But their crowning triumph was the huge production of the popular Soviet masterpiece by Prokofiev, *War and Peace* . . .'

Opera is also an important element in the Edinburgh Festival of Music and Drama in August, and something more must be said of the Glyndebourne Festival, which John Christie started with Fritz Busch as musical director, Carl Ebert as producer, Caspar Neher as stage designer and Rudolf Bing (later director of the Met) as organiser. In 1934 the first improvised Mozart stage was in action. Its success led to the construction of a permanent theatre seating about 600 and closely connected with the surrounding countryside. Those who sing at Glyndebourne have to be of international standard and also need to possess an accomplished chamber-opera style. As the years have passed, besides Mozart the repertoire has included *Fidelio* –

an outstanding production – works by Cimarosa and Donizetti, Richard Strauss's *Capriccio* (model of a modern chamber opera), Busoni's *Arlecchino*. In these days of musical mass-consumption opera can all too easily lapse into the coarsely lavish and spectacular. Attempts have often been made to revert to the gracious living of earlier days, but they may succumb to the other extreme of snobbish superiority. Like some of the small continental opera-houses – the Cuvilliés-Theater at Munich, Vienna's Redoutensaal and Castle Theatre at Schönbrunn, Schwetzingen-Mannheim, and Stockholm's Summer Opera – Glyndebourne succeeds in providing truly civilised high-level entertainment in a delightful setting.

Until after the war, despite London's long-standing reputation through Covent Garden, Britain was one of the less important countries, operatically speaking. But the country as a whole has long had a special tradition for oratorio. This may be the place, then, to say a few words about an art-form which is immensely popular with professionals and amateurs alike, and to which some British singers have devoted a large part of their working life. A few, indeed, do not appear in opera at all, which is rarely the case with leading singers in Europe.

The word 'oratorio' has ill-defined boundaries, for it has sometimes impinged on opera or secular cantata on the one hand and on purely liturgical music on the other. Grove's Dictionary of Music and Musicians (5th edition) defines it as 'a dramatic poem, usually of a sacred but not liturgical character, sung throughout by solo voices and choruses, to the accompaniment of a full orchestra, but – at least in modern times – without the assistance of scenery, dresses, or action'.

It is often traced back to the Church Oratorians of the sixteenth-century Italian saint, Philip Neri. In Britain its popularity has been mainly bound up with Handel (especially *Messiah*), Bach (assuming that the *St John* and the *St Matthew Passions*, definitely liturgical, can properly be called oratorios), Haydn's *The Creation and The Seasons* (which is partly religious, partly secular), Mendelssohn's *St Paul* and *Elijah*, and more recent works by British composers such as Elgar's *The Dream of Gerontius* (pre-eminently), *The Apostles* and *The Kingdom*, Holst's *Hymn of Jesus*, Vaughan Williams's *Sancta Civitas*, William Walton's *Belshazzar's Feast* and Herbert Howell's *Hymnus Paradisi*. These composers have recognised the existence of a reservoir of good singers eager to perform in their works, and conversely the singers have been inspired to further excellence of performance.

Notable singers in concert and oratorio at the end of the last century included Sims Reeves, Santley and the very fine tenor, Edward Lloyd. Among the great oratorio soloists who could have been heard by older readers of this book are Agnes Nicholls, Phyllis Lett, Muriel Foster, Dilys Jones, John Coates, Gervase Elwes, Campbell McInnes, Keith Faulkner; of the more recent ones Norman Walker (wonderful in *Messiah* and *Gerontius*), Heddle Nash, Peter Pears (called 'the Archangel of Evangelists' in Bach's *Passions*), Benjamin Luxon (another glorious soloist in the *Passions*), John Shirley-Quirk, Elsie Morison, Marjorie Thomas, Helen Watts, Kathleen Ferrier (unforgettable especially as the Angel in *Gerontius*), Heather Harper and Janet Baker. Few operatic stars, even in their noblest passages, can surpass the exciting, soul-stirring beauty of sound, enhanced by the religious context and musical inspiration, of some of these great singers in oratorio.

Scandinavia and Holland

Stockholm's early operatic history is connected with the name of two kings. Adolf Friedrich built a theatre in the castle grounds at Drottningsholm, which today, two hundred years after its foundation, is the scene of a delightful festival, an essential part of Scandinavia's summer music. In 1773 the King's son, Gustav III, created the first opera-house in his residence. That Gustav was murdered during a ball is familiar not only to historians but to opera-lovers through Verdi's *Masked Ball*, though to avoid censorship Verdi had to change the locale to seventeenth-century Boston with the fictional Governor (Riccardo) representing Gustav III.

In 1782 the Stockholm Opera acquired its own building, where it played for over a century. This was demolished in 1891, to be replaced in 1898 by the present elegant red-and-gold opera-house with 1200 seats.

Scandinavia, especially Sweden, has produced a large number of famous names, starting, of course, with Jenny Lind; Christine Nilsson, Eidé Norena, Ellen Gulbranson, Lilly Hafgren, Sigrid Arnoldson, Olive Fremstad, Nanny Larsen-Todsen, Karin Branzell, Kirsten Flagstad, Kerstin Thorborg, Elisabeth Söderström, Kerstin Meyer, Birgit Nilsson, Sigrid Onegin, Astrid Varnay, John Forsell (from 1924–1939 director of the Stockholm Opera), Lauritz Melchior, Set Svanholm (also director of the opera-house at the end of his brilliant career), Jussi Björling (for some record-lovers the finest tenor voice of our time), Joel Berglund, Sigurd Björling, Torsten Ralf, Axel Schiötz, Nicolai Gedda, Martti Talvela. Besides these, there are many others whose fame has not spread beyond their own country but who can still be rated as distinguished singers in their own right.

Oslo and Copenhagen are also flourishing musical capitals, where there has lately been a much increased interest in opera, no doubt partly due to the appearance of important Scandinavian works; Blomdahl's space opera, *Aniara*, for instance, is the first Scandinavian opera to be performed internationally with striking success.

Holland, despite its historical importance in music, has no opera to speak of. The annual Holland Festival organised throughout the country gives an extra impulse towards opera production, but it is still a big step from there to the establishment of permanent opera-houses. Even so, there are some fine voices to promote Dutch pride; I would especially pick out Gré Brouwenstijn, Gerry de Groot and Maria van Dongen.

France and Belgium

French operatic history begins in 1669, Lully and Rameau are its first enduring names. Afterwards came the clashes between those for and against *opera buffa* over Pergolesi's *La serva padrona*, and later between the followers of Gluck and those of Piccini. In the course of the centuries the Paris opera-house has been called Opéra National, Théâtre des Arts, Théâtre de la Republique et des Arts, Académie Impériale, Académie Nationale de Musique, till finally the popular name Grande Opéra was left. All the earlier opera-houses burned down. At the re-opening of one of them Noverre's ballet *Les petits riens* was staged, with some (anonymous!) musical numbers contributed by Mozart, who had just arrived in Paris.

The continual fires and rebuildings were perhaps symbolic of the continual social and political changes through revolution, terror, restoration, Napoleonic era, Empire, Republic. But all classes seemed to have one thing in common, an enthusiasm for the brilliant virtuoso singers who were constantly arriving in Paris. We have seen Malibran celebrating her triumphs there, and her sister Pauline Viardot-Garcia dominated Paris opera for many years. In the eighteen-thirties and forties Paris was the centre of international musical life, and it retained much of this glory for several more decades. Most of the famous operatic composers of the time lived there, not only Frenchmen like Berlioz, Méhul, Gounod, Halévy, Thomas and Bizet, but also other illustrious names, mainly Italian; Cherubini, Spontini, Bellini, Donizetti, Rossini, Meyerbeer and Offenbach. The distinction between the two groups was easily set aside or blurred in this most cosmopolitan of cities.

The building of the new Grande Opéra testifies more clearly than anything else to the style of the Second Empire. After Vienna opened its magnificent new opera-house in 1869, Paris had to come up with something still more splendid. The architect Charles Garnier designed a palace which became a centre of musical life almost more than a temple of the muses. It was fourteen years in the building, and with its area of over 13,000 square yards gave Parisians the heady feeling of having the biggest opera-house in the world. When the Empress Eugénie entered it for the first time, she asked in amazement: 'What style is this?' Garnier answered: 'Napoleon III style'.

It was the thirteenth home of Paris opera. The ceremonial opening took place on 5th January 1875, with a mixed programme which did not augur too well for its artistic future; the first and second acts of *La Juive*, the *William Tell* overture, a scene from *Les Huguenots*, a Délibes ballet and the overture to Auber's *La Muette de Portici*. Nevertheless, towards the end of the century and the beginning of our own century, the opera-house provided a stage for such a host of glorious voices that for the historical record they justify a long list of names; Francesco Tamagno, Jean de Reszke, Jean Lassalle, Pol Plançon, Adelina Patti, Nellie Melba, Rose Caron; Célestine Galli-Marié (the first Carmen and Mignon), Hélène Bouvier, Lucienne Bréval, Emma Calvé (world-famous as the 'best' Carmen), Marguerite Carré, Emma Luart, Germaine Lubin, Janine Micheau, Gabrièlle Ritter-Ciampi, Ninon Vallin, Geneviève Vix, Rita Gorr, Fanny Heldy, Suzanne Juyol, Ketty Lapeyrette, Lily Pons, Régine Crespin; Ernest Blanc, Edmond Clément, Lucien Fugère, Jacques Jansen (the best Pelléas of his time), Raoul Jobin, Marcel Journet (a leading bass), René Maison (one of the few French Wagner tenors), Adolphe Maréchal, Gaston Micheletti, Pierre Mollet, Jean Noté, Jean Périer, Maurice Renaud, Léon Rothier, Edouard Rouard (Amfortas in the first Paris production of *Parsifal*), Charles Rousselière, Félix Vieuille (first Bluebeard in Dukas's *Ariane et Barbe bleu*), Georges Thill (a tenor of world class), Charles Panzéra and Gérard Souzay (more of these two when we talk of Lieder-singers); Emile Scaremberg, a gifted tenor who at thirty-four suddenly lost his voice, and Gabriel Soulacroix, who saved the lives of many people during a fire at the Opéra Comique in 1887, still wearing his costume of Laertes in Thomas's *Hamlet*, which was being performed that evening.

The Opéra Comique, Paris's second opera-house, probably goes back to the markets of Saint-Germain and Saint-Laurent, which in

the eighteenth century performed bawdy parodies of the operas of
the official company; the expression 'opéra comique' was used in this
connection in about 1715, and was retained for the genre, which was
related to the Italian opera buffa. A vaudeville theatre then merged
with a theatre called 'Comédie Italienne', and in 1783 this combination acquired its own building called 'Opéra Comique'. Here too
there were many changes of name, until it was eventually fixed as
Théâtre de l'Opéra Comique, although the name no longer corresponded with the programme of the opera-house – which, for instance, staged the premières of *Carmen*, Charpentier's *Louise* and
Pelléas et Mélisande. The Scottish girl Mary Garden, later world-
famous, was the first Mélisande, and her greatest successor, curiously
enough, was an English girl, Maggie Teyte, who was trained in
Paris and was a pupil of Jean de Reszke – we shall meet her again in
the section on solo song. Many of the singers mentioned above came
from the *Opéra Comique*. The building burned down in 1887 and the
new opera-house as we see it today, opened in December 1898. It
seats about 1700 and although a good deal less grand than the
Garnier 'palace', is often musically superior.

For a long time France's other opera-houses were overshadowed
by the two at Paris, but the situation changed decisively after the
Second World War, and it would be unfair not to mention some of
the other French towns where opera thrives today, such as Stras-
bourg, Lyons, Bordeaux, Marseilles and Aix-les-Bains with its
summer theatre. I must also refer to two French-speaking centres
outside France, Monte Carlo and Brussels. The Prince's Opera at
Monte Carlo, a sort of annexe to the casino, is a neo-baroque building which seats 600 and was opened in 1879 by Sarah Bernhardt. It
often housed great singers, who were even to be heard there in
world premières, notably the first stage production of Berlioz's
Damnation of Faust, Massenet's *Le Jongleur de Notre Dame* and *Don
Quichotte* (with Chaliapin in the title rôle), also works of Fauré and
Honegger, and Puccini's *Rondine*.

In 1685 there was a battle in the heart of Brussels between Haps-
burgs and Bourbons, during which over 4,000 buildings were destroyed, among them one known as 'Hotel des Monnaies'. Fifteen
years later an opera-house was opened on this site and was named
after it. In 1819 a new building went up with the same name, by the
wish of the government of Holland, which then ruled a large part of
today's Belgium, including Brussels. But Belgian independence was
to be particularly associated with this opera-house, for a performance
of Auber's *La Muette de Portici*, with its revolutionary mood, helped

to inspire the rising of 1830 which led to the Flemish gaining their independence as part of Belgium.

That particular 'Monnaie' burned down in 1855, and Brussels obtained its third opera-house, the present building, which after many changes of name is now definitively Théâtre Royal de la Monnaie. Neo-classical in exterior, its interior is red, white and gold, in Louis XIV style, and seats 1800. Opened in 1856, 'La Monnaie' within a few years became one of Europe's important opera-houses. There were world premières (eg Massenet's *Hérodiade* in 1881), and many famous singers appeared there; Melba (who made her stage début at La Monnaie), Patti, Rose Caron, Marie Brema, Emma Calvé, Emma Albani, Ernest van Dyck, Marcel Journet, Maurice Renaud; later Caruso, Chaliapin, Anselmi, Bahr-Mildenburg and Hempel; also three Belgians who achieved international fame from there, Fanny Held, Fernand Ansseau and Armand Crabbé. Today the 'Ballet of the 20th-century', under the direction of Maurice Béjart, which is incorporated with La Monnaie, may have a greater international reputation than its opera, but the theatre is still important operatically as well, especially after the world premières of works by Milhaud and Prokofiev.

Eastern Europe

New York, Buenos Aires and London can regularly offer about 4500 seats to opera-lovers on a winter evening; the figure is about 3800 for Paris, Vienna, Milan and Munich (when Munich's three opera-houses are all playing). These are the largest numbers for the western world, and not very impressive considering the millions of inhabitants in its various capitals, although we should not forget the additional facilities through records, radio and television.

But undeniably the number of those who go to opera in the west is far surpassed by the numbers for eastern Europe. Moscow has 10,000 seats every evening for lovers of opera and ballet, and there are proportionately similar figures for the other big cities in eastern Europe. This is not the place to discuss the basic differences between opera in Europe's two main 'sectors', or the conservative ideas prevailing in Moscow's state theatre, the old 'Bolshoi', especially as regards production and choreography, which are such a remarkable contrast with the revolutionary experiments of, say, West German opera. Nor shall I do more than mention that the Soviet Union's contemporary composers are in direct continuity with the tradition, rather than rejecting it and trying to break it as in the West. In the

Bolshoi, for instance, and elsewhere in Eastern Europe, Prokofiev, Shostakovitch, Muradeli, Shaporin, Shebalin, Shigenov and Dzershinski can be played with no greater difficulties than Tchaikovsky, Moussorgsky and Rimsky-Korsakov; whereas in Western opera-houses there are enormous differences between Weber, Wagner, even Richard Strauss on the one hand and Schönberg, Klebe, Zimmerman and Nono on the other. In this book we are concerned only with singers, and in the West very few of today's famous opera-singers are involved with *avant-garde* works. This is not only because rôles in these are so difficult musically that studying them takes up a disproportionate amount of time, but also because the contemporary composers mostly demand a completely different type of interpretation from the singer's point of view. Beauty of tone, phrasing, legato singing – all these former virtues are thrown overboard to do justice to the powerful expression of a present-day work. The singer in Eastern Europe is not faced with this dilemma, or to a far smaller extent.

Some top singers from behind the iron curtain have found their way to the greatest opera-houses in the West, Boris Christoff, Nicolai Ghiaurov, Ludovic Spiess, Hanna Yanku, Danisa Mastilovic, Raina Kabaivanska, Miliza Korjus, Sandor Konya, to name only a few; but the music-lover in the West learns little of the wealth of splendid voices to be heard in the opera-houses of eastern Europe. In succession to the generation of the giants – Baklanoff, Kipnis, Didur and above all, of course, Chaliapin – there were the bass Ivan Petrov, the soprano Tamara Milashkina, the mezzo-soprano Larissa Nikitina; and of many other beautiful voices the most prominent were Eleonora Andreyevna, Galina Vishnevskaya, Irina Archipova, Larissa Avdeyeva, Pavel Lissizian and Yevgeni Kibkalo. Russian voices often have their own special sound, a 'colour' not to be found anywhere else in the world. This seems to be particularly the case with deep men's voices, even a distant Russian ancestry often reveals itself in such a voice. Two well-known examples of this are the Italian bass Nicola Rossi-Lemeni and the Swiss bass Peter Lagger.

By old custom, ballet enjoys the same treatment as opera, indeed is sometimes even more popular with the public, in Moscow's five 'music theatres'. The most famous of these was, and is, the 'State Academic Great Theatre of the USSR', called 'Bolshoi Theatre'. But in fact the largest is the Congress Palace in the Kremlin, opened in 1961, which seats 6000.

Leningrad's opera in relation to Moscow's is a little like the Teatro Fenice in relation to La Scala; it is quieter and lives more off the past. The comparison also applies, by accident, in a further point; the interiors of La Scala and Bolshoi are in red and gold, while blue and silver are the colours of Fenice and Leningrad's State Academic Opera and Ballet Theatre, also called Kirov Theatre. As early as the second half of the eighteenth-century, in the time of Tsar Peter III, there was opera to be heard in St Petersburg, mainly Italian opera with Italian singers. Nicholas I built the former opera-house in 1836 and had it opened with the first Russian national work, Glinka's *A Life for the Tsar*. In 1832 another opera-house was opened, and in 1850 there was a third, called the Circus Theatre, where many musical entertainments were given. This burned down in 1859; but the following year, now as the Maryinsky Theatre, it became the seat of the Imperial Opera. In 1862 Verdi directed there the first production of his *Force of Destiny*, Moussorgsky's *Boris Godunov* was launched there in 1874, and in 1890 Tchaikovsky's *Queen of Spades* was sung there for the first time. After the Revolution the Maryinsky Theatre became the Kirov Theatre, and 1918 saw the opening of another theatre, the 'Little Academic Opera-House', where Shostakovich's *Lady Macbeth of Mdensk* and works by Prokofiev had their premières. The voices heard in the former St Petersburg and today's Leningrad have been among the finest in the world; for examples in the present I would mention the contralto Sofia Preobrashenskaya, the tenor Vladimir Atlantov and the bass Nikolai Krikulya.

Simply for the record I give the names of some of the other Soviet cities which have notable opera-houses; Alma-Ata, Ashkabad, Baku, Kharkov, Frunse, Gorki, Yerevan, Kazan, Kiev, Kishinev, Kuibyshev, Lvov, Novosibirsk, Odessa, Perm, Riga, Saratov, Stalinabad, Stalino, Sverdlovsk, Tallinn, Tashkent, Tbilisi, Tchelyabinsk, Ufa, Ulan-Ude and Vilna. So there is a whole world of intensive opera production, of which we know almost nothing in the West, but in which there must be hundreds of beautiful and well-trained voices, and even potential 'greats'.

Warsaw's opera-house, Teatr Wielki (Great Theatre), really deserves to be called 'great'. Completely destroyed in the Second World War, it rose in 1965 more spacious than before, larger than any other opera-house in the world, including the Grande Opéra at Paris. Something in its basic concept is reminiscent of the original plan of the Munich opera-house; the pillars and the building's extensive sides give it a classic majesty. In addition to the auditorium in white and red, with its 2000 comfortable seats, there are other halls, a theatrical museum and a drama school.

Poland's opera is probably older than any other country's (except of course Italy). In 1613 a big Polish land-owner invited an Italian opera company to come and perform on his estate, although admittedly this was only an isolated occasion. Still, there was a first operatic performance in Warsaw fifteen years later. In 1725 the first opera-house was opened there, in 1778 – after the long predominance of Italian opera – the first Polish work was staged, and in 1833 the Teatr Wielki was built. It was gutted in 1939 under the German conquest, the walls collapsed in 1945 during the Warsaw Rising. Today, in the magnificently restored opera-house, opera is flourishing vigorously, although as it is mostly performed in Polish, little international exchange of singers is possible. Besides Warsaw, Bydgoszcz, Bytom, Gdansk, Cracow, Lodz, Posnan and Vroclav have regular opera-houses, and all depend on their own companies. Their stars are Halina Slonicka, Krystina Szostek-Radkova, Bogdan Paprocki, Andrei Hiolski, Bernard Ladysz; and there are also singers who have become known in the West through records – Teresa Zylis-Gara, Stefania Voytovics, Urszula Koszut and Vieslav Ochmann.

Prague's musical life must be regarded as one of the most intensive of all for the size of the city. Three opera-houses are playing regularly to audiences of 4300 altogether. The oldest of them, one of Europe's oldest opera-houses still in operation, is the former Assembly Theatre, today Kajetan-Tyl Theatre. It experienced one of its early peaks through Mozart's glorious stay in Prague, with *The Marriage of Figaro* which he conducted here, and the world première of *Don Giovanni*, also under his baton. It had been completed a few years earlier in 1783. A century later, with the building of the Narodni Divadlo, a national theatre in the fullest sense of the word, Prague acquired the desired home for Czech opera. In 1868 the foundation stone was laid, after a popular assembly had voted in favour of the new building on the Moldau bank, but just before its opening in 1881 this burned down. A new effort by the whole population realised the apparently impossible; the Narodni Divaldo opened on 18th November 1883 with *Libuse*, a celebratory opera which Smetana, 'father of Czech music', had written for this purpose a long time before – but tragically the composer by then was stone deaf.

About this time Prague's German-speaking citizens, with a strongly Jewish element, set about putting up a new opera-house. This 'German Theatre' did valuable work for German culture, and in its heyday saw many great singers and conductors. After the Second World War its days were naturally numbered; renamed the

Smetana Theatre, it became the third of Prague's opera-houses, all under joint direction. Seating about 1500, it is little smaller than the National Theatre and rather bigger than the Kajeta-Tyl, the historic Assembly Theatre.

Brno has an old City Theatre from which many great singers – most notably Maria Jeritza and Leo Slezak – started on their world career. Today, named after the great Czech master Leos Janacek, it is a serious rival to Prague. The other important opera-houses in Czechoslovakia are at Banska Bystrica, Bratislava, Ceske Budejovice, Kladno, Liberec, Olomouc, Opava, Ostrava, Plzen, Usti. The outstanding singers between the wars were Marta Krasova, Drahomira Tikalova, Maria Tauberova, Jarmila Novotna, Maria Podvalova, Zdenek Otava, Beno Blachut, Eduard Haken. Their successors today include Alena Mikova and Ivo Zidek, the lyric sopranos Milada Subrtova and Libuse Domaninska, both lovely voices, and Hanna Janku, a dramatic soprano of the highest class with tremendous vocal powers which can soar above even the largest ensemble. They encompass an immense range, and are as suited for *Turandot* as for the native *Dalibor*.

Budapest has a long and honourable operatic history. In 1837 the National Theatre opened its doors, and the works of its director, Ferenc Erkel, were heard there, using Hungarian motifs for the first time. When in the seventies the opera-house had become too small, the Hungarian architect Miklos Ybl's design won the prize for a new building, which was clearly based on the magnificent Viennese opera-house. The first performance there was given in September 1884. Although only seating 1300, it had a certain regal splendour, especially in its foyers and the marble steps outside. By 1911 this also had become too small, and the city put up the Magyar Allami Operahaz, a theatre seating 2200. Many superb voices originated from Budapest: Maria Nemeth, Ester Rethy, Maria von Ilosvay, the important Lieder-singer Ilona Durigo, Koloman von Pataky, Alexander Sved, Maria Basilides, Sandor Konya (one of the best Lohengrins in the world after the war), Robert Ilosfalvy; Elsa Szamosi, Maria Gyurkovics, Erszebet Komlossy, Paula Takasz, Maria Matyas, Klara Palankay, Joszef Simandi and Mikaly Szekely.

Yugoslavia's opera-houses have earned a great reputation, especially the Belgrade Opera with its highly gifted company which has been on many world tours. Miro Changalovich is a towering Boris Godunov, eloquently combining the power of his majesty and the torment of his downfall, also a notable Dosifei in Moussorgsky's *Khovantchina* and Gremin in Tchaikovsky's *Eugene Onegin*. He is surrounded by an abundance of outstanding artists: Valeria Hey-balova, Melanie Bugarinovich, Bogdana Stritar, Sofia Yankovich, Tatiana Slastenko, Nada Tonic, Bjanka Dezman, Miro Brajnik, Drago Startz, Nichalos Tzyvech, Alexander Marinkovich, Dushan Popovich, Latko Koroshetz, Milenko Grozdanic, Ana Lipsa, Marija Glavasevic, Miltza Miladino.

Rumania and Bulgaria are younger countries operatically, but in the last years have also produced a good stock of splendid voices. The first Rumanian to have a world career was Hariclée Darclée; Ludovic Spiess, a heroic tenor who quickly advanced to the highest class, and the remarkable lyric tenor Ion Buzes also come from that country. Two Bulgarian basses are among the great singers of our century, Boris Christoff and Nicolai Ghiaurov, nor should the wonderful voice of Dimitri Uzunov be overlooked. But the majority remain at home, in the Bucharest and Sofia operas in the latter especially, productions can occasionally be seen which, for vocal accomplish-ment, might be the envy of many world-famous opera-houses.

Spain and Portugal

For various reasons which I cannot consider here, as they are certainly outside the sphere of singing, the achievements in opera of Spain and Portugal have been conspicuously irregular and for the most part very scanty. They have, however, produced large numbers of quite outstanding voices; Manuel Garcia with his two daughters, Maria Malibran and Pauline Viardot, Adelina Patti, Maria Barrien-tos, Mercedes Capsir, Regina Pacini, Miguel Fleta, Francisco d'Andrade, Lucrezia Bori, Hippolito Lazaro, Teresa Berganza, Pilar Lorengar, Victoria de los Angeles, Conchita Supervia, Conchita Badia and Montserrat Caballé.

The singers who stay in Spain were, and are, thoroughly absorbed in the native form of operetta or comic opera called *Zarzuela*, which has provided some excellent works and enjoys immense popularity; it has often involved a great many fine singers (Sagi Barba and Sagi Vela, to name only two) who could have helped build a national opera, something which in fact has never become a permanent institution. In 1818 the Spanish king decided to put up an opera-house in Madrid, but it took more than thirty years to build, and the result was a disappointment, at first architecturally and later artis-tically. Still, from its opening in 1850, there were good periods. Its connection with Italy was so close that instead of creating a national opera Madrid became an Italian subsidiary. Except for the productions of a *zarzuela* or one of the few Spanish operas, performances were almost all in Italian. In 1925 the Teatro Real (Royal Opera-house) was closed for structural repairs, and it was over forty years before it was re-opened, in October 1966.

Barcelona has always been Spain's real operatic capital. It has had a theatre since 1587, and the first opera, naturally an Italian one, was produced there in 1708. Then various theatres for opera were built, until in 1847 the opera-house was opened. It burned down in 1861, but was duly restored and after restoration has remained in its present form one of the most beautiful and imposing in Europe. Its name, Teatro del Liceo or simply Liceo, is derived from the lay society which from 1838 on, as 'Liceo Filarmonica-dramatico de la reina Isabel II', could claim many fine achievements, especially in the field of artistic training. The Liceo with its 3800 seats (which make it one of the most capacious theatres in the world) is devoted exclusively to opera, but only in short annual seasons and almost entirely performed by prominent international companies. With its painted ceiling and hundreds of chandeliers and private boxes, this baroque palace caters for a high-society audience. Opera is sung in the original language, and there is a striking Wagner cult, which takes many distinguished German singers across the Pyrenees every year.

Our Century of Festivals

Among the countless festivals which fill the musical year, and the engagement diaries of famous singers, Bayreuth has a special place. It is the oldest of those which are still running today, and is unique in being devoted exclusively to the works of a single master for nearly a century.

In 1876 when Wagner launched 'his' festival, the summer meant a rest period for all musical and theatrical activities. June, July and August gave the European opera-singers a much appreciated holiday. There were no records to make, and South America, still 'undis-covered', was not yet recognised as an ideal place for guest per-formances during the summer months because the seasons were reversed there. Nor as yet were there festivals in today's sense. Those summoned by Wagner to Bayreuth sacrificed their holidays, but in compensation received something more; a sort of initiation. Anyone who sang merely one of the Valkyries, a Rhine maiden or a Norn, was thereafter considered to have 'arrived'. Anyone who had the chance to sing Siegfried, Tristan, Brünnhilde or Isolde had advanced to the highest ranks of singing.

Of course, not all Bayreuth seasons throughout the century were of the same quality. Here too there were both singers with ephemeral glory and the great figures who became 'owners' of important rôles over many years and in them set standards which became valid for Wagner productions everywhere else. Let us skim through the Bayreuth annals.

It is well-known that the festival building on the green hill opened in 1876 with *Der Ring des Nibelungen*. Franz Betz was the first Wotan and Wanderer, Albert Niemann Siegmund, Josephine Schefsky Sieglinde, Amalie Materna Brünnhilde, Georg Unger was Siegfried. Lilli Lehmann, not yet world-famous, sang the Woodbird in *Siegfried* and was also one of the Valkyries with her sister Marie.

The Bayreuth Festivals were twice suspended; from 1914 to 1924 in the train of the First World War and its chaotic after-effects, and from 1944 to 1951 when Europe's tragedy was repeated in even more intense form. The second break meant for Bayreuth a profound change of attitude, of which there will be more to say later.

The successors of Franz Betz as Wotan were Hermann Bachmann, Karl Perron, Anton van Roy, Theodor Bertram, Walter Soomer, Karl Braun, Friedrich Schorr, Josef Correk, Rudolf Bockelmann, Jaro Prohaska, Hans Hotter. The list of tenors, up to 1944, includes Emil Gerhäuser, Heinrich Vogl, Alois Burgstaller, Wilhelm Grüning, Ernst Kraus, Alfred von Bary, Erik Schmedes, Rudolf Ritter, Peter Cornelius, Jakob Urlus, Lauritz Melchior, Gotthelf Pistor, Paul Wiedemann, Gunnar Graarud, Franz Völker, Max Lorenz, Set Svanholm. Those who sang Sieglinde were Rosa Sucher, Marie Wittich, Katharina Fleischer-Edel, Martha Leffler-Burkhard, Minnie Saltzmann-Stevens, Helena Forti, Emmy Krüger, Henny Trundt, Maria Müller, Kirsten Flagstad (who soon afterwards grew into one of the greatest Brünnhildes); other Brünnhildes were Ellen Gulbranson, Lilli Lehmann, Olga Blomé, Nanny Larsen-Todsen, Frida Leider, Marta Fuchs, Paula Buchner. Tristan and Isolde had the following interpreters; Heinrich Gudehus and Therese Malten, Heinrich Vogl and Rosa Sucher, Alfred von Bary and Marie Wittich, Gunnar Graarud and Emmy Krüger, Gotthelf Pistor and Emmy Krüger, Gunnar Graarud and Nanny Larsen-Todsen, Lauritz Melchior and Nanny Larsen-Todsen, Karl Hartmann and Martha Fuchs, Max Lorenz and Frida Leider, Max Lorenz and Germaine Lubin.

With the re-opening in 1951 under the Wagner grandsons Wieland and Wolfgang, a new generation came into prominence. Otto Edelmann took over Hans Sachs, succeeding Jaro Prohaska and Paul

Schöffler, and the Swede, Sigurd Björling, became Wotan; Elisabeth Höngen sang Waltraute and Fricka (until 1944 taken by Sigrid Onegin and Margarete Klose); Hans Hopf succeeded Lorenz and Suthaus as Stolzing, and Paul Kuen succeeded Erich Zimmermann as Mime. Erich Kunz sang Beckmesser as he had already done in 1943, Wilma Lipp sang the Woodbird, George London made a powerful Amfortas, Martha Mödl a stirring Kundry and also Gutrune. Ira Malaniuk sang Magdalene, Arnold van Mill four of the great bass rôles. Leonie Rysanck became Sieglinde, Elisabeth Schwarzkopf Eva (in *Meistersinger*) and Woglinde (*Ring*). Gerhard Stolze sang small rôles at first, but soon grew out of them and became one of the most magnificent interpretative singers of rôles like Loge and Mime (*Ring*). Bernd Aldenhoff, with his brilliant high notes, and Günther Treptow took over Siegmund, Hermann Uhde Gunther and Klingsor. Astrid Varnay became a fine Brünnhilde, Ludwig Weber Fasolt and Hagen in *The Ring* as well as Gurnemanz in *Parsifal*. Windgassen, who became the leading Wagner tenor, started as Parsifal. Then there were two *Spieltenors*, Erwin Wohlfahrt and Gerhard Unger, Birgit Nilsson, the great Flagstad's worthy successor; Josef Greindl, a sonorous and versatile bass; Gustav Neidlinger, an unforgettable Alberich. In 1961 there was a sensation caused by the appearance of Grace Bumbry, the first black singer at Bayreuth, in Wieland Wagner's sensual production of *Tannhäuser*. She was breaking one of the last taboos of the Wagner temple, to which many thousands make their way every year, as if it were a real pilgrimage.

Salzburg's musical history began long before Mozart father and son; in a very beautiful baroque theatre, which is still one of the sights today. Festive music in the name of Wolfgang Amadeus was already heard in the last century. Then, at the beginning of our century, there were two commemoration days for this greatest of Salzburg's musical sons. In hard times – post-war revolution and impoverishment – far-seeing people (the singer Bahr-Mildenburg with her writer husband Hermann Bahr, the poets Hofmannsthal and Zweig; Richard Strauss, Bruno Walter, Vienna's opera director Franz Schalk, the producer Max Reinhardt) planned to hold an annual festival during the summer months. In 1920 it began with a performance of *Everyman* in front of the Cathedral, one of the city's many glorious squares and one of the most impressive in all Europe. Two years later the first opera was presented. Mozart of course; *Don Giovanni* under Richard Strauss in the Landestheater (Province Theatre), for there was not yet a festival building. Two casts were mustered, both from Vienna: Alfred Jerger, Gertrud Kappel, Claire Born, Lotte Schöne, Richard Tauber and Richard Mayr formed one; the other had Hans Duhan, Felicie Hüni-Mihacsek, Rose Pauly, Georg Maikl, Karl Norbert, Editha Fleischer and Julius Betetto. Mayr and Elisabeth Rethberg shone in *The Marriage of Figaro*, and there was a brilliant *Entführung* with Selma Kurz as Constanze and Tauber as Belmonte.

After that there was no opera again until 1925, when Ivogün sang Zerlina in the festival *Don Giovanni* and, with Mayr, Donizetti's *Don Pasquale*. For the repertoire was no longer confined to Mozart, in fact the festival programme became more and more comprehensive. In 1926 Tauber, who was at the height of his powers, sang Belmonte, Ottavio, and Eisenstein in *Die Fledermaus*. For the first time Salzburg had a Strauss opera, *Ariadne auf Naxos*, with Lotte Lehmann's superb voice for the title rôle. The summer of 1927 saw a combination of four stars in *Fidelio* which would be hard to surpass; Lotte Lehmann, Alfred Piccaver, Richard Mayr, Elisabeth Schumann. Lehmann became Salzburg's permanent Fidelio, and for her benefit something happened which sounds almost incredible to the connoisseur; as she was no longer in full possession of her top notes, Toscanini, usually so inexorable in artistic questions, transposed her great aria down a semitone, simply so that he could go on putting her in this rôle, in which she had previously given such wonderful performances. She had different partners then; Kalenberg sang Florestan, Luise Helletsgruber Marzelline, Wilhelm Rode Pizarro and Josef von Manowarda Rocco.

A new magnificent Festival Theatre was built at the foot of the Mönchsberg, and more and more foreign visitors began to make their pilgrimages to Salzburg. They were stirred to the depths by Lotte Lehmann as the Marschallin, overflowing with warm-hearted humanity; Vera Schwarz, an outstanding artist, was Oktavian, Adele Kern an enchanting Sophie, so complete and effective a contrast to the noble Marschallin, and Mayr, naturally, was Baron Ochs – a model, even today, for every interpreter of this rôle. In 1930 Viorica Ursuleac shared the Marschallin's rôle with Lehmann, a difficult task. She has been followed by Maria Reining, Elisabeth Schwarzkopf and most recently Sena Jurinac, all four remarkable by any other standards than comparison with the unique Lehmann; unique not so much in her singing, where the others might have matched her, as in the radiance of her personality. The charming Oktavian in 1930 was Margit Angerer, who came swiftly into the limelight but very soon disappeared again.

Karl Hammes and John Forsell were now singing the title rôle in *Don Giovanni*, both with great distinction. Maria Nemeth was a powerful Donna Anna, Luise Helletsgruber had great beauty of tone as Donna Elvira, Adele Kern and Lotte Schöne were equally delightful as Zerlina. In 1932 Tauber was succeeded in all his rôles by Koloman von Pataky, who had for years been successful at Salzburg, and again one must say that though Pataky was a brilliant bel canto and legato singer, Tauber was unique. There was also a new tenor, discovered by Clemens Krauss and transformed from a bank-clerk to a juvenile lead of the operatic stage; Franz Völker. No other heroic tenor of the time could match him for nobility, artistry in phrasing and melting beauty of tone, even in the most exciting forte passages. Gluck's *Orpheus and Eurydice* had a wonderful cast – Sigrid Onegin, Maria Müller, Maria Cebotari, and with Bruno Walter conducting. Three of the most splendid voices of the age were together here, and to rival this 'Nordic' combination, an Italian company came to Salzburg for the first time, to sing Rossini and Donizetti. They were led by Dino Borgioli, Mariano Stabile and Fernando Autori, all wonderful singers but capable of the most side-splitting comedy as well.

The Festival's international reputation was increasing all the time; so were the audiences. The 1933 programme contained ten operas, including two works new to Salzburg: Strauss's *Die Ägyptische Helena* (which had been produced for the first time a few years before) with Ursuleac, Völker, Roswaenge, Jerger and Gertrude Rünger; and *Tristan und Isolde*, first with Dorothea Manski and Hans Grahl, under Toscanini's baton, and then Theo Strack and Anni Konetzni; Rosette Anday, Vienna's leading contralto, alternated with the dramatically impressive Gertrude Rünger as Brangäne.

Don Giovanni that year had another superb cast: Ezio Pinza, Maria Müller, Dusolina Giannini, Lotte Schöne, Dino Borgioli, Emanuel List, Virgilio Lazzari, Karl Ettl. In 1935 Mariano Stabile sang his famous Falstaff, brilliantly supported by Borgioli, Autori, Maria Caniglia (alternating with Dusolina Giannini) and Piero Basini. Hugo Wolf's *Der Corregidor*, a sadly neglected opera, did not, unfortunately, fare any better through its performance at Salzburg, even with the voices of Graarud, Jerger, Jarmila Novotna and Kerstin Thorborg.

1937 was the last Salzburg Festival before the German occupation and the war. *Die Meistersinger* was performed here for the first time, with Henk Noort as Stolzing, the delightful Maria Reining as Eva, and a cast which included Hans Hermann Nissen, Herbert Alsen,

Georg Maikl, Ralph Telasko, Hermann Wiedemann, Viktor Madin and Anton Dermota. Italian operas were on the programme more and more, sung increasingly in the original language, and besides *Don Giovanni* and *Falstaff* there was a star cast that year for Mozart's *Figaro*; Mariano Stabile, Ezio Pinza, Ester Réty, and the Finnish soprano Aulikki Rautawara, who made an outstanding Countess.

After the arrival of the Nazis, Salzburg lost many leading personalities – Toscanini, Bruno Walter, Lotte Lehmann, Max Reinhardt, another notable producer, Margarethe Wallmann, and many others. The Festival continued, and still had some great artists taking part, including Julius Patzak, Hans Hotter and Paul Hörbiger, who sang Papageno for the first time, but by 1944 there was only a semi-public 'dress rehearsal' of the Salzburg première of Strauss's *Liebe der Danae*, with Viorica Ursuleac, Maud Cunitz, Horst Taubmann, Hans Hotter, Franz Klarwein and Karl Ostertag.

A modest new start was made the following year in the small though very pleasant Landestheater (the Festival building was seriously damaged). Only one opera, *Die Entführung*, was performed, but this had a real Festival cast; Maria Cebotari, Julius Patzak, Ludwig Weber. After that a new generation began to move in, and often proved worthy successors to the great names hallowed for decades by Salzburg audiences. Hans Hotter now sang Don Giovanni, Dermota was Ottavio, Georg Hann Leporello. While these three, long recognised as masters of their craft, now reached the peak of their careers, three women's voices were coming strongly to the fore; Maud Cunitz, Hilde Güden (a future coloratura diva of international stature) and Ljuba Welitsch, a gifted Bulgarian with a radiance like Jeritza's, who after several years as a bright star disappeared much too soon. Erich Kunz, a modern singer-actor, took over Mozart's Figaro with charm and deep musical sensitivity; Irmgard Seefried was an equally attractive Susanna, while Maria Cebotari made a beautiful Countess both in voice and appearance. Hilde Konetzni, now a fully mature artist, presented a noble, melodious – and very Viennese – Marschallin.

Arabella, the last of the glorious heroines created by the poetic genius of Hofmannsthal and the musical genius of Strauss, was now firmly anchored in the Salzburg repertoire. Maria Reining was passionate, charming, full of humanity in this rôle, which she sang exquisitely. Arabella's younger sister Zdenka was sung by Lisa della Casa, who here reached the first peak of her steeply rising career; she was soon to become herself an ideal Arabella.

In 1947 there was a big new feature, the world première of a contemporary opera. A century earlier such a thing would have been nothing out of the ordinary; now it took long discussions and showed a distinctly progressive attitude. The work in question was *Danton's Death* by Gottfried von Einem, triumphantly launched by Paul Schöffler, Julius Patzak and Maria Cebotari, with the young Ferenc Fricsay conducting. 1948 saw another successful première, *Le Vin Herbe*, by the distinguished Swiss composer, Frank Martin, with Patzak, Cebotari, Endré Koréh, Hilde Zadek, Maria Ilosvay, Dagmar Hermann, Alfred Poell, Kark Dönch and Wilhelm Friedrich.

The following year Orff's *Antigone* was heard for the first time, in the *Felsenreitschule* (mentioned before for its open-air stage) with Res Fischer – a fine contralto – Hermann Uhde, Benno Kusche, Lorenz Fehenberger, Ernst Haefliger, Josef Greindl, Hilde Zadek, Maria Ilosvay and Helmut Krebs. Haefliger, an excellent Swiss tenor, sang Tamino at the 1949 Festival, Wilma Lipp produced brilliant coloratura as the Queen of the Night, and Irmgard Seefried, climbing towards the summit of her successful career, made a fine Pamina. For Leonore, the greatest dramatic soprano of the era was once more in action – Kirsten Flagstad. There was a new, outstanding cast for Gluck's *Orpheus*; Elizabeth Höngen, a mellifluous and extremely expressive contralto, the delightful Jarmila Novotna, and Hilde Güden with her great vocal purity and lightness.

Jaro Prohaska became Salzburg's Baron Ochs, Tito Gobbi was *Don Giovanni*, unusually compelling for his acting of the part as well as its singing. Who can talk of decadence in a generation which could fill this key rôle with artists like Gobbi, George London, Eberhard Wächter, Hans Hotter and soon Cesare Siepi, and interpreters of the seducer's victims like Ljuba Welitsch, Elisabeth Schwarzkopf, Irmgard Seefried, Elisabeth Grümmer and Erna Berger? Erich Kunz as Leporello was in the same international class as Baccaloni and Geraint Evans. Dermota's noble singing line as Ottavio was worthy of his predecessors, Tauber, Borgioli, Roswaenge, Pataky, Patzak, while his singing of Mozart was on a lonely bel canto height, attained a little later by the young Fritz Wunderlich before his tragic early death.

Hilde Güden made a magnificent Zerbinetta in *Ariadne auf Naxos*, Lisa della Casa sang a perfect Countess in *Capriccio*, with Schöffler an inimitable La Roche. In 1950 the range of Mozart operas was extended with *Idomeneo*; Rudolf Schock, a German tenor favourite with a superb voice, sang the title rôle, Hilde Güden, Jane Lawrence, Richard Holm and Kurt Böhme formed a homogeneous company.

Alban Berg's *Wozzeck*, twenty-five years after its creation, now entered the Salzburg programme, with the principal rôles sung by Josef Hermann, Hans Beirer and Christl Goltz. A tremendous impact was made by the production of *Otello*, with the powerful Chilean tenor Ramon Vinay as the Moor, Paul Schöffler, confirming earlier triumphs as Iago, and Dragica Martinis as Desdemona. (Like Ljuba Welitsch and several others, after a sensational rise she soon faded.)

In 1953 Cesare Siepi began his own triumphs as Don Giovanni, though at the same time at Salzburg of all places, a strong rival was appearing in Eberhard Wächter. The Italian filled this rôle for over twenty years with his youthful *élan*, his coquetry, his playful, almost too light-hearted elegance and high spirits (where many critics from northern Europe expected inner torment), and his passionate singing.

1954's *Ariadne* brought together Lisa della Casa, Hilde Güden, Irmgard Seefried, Rudolf Schock and Paul Schöffler. The young bass Oskar Czerwenka began to attract attention, his Truffaldino was a rarity now almost regarded as a museum piece, and a good reason for his being called to the Met where he soon afterwards sang an amusing Baron Ochs. Rolf Liebermann's *Penelope* had its world première at Salzburg, with Christl Goltz and Annaliese Rothenberger, the former at the height of a brilliant international career, the latter just breaking through as a star of the first rank. Pfitzner's *Palestrina* was performed that year, with a surprising choice for the title rôle; Max Lorenz, for many years a wonderful Tristan and Siegfried, sang the part of the quietly devoted Roman composer of church music, accepting his lot. It was a part 'out of character' and voice, but the radiant heroic tenor had become an extremely profound artist as well. Jean Madeira, American mezzo-soprano of the new generation, made a name as Waltraute in *The Ring*, even Erda in the same work, but above all as a highly seductive Carmen. That summer's new opera had in its cast singers of the rank of Lorenz, Kurt Böhme, Walter Berry, Laszlo von Szemere, Margarete Klose, Hilde Rössl-Majdan (a very melodious contralto) and Inge Borkh. Striking in voice and appearance, the last-named had a fascination which carried her later to triumphs at the Met, especially as Salome.

1956, second centenary of Mozart's birth, was naturally devoted to his works, six of which were produced with a host of top singers. Dietrich Fischer-Dieskau, who had made a meteoric rise to become the most famous of Lieder-singers, indeed to win large audiences for this art long neglected by the wider public, here turned into a stage star as well. His masterly diction, exemplary phrasing and subtle variation of dynamics were most effective in the part of Count Almaviva. Christa Ludwig, first heard at Salzburg the year before, sang a delightful Cherubino and a seductive Dorabella; her rapid rise took her by way of Oktavian (one of the best ever) to the Marschallin, and even to dramatic soprano rôles like Leonore. Rita Streich was Zerlina and a Queen of the Night with glittering coloratura; Erika Köth shone in the even more demanding rôle of Constanze in *Die Entführung*. Rudolf Schock was there again, also Cesare Siepi, Eberhard Wächter and Walter Berry, husband of Christa Ludwig and, like her, heading for international fame. He had taken over several rôles formerly sung by Kunz, now a bel canto Guglielmo (in *Così*). Fernando Corena, a cosmopolitan from Geneva, was swiftly rising to the top in Italian opera, his Leporello at Salzburg was an important step on the way. As Ottavio in *Don Giovanni* Dermota's successor was the young Canadian Leopold Simoneau, a lyric tenor with extreme beauty of tone, which comes out particularly clearly on records.

Salzburg was Karajan's home town, and in 1957 he started there on his rise to world pre-eminence. One of his greatest achievements was the collaboration between German-speaking and Italian singers, which became extraordinarily intensive. *Fidelio* was staged with Christl Goltz, partnered by the Italian tenor Giuseppe Zampieri. Elisabeth Schwarzkopf, whose name was now being compared with Tebaldi, was put into the Italian company performing *Falstaff*; Tito Gobbi, Rolando Panerai, Luigi Alva (a Peruvian with one of the finest lyric tenors of the Italian bel canto school), Renato Ercolani, Anna Maria Canali, Giulietta Simionato, and the young Anna Moffo, soon to win rapid fame. A year later Karajan conducted a glorious Italian *Don Carlos* with Siepi as King Philip, Eugenio Fernandi in the title rôle, Ettore Bastianini as a very noble Posa; Christa Ludwig alternated as Eboli – no small honour for a young artist – with the great Simionato; Anneliese Rothenberger was the Voice from Heaven, Sena Jurinac a very powerful Queen. Lisa della Casa, a flawless Arabella, was supported in this opera by Fischer-Dieskau and Rothenberger.

The new work in 1957 had been composed by Rolf Liebermann for America; *Die Schule der Frauen* (The School for Women). It was a resounding success at Salzburg with an all-star cast; Rothenberger, Christa Ludwig, Nicolai Gedda (on his way to becoming one of the leading tenors of our era), Walter Berry, Kurt Böhme and Alois Pernerstorfer. In 1959 Samuel Barber's *Vanessa* was equally successful, with the glorious voices of Eleanor Steber and Nicolai Gedda.

There was a splendid company performing *Così*. Elisabeth Schwarzkopf and Christa Ludwig sang the two sisters, Rolando Panerai and Luigi Alva the deceiving and deceived wooers; the charming Grazella Sciutti from Milan made a brilliant Despina; she was soon to become in Vienna one of the best coloratura soubrettes in the world. She also took over Papagena, for which Annaliese Rothenberger was now too old; with Walter Berry's equally merry Papageno, they were a pair who would have delighted Mozart and Schikaneder. Hotter gave a masterly interpretation of the old grumbler Sir Morosus in the Stefan Zweig–Richard Strauss work, *Die schweigsame Frau* (The Silent Woman); and in this production Salzburg made the acquaintance of Fritz Wunderlich, a lyric tenor with a rare beauty of tone. Gluck's *Orpheus*, a traditional Salzburg showpiece, blossomed to a new beauty under Karajan, in the voices of Simionato, Jurinac and Sciutti.

The new festival theatre, four years in building, was opened in 1960. The architect, Clemens Holzmeister, had dug it deep into the Mönchsberg, and it did him credit in every way. His name, which in German means 'wood-master', was appropriate enough as regards the auditorium, for wood-panelling formed the keynote of this hall designed like an amphitheatre with its 2200 seats; monotone in the contemporary style, it still has a festive and inviting look. For its opening under Karajan there was a voluptuous feast of sound in *Rosenkavalier*, with Lisa della Casa and Elisabeth Schwarzkopf alternating as the Marschallin, Sena Jurinac as Oktavian, Hilde Güden and Anneliese Rothenberger alternating as Sophie, and Otto Edelmann as Baron Ochs. This production – though with two changes in the cast (Christa Ludwig and the silvery soprano of Teresa Stich-Randall as Oktavian and Sophie) – was carried round the world on records and film.

Boris Christoff was one of the worthiest of Chaliapin's successors as Boris Godunov; perhaps less a creature of impulse, but psychologically elaborated down to the deepest recesses of a sick heart, and vocally of wonderful quality, with pianissimo notes which brought shivers to the spine. His King Philip, too, was a historic achievement, showing the lord of an empire bowed not with age and responsibility but with loneliness; who does not believe in love and yet longs for it. Once, in the massive Teatro Colón, crammed full to the top of the gallery, there were overwhelming ovations for Christoff as he took a curtain call on his own in the costume of the sorrowful king. The tumultuous applause swelled to hurricane force and went on and on. Then Christoff slowly knelt and spread out his arms, in a truly Slav gesture of humility. It was one of the great moments of opera.

Leontyne Price had appeared when quite young as Gershwin's Bess on a world tour by a Negro company. It was easy enough to 'discover' her. Her extraordinary physical beauty, the sensual timbre of her voice, effortlessly overcoming every difficulty, her deeply convincing acting, made her a perfect Aida, a noble Donna Anna, a touching Liù and a lyrical Carmen.

With all its world fame and the immense singing talent heard in Salzburg's Festival Theatre, it is no wonder that, hard on the heels of their triumphant predecessors, the next generation have been moving in to make *their* names just as well known; for instance Waldemar Kmentt, a splendid lyric tenor; Ingeborg Hallstein, one of the most passionate of sopranos, Murray Dickie from Scotland with his gift for hilarious comedy; Mimi Coertse from South Africa with her caressing coloratura; the American, Teresa Stich-Randall, noted for her brilliant top notes, at first mainly a concert performer but then transferring to opera.

One of the most versatile of all the great singers, Tito Gobbi, could present with complete conviction the mischievousness of Gianni Schicchi, the villainy of Scarpia, the exuberance of Rossini's Figaro, the pathetic but somehow disarming remains of Falstaff's gallantry, the nobility of heart and mind in Simon Boccanegra. In that lovely opera he was partnered by the young Turkish soprano Leyla Gencer. She had first made a name at La Scala in the world première of Poulenc's *Dialogue des Carmelites*, and then won fame quickly thanks to her dramatic but also very mobile voice, capable of all coloratura acrobatics. *Macbeth* brought outstanding performances from Fischer-Dieskau and Grace Bumbry, while Peter Lagger's Banquo gave due notice of greatness to come. In *Trovatore* at Salzburg, the young American heroic tenor James McCracken and Leontyne Price were a pair whose voices could fill the spacious Festival Theatre with ease.

The unforgettable Rose Pauly had for a long time been the supreme embodiment of the tragic figure of Elektra. She now had brilliant successors in Gladys Kuchta and Astrid Varnay. The smart Festival audiences were brought a new dimension of pity and terror by a production of the opera for which Karajan had collected a superb cast; Astrid Varnay in the title rôle, Martha Mödl as Klytämnestra, Eberhard Wächter as Orestes, Hildegard Hillebrecht as Chrysothemis. Martha Mödl, formerly one of the most radiant of Isoldes, had now become a tremendous interpreter of the strongest dramatic rôles. Most notable of these were Jenny Begbick in the

Weill-Brecht opera *The Rise and Fall of the City of Mahagonny* –
adventuress, procuress, ice-cold in business deals, connoisseur and
exploiter of human weaknesses – and the horrific Klytämnestra, ruin
of a woman, harassed by the Furies, who would have given her soul
to be free from the ghastly dreams which brought her to the borders
of madness. Both these parts Martha Mödl filled with uncanny intensity, and in both the characterisation was amazingly enhanced by
the roughness, even brittleness of that once so lovely voice. As
Elektra, Astrid Varnay held the audience in her spell throughout the
opera from her first distracted digging for a hatchet, through her
dream-like reaction to the return of her avenging brother whom she
had thought dead, to the outburst of madness in her dance of
triumph. The early scene between Varnay and Mödl was one of the
dramatic peaks of opera, which made the audience hold their breath
and doubt whether the sun would ever rise. But it does rise once
more (in Elektra's soul) when she hears Orestes – sung then by
Wächter with such gentleness and warmth – ask: 'I am known by
the dogs in the yard, does my sister not know me?' And light breaks
through, the atmosphere of suffocating obsession clears for a
moment, as Chrysothemis (in the voice of Hildegard Hillebrecht)
sings her cantilenas of love and desire for motherhood.

For his Salzburg *Boris Godunov*, sung in Russian, Karajan had the
majestic voice of the Bulgarian, Nicolai Ghiaurov, whose voice
probably surpassed all other successors of Chaliapin, Baklanoff and
Journet. He was one of the many fine basses who came to the fore in
a very short space of time; others were Pinza, Christoff, Siepi,
Petrov, Greindl, Frick, Weber, Böhme, Jerome Hines, Rossi-
Lemeni, London, Wildermann, Ernster, Crass, Ridderbusch, Talvela
and Lagger. Ghiaurov is perhaps not so subtle as Christoff, his more
intellectual fellow-countryman, but few voices at once so exhilarating and so exciting can have been heard on the operatic stages of our
time.

Salzburg offers many examples of 'classic' productions; the casts
were gradually changing but always maintained their high quality.
Just a year or two ago, *The Magic Flute* had Walter Kreppel (Saras-
tro), Franz Crass (Speaker), Waldemar Kmentt (Tamino), Roberta
Peters (Queen of the Night), Pilar Lorengar (Pamina), Walter Berry
and Anneliese Rothenberger (Papageno and Papagena). *Die Ent-
führung* had Erika Köth (Constanze), Renate Holm (Blondchen),
Donald Grobe (Belmonte), Gerhard Unger (Pedrillo), Ludwig
Weber (Osmin). *Figaro* had Fischer-Dieskau, Hilde Güden, Geraint
Evans, Graziella Sciutti, John van Kesteren, Evelyn Lear. *Così* had

Elisabeth Schwarzkopf, Christa Ludwig, Graziella Sciutti, Hermann Prey, Waldemar Kmentt, Karl Dönch. *Iphigénie en Aulide* had Inge Borkh, Christa Ludwig, James King, Otto Edelmann, Lucia Popp, Walter Berry, Alois Pernerstorfer. Elisabeth Schwarzkopf, now in her full maturity, has become the ideal Marschallin; young opera-lovers assume there has never been anyone else anywhere as good.

When I refer to the abundance of good or even great singers, it must be admitted that there has been a dearth of heroic tenors for Wagner operas and of dramatic contraltos; I shall consider the reasons for this later. The position has been ameliorated by two tenors from America, James King and Jess Thomas. The former made his Salzburg début as Achilles in *Iphigénie en Aulide*, the latter as Bacchus in *Ariadne auf Naxos*; two fine voices with great dramatic power, extremely reliable – like all American singers – ready to tackle almost any rôle, since they are largely free from European specialisation. Jess Thomas studied psychology before he thought of a career in singing. It was by way of Verdi and Puccini that he came to Wagner, of whom he was soon a splendid interpreter. James King started as a baritone, but achieved increasing brilliance in the high range. After training under Martial Singher, a prominent French baritone with an international career, he was converted into one of the most outstanding heroic tenors. He is now a singing teacher himself.

In 1967 Karajan started his own international Easter Festival at Salzburg. He surrounded himself with a company of singers, choosing them – perhaps for the first time in such a context – on new principles adapted to the technological developments of our time. Till now the vocal powers which singers can produce on the stage has always been the basic criterion. Here their suitability for the microphone was to play an equally important part, since Karajan's magnificent and costly undertaking is aimed almost exclusively at the mass media of records and television. In the first four Easter Festivals (1967–70) he produced the complete *Ring* cycle, showing that by the subtlest treatment of the orchestra he could reach a clarity almost as great as in chamber music, so that even smaller voices made their full effect. The chief requirement was beauty and expressiveness through a microphone; the great conductor was simply acknowledging the facts of modern musical life.

Gundula Janowitz was one of Karajan's happiest discoveries. She was already a good Mozart singer when he cast her as the Empress in *Die Frau ohne Schatten* at the Vienna Opera. Her love duet with the

Canadian tenor Jon Vickers, an equally fine singer then at the height of his international career, was a memorable experience for those who heard it – and the same quality is confirmed on the subsequent recording. Janowitz's voice has the radiant warmth of the great sopranos; carried by the orchestra, she spreads a sense of harmony and exhilaration. And Helga Dernesch, the Easter Festival Brünnhilde, has gifts which may one day make her the equal of Birgit Nilsson, the greatest, in fact possibly the only dramatic soprano who is in the highest international class today. Thomas Stewart, American husband of the equally famous Evelyn Lear, sang Wotan and the Wanderer. He is very much the 'modern'singer, and was originally fascinated by electronic music, but has learnt to tackle other artistic tasks as well with a keen intellect. His career began, incidentally, at Bayreuth, where he had to step in as Amfortas almost overnight. His wife acquired her reputation in a similar way, brought in quite unexpectedly, with only a few days' study, to sing Strauss's difficult 'Four Last Songs' at a London concert. Karajan's Hunding and Fasolt were sung by the Finnish bass Martti Talvela, who looks like a prehistoric giant and has a magnificent voice. Gerhard Stolze's genius as an actor has several times been mentioned with admiration; his Loge (*Rheingold*) at Salzburg was a masterpiece of deep insight into the spiritual complexities of Valhalla. Other examples of his achievements as a singer-actor are his Oedipus at Stuttgart in Orff's opera of that name and his Captain in *Wozzeck* at Vienna.

He is a good illustration of the difficulty of defining the 'great' singer. So long as operatic singing aspires to perfection within a stage framework, the singer-actor will have a place by the side of the artist who is 'merely' a singer. An authority on opera once called Stolze 'the greatest singer without a voice', a witty exaggeration. He has, of course, a fine voice, though its quality is certainly not in the highest class; but this seems insignificant in an artist of such genius.

One of the singers who came quickly into prominence under Karajan was his Fafner and Hagen, Karl Ridderbusch, an accomplished bass with a strong personality. Those who saw the production by Zoltan Kelemen will remember Ridderbusch particularly in the masterly scene of his dialogue with the sinister Alberich – the recitative has an eerie, somnambulistic flavour, as if the deepest feelings were streaming from the unconscious; and in the mighty vocal outburst when he summons the vassals to the wedding in the Hall of the Gibichungs. The possibilities for a really great singer in shorter rôles were shown by Christa Ludwig in her scene as Waltraute in *Götterdämmerung*; through gesture and voice she made a shattering reality of all the misery of Valhalla, waiting for its irresistible fate.

Salzburg's Easter Festival is now one of the important festivals in the crowded musical diaries of the present world. I have given it space in this section because it is a focal point for great singers and those who give promise of achieving this quality.

America

Consideration of the important opera-houses would be incomplete if confined to Europe, although the United States – greatest reservoir of singers for all opera in the Western world – has very few cities with special opera seasons. Anyone who talks of opera there thinks first of the Met, so rich in tradition, where every prominent opera-singer aspires one day to perform. The Met now has a few rivals. In New York itself there is an excellent second opera-house, the City Center, and some other cities in the USA, as in Canada, have opera seasons of varying duration, which reach quite a high level of performance. These are based more on well-known guest artists, however, than on local companies. The position is much the same in Latin America; one dominating opera-house, the Teatro Colón in Argentina's capital, Buenos Aires, and otherwise only sporadic productions in various places.

New York's operatic history begins in 1825, when Manuel Garcia crossed the Atlantic with his company, which included his daughter Maria (the future Malibran). So here were two authentic stars to launch opera in this fast-growing city, an omen, perhaps, for the future 'starriness' of the Met. In 1854, New York's first permanent opera-house opened with Bellini's *Norma*. Despite a fire in 1866 it kept in business for many years. Guest artists from Europe came with increasing frequency, like Patti and Christine Nilsson, and Nilsson had the privilege of starring in the first production at the new building (as Marguerite in Gounod's *Faust*).

This was a huge theatre with nearly 4000 seats. Its exterior was remarkably simple and unornamented, the interior more and more brilliant with each new addition or improvement. Eventually it came to be called 'The Golden Horseshoe', as well as its official name, the Metropolitan Opera House – soon shortened by New Yorkers to 'the Met'. From 1903 the auditorium had imitation baroque decorations in 'Edward VII' style; the colours were gold, red and a brownish ivory. Anyone who ventured to find it less than superb would have been despised by the New Yorkers. With buildings as with people we love, faults often go unnoticed. The Met was certainly not ugly, though less beautiful than the European opera-houses, on which it was modelled (Covent Garden in particular, and to a lesser extent La Scala); and it became a symbol deeply loved by millions. The opening night every year was the assembly point for 'high society', admittedly a rather blatant display of luxury and snobbery. But on the other evenings, after all the overwhelming majority, genuine love of music was predominant.

The Met was the one great opera-house completely independent of public funds, receiving no subsidies of any kind. Despite (or because of) that, it was the richest of them all, able to afford all the prima donnas in the world, all the most expensive tenors – and not only at specially promoted guest performances but within the framework of ordinary productions. There was no other opera-house, except sometimes the Teatro Colón, where this happened to the same extent. On the second opening night Marcella Sembrich sang Lucia di Lammermoor. In 1886 there was the American première of *Tristan und Isolde* with Albert Niemann and Lilli Lehmann. After that there was an unending procession of great artists; Emma Eames, Emma Calvé, Nellie Melba, Lillian Nordica, Ernestine Schumann-Heink, Emmy Destinn, Geraldine Farrar, Louise Homer, Olive Fremstad, Johanna Gadski, Milka Ternina, the de Reszke brothers, Francesco Tamagno, Victor Maurel, Jean Lassalle, Pol Plançon, Antonio Scotti, Chaliapin and Titta Ruffo. Caruso, treated like a demigod in other cities and performing for two or three evenings only, usually gala performances with subscription tickets at astronomical prices, was 'at home' here – and sang 36 different rôles on 607 evenings.

In 1906 the Manhattan Opera House opened with Alessandro Bonci, Caruso's famous rival, in Bellini's *I Puritani*. Mary Garden and Tetrazzini sang there, and so did Melba – but for only four evenings. After that the house closed, in 1910, and the Met reigned supreme once more. Wealthy patrons dug deep into their pockets every year to cover the deficit, and they did it proudly and gladly. The Met was naturally an opera for stars, which had to present singers of world renown every evening. But this did not result in mere guest performances or a *stagione* system; astonishingly enough, the stars formed something like a company. Nationality was unimportant. No one thought of a 'native' company, or guessed that one day American singers might play a leading part in world opera.

Operas by American composers were already being performed (in English, naturally), and so American singers were getting heard. But for a long time their names paled besides those of the world-famous singers, who now included Lucrezia Bori, Frieda Hempel, Amelita Galli-Curci, Maria Jeritza, Elisabeth Rethberg, Frida Leider, Claudia Muzio, Margarethe Matzenauer, Frances Alda, Lotte Lehmann, Florence Easton, Lily Pons, Kirsten Flagstad; Martinelli, Gigli, Slezak, Didur, Schorr, Schipa, Lauri Volpi and Melchior. By now, however, there were several native Americans, like Rosa Ponselle and Grace Moore, who had sung themselves to fame in Europe, and one could also count Emma Eames, with American parents but born in Shanghai, who had already become almost legendary. Then there was Lawrence Tibbett, one of the first to make his career only in America, winning Europe's appreciation mainly in the form of massive audiences at his films. He lost his powerful baritone through a sudden vocal seizure, and was soon afterwards killed in a car crash.

The Met, under its various directors, remained a singers' opera-house *par excellence*. Here are some of the most notable names from the thirties and forties – with the number of American-born singers rising steeply: Zinka Milanov, Bidu Sayao, Licia Albanese, Helen Traubel, Eleanor Steber, Risë Stevens, Jarmila Novotna, Jussi Björling, Richard Tucker, Jan Peerce, Leonard Warren, Robert Merrill. Perhaps special mention might be given here to that glorious tenor, Richard Crooks, born in New Jersey in 1900, who retired from the stage relatively young. He was a star at the Met from 1933 to 1946, had well-earned triumphs in Europe too, and his voice was particularly effective in the recordings of those days.

After the war the Met soon gained an immense throng of world-famous singers; among the women, names like Callas, Tebaldi, Barbieri, de los Angeles, della Casa, Schwarzkopf, Sutherland, Moffo, Anderson, Nilsson, Crespin, Güden, Gorr, Price, Farrell, Rysanek; among the men, Bergonzi, del Monaco, Gedda, Gobbi, Domingo, Tagliavini, di Stefano, Taddei, Christoff, Rossi-Lemeni, Hines, Siepi, MacNeil, Milnes – the list could be prolonged almost indefinitely.

While the stock of great singers was continually being renewed, the well-loved opera-house amidst New York's roaring traffic had grown out of date. The echo of countless wonderful evenings might be stored invisibly within the walls of the Met, but its installations were no longer adequate for modern opera production. For a long time plans for a new building were on the board, though nobody could bear the thought of New York without the old Met. But its last day came, 16th April 1966; over sixty of the most famous singers appeared on the familiar stage and sang arias and duets, and finally a scene from *Faust*, with which the Met had opened eighty-three years before. It was an unforgettable evening, melancholy but splendid. There were petitions and demonstrations for the building to be preserved, but they had no chance against the millions of dollars represented by this piece of real estate in the heart of Manhattan. The old Met 'fell a victim to the axe', as the saying goes – though there are now quicker demolition methods!

Five months later, on 16th September, the new opera-house opened, a showpiece in the gigantic Lincoln Center, one of the most magnificent theatrical complexes which city architects have ever designed and realised. The new Met is a 'classic' opera-house, and yet completely modern; also, with its 3800 seats, one of the largest in the world. Full of the most up-to-date technical equipment, it has murals by Chagall and Raoul Dufy; on the 'classic' side the gleam of its red and white colours is magically enhanced by a fairyland glitter of light and reflected light.

It has remained a singers' opera-house; no place for contemporary music but rather what enemies of conventional opera have called 'a museum of sound'. For it continues to be under private management and the rising 'social' costs – fees for orchestra, chorus, ballet, staff – have pushed the budget up to dangerous heights. Contemporary works mean a risk of small audiences which only an opera-house subsidised by public funds can afford to take, and then only to a precisely fixed point. So the Met stays with Mozart, Gluck and Beethoven, with Rossini, Bellini and Donizetti, with Verdi and Wagner, plus some dead certainties like *Faust*, *Cav* and *Pag*, *Fledermaus* and a few more; but all, literally all, with star casts. Of course a city like New York is large, young and lively enough to carry other operatic enterprises, especially those where a public concerned with modern music can get to know more recent works. In this connection I would pay a tribute to the New York City Opera, also housed today in the Lincoln Center, which stages some quite outstanding productions.

Outside New York there is little worth mentioning. San Francisco has a very good short season of opera, and Dallas is trying to establish something similar. Many other big cities have a few weeks of opera every year built round world stars, expensive guest artists in productions made possible because of an affluent society; and audiences thoroughly enjoy these productions, though with very naïve appreciation. But there is scarcely anything in the way of a real operatic company with systematic planning and a sizeable repertoire. Nothing organic, closely connected with the locality, has grown up.

The real cultivation of opera takes place elsewhere. To see and admire it one must go to the hundreds of universities which have built up a very valuable musical life. As well as having their choirs, symphony concerts and chamber music, they work hard and seriously at operatic performances without the haste and pressure of time affecting commercial stages. One should also visit the 'workshops', where modern opera is performed and often surprisingly well sung. Everything is very lively, and there is enthusiastic co-operation from all. This kind of experimental stage and school (*ie* university) opera, according to Herbert Graf, one of the great international experts on the musical theatre, is perhaps, at least in America, 'the only possibility for the development of a contemporary operatic style. It is relatively independent of the cares of insufficient subsidies and trade union handicaps, from which the great opera-houses suffer, and all thought and effort can be focused on the accomplishment of the artistic task. This includes, above all, having enough rehearsals. Fifty to sixty rehearsals on the stage for an operatic production here are no rarity . . .' Then he continues: 'So America's opera workshop offers quite exceptional opportunities not only for singers . . . to acquire the craft of opera and develop a new style. But this does not solve the one great problem: where can the many young operatic artists find an appropriate field of professional activity? They all look first, of course, towards the Metropolitan and a few other big opera-houses, but these have room for only a few new members. Many eventually find their livelihood in the church, the concert-hall, a choir, a school – or on a European stage.' This is just what we shall find borne out in a later chapter. The American workshops and university theatres have become an almost inexhaustible source of singers for Europe's opera-houses.

The only place missing in our round-up of opera-houses is one of the most glorious in the world, often mentioned already in this book; the Teatro Colón, opened on 25th May 1908. Buenos Aires had previously had the Teatro Coliseo, built in 1804; and there, in 1825 – coincidentally the same year as Garcia's company arrived in New York – the first operatic production in Latin America took place; Rossini's *Barber of Seville*, then nine years old. In 1838 the city also acquired the Teatro Principal de la Victoria, but both gave way to the first Teatro Colón, which opened on 25th May 1857 with Verdi's *Traviata* (written four years previously). There were two guest artists from Italy, the famous tenor Enrico Tamberlick and the soprano Sofia Lorini, as yet scarcely a name. Buenos Aires was quite a small city at the time, but it was gripped by a real opera fever. In

1872 another opera-house was built (called La Opera), but other theatres, too (Politeama and San Martin), often staged operatic productions with companies from Italy. After the re-building of the Colón, the performance of opera rose to a good level and soon afterwards to the highest of international standards.

The capacity of the Colón is officially given as 3000 seats; but on great evenings the massive seven-floor arena gets in many hundreds more, which is always possible, of course, in theatres with boxes and where there is careful supervision. The Colón's acoustics are as famous as its enthusiastic and knowledgeable audiences. With a magnificent auditorium in red and gold, it is a Mecca for European singers, all the more because the main season in Buenos Aires coincides with summer recess in Europe.

In the early days all works, including the French and the very few German operas, were sung in Italian, mother tongue of the overwhelming majority of the singers. Then French too became a more current operatic language – though *Carmen* continued for a long time to be the domain of the Italians! – but it was not until 1917 that an Argentinian opera was sung in Spanish. Opera in German was heard for the first time at the Teatro Colón, and in Latin America as a whole, with the memorable guest season by the Viennese Opera after the First World War. This led to the innovation a few years later of having the opera season divided into an Italian, a French and a German section, with singers and conductors from the countries concerned. Sometimes there was even a Russian section as well. So opera-lovers not only had the chance to hear every important work in the original language, but also to enjoy the singing of the best artists – as if they were spending some evenings in the Paris Opera, some in La Scala, and some in Vienna, Berlin, Bayreuth or Salzburg. In the years of the Second World War, rather the same as in the United States, there was a significant change; singers could not be drawn from all over the world as in peace-time, and that favoured the formation of a native company, for which there had long been a surprisingly good basis. Two great conductors, refugees from Germany, Erich Kleiber and Fritz Busch, set about this rewarding task, which has led to the existence today of a large number of outstanding Argentinian singers. I will name only a few out of a list which now goes back two or three decades; Hina Spani, Pedro Mirassou, Elena Arismendi, Angel Mattiello, Renato Cesari, Viktor de Narké, Mirta Garbarini.

To go through the world stars who have appeared on the Colón stage, I should have to repeat the list for the Met and add a number of other famous names. There is a skilfully administered *stagione* system, which has continued to ensure a high standard of performance in an extensive repertoire including operas from all countries. But the home company is appearing more and more frequently; and their performances too, especially after the foundation of an affiliated 'chamber opera', are on the level of a very good European opera-house.

No other opera-house in Latin America comes anywhere near the history and achievements of the Colón. But there are places with seasons of varying length; for instance, Mexico City, Caracas, Santiago, Rio de Janeiro, São Paulo, Montevideo, La Plata and Rosario. Some of these cities have extremely talented native singers. Mexico City in recent years has produced international stars like Oralia Dominguez, a contralto rated very highly in Europe's festivals, and the outstanding lyric tenor Placido Domingo. Santiago (Chile) can boast the distinguished heroic tenor Ramon Vinay and the equally brilliant Renato Zanelli. São Paulo (Brazil) has sent some glorious voices into the world of opera; Bidu Sayao, Paulo Fortes, Rio Novello, Aurea Gomes, Neide Thomas. Montevideo (Uruguay), after José Oxilia (one of the most famous singers of his time), has come up with magnificent voices like those of Victor Damiani, Virginia Castro and Jorge Algorta. For the moment none of the cities mentioned here plays any important part in international opera, except perhaps as a quick stop during an extensive tour or a place which can be taken in on the way to or from the Teatro Colón.

There is still less to report from other continents. Sydney has built one of the most fantastic opera-houses in the world, a sign of the very intensive promotion of opera in Australia during the last few years. An opera-house has been established in the Persian capital, Teheran. Several Japanese theatres have large stages on which guest performances by European companies are very popular. But it will be some time before any of these countries provide singers with opportunities for permanent and worth-while activity.

VIII

Singing and Singers

The Great Rôles

Great rôles belong to great singers, as do great opera-houses. The latter are the focal point from which their brilliance can radiate. The rôles are the medium through which their personality is expressed. Perhaps for the true artist there is scarcely any difference between great and small rôles; he can make a cameo into a masterpiece. Still, there are rôles, of course, which give special opportunities for his voice and personality as well as his various abilities.

The opera-singer, and to a certain extent the Lieder-singer as well, transforms himself with each interpretation. When Lotte Lehmann sang Sieglinde, she became the character. Tauber could on one evening be Don José, the poor farmer's son falling into ruin in an alien environment, and the next evening he would be Tamino, the glorious prince for whom no ordeal is too great if it brings him to the truth and the woman he loves. When Maria Callas sang her now legendary Traviata, throughout the evening, apart from one short vocal outburst, there was a complete absence of the 'loud' singing to which one is accustomed. She had thought out the rôle of Violetta or 'composed' it (to use a justifiable exaggeration) so fully, that almost from the first moment of the opera you could feel the constant and ever-increasing threat of death hanging over the young girl, until the actual moment of death in the last scene. All Traviatas cough to indicate consumption. Callas didn't. Her singing merely had a softness and delicacy, mingled with a frail and muffled quality; a supreme performance which demanded not only self-denial, especially for one blessed with a voice of such powerful radiance, but also the highest technical ability. That few in the audience or even among the critics understood this is another matter.

The basic division of human voices into high, middle and low – respectively sopranos and tenors, mezzo-sopranos and baritones, contraltos and basses – is a natural phenomenon; only nature does not always provide a neat dividing line and there are voices which straddle two of these compartments. Baritones sometimes develop into tenors, as we have already seen, and I shall be discussing some more cases; mezzo-sopranos into dramatic sopranos. At all times, though less so today, there have been voices equally at home in different registers. Some women have been able to sing both soprano and contralto rôles, and – more rarely – men have sung tenor, baritone and bass. Today these phenomena are exceptional. Centuries of operatic practice have set boundaries, and in creating their works the composers have in mind a particular register for each rôle; indeed there is a more closely defined category within each register.

Before discussing these sub-divisions, let us have a brief look at voice-range. The good singer can consider as a desirable norm a range of up to two and a half octaves with each note well-formed and perfectly controlled. Freak voices possess a range of three, three and a half and allegedly even four octaves, but their importance is extremely small. In modern opera and concert-singing a person with such an extraordinary larynx might well have no opportunity during his lifetime to exploit this special faculty. The greater specialisation common in all fields today has limited voices more and more, although on the whole singers today within each range are expected to have a more comprehensive training.

Among sopranos there are soubrettes, lyric and dramatic coloratura sopranos, lyric sopranos, juvenile dramatic sopranos and character sopranos; five or six types, in fact, a degree of specialisation which is doubtless exaggerated and is often enough ignored. There are two kinds of mezzo, lyric and dramatic, and contraltos are either 'character' or dramatic. There are as many different kinds of tenor as of soprano; *spieltenor* or tenor buffo, lyric tenor, two types of heroic tenor – the 'young hero' type, with a less strenuous vocal line, and the heavier, Wagner tenor (usually called *Heldentenor* from the German original) – and character tenor, vocally akin to the lyric tenor but with a special talent for characterisation. Baritones are generally divided into lyric, character and heroic voices. The bass can be buffo, *ie* comic, or serious. These classifications are really only important to the manager in his capacity as casting director for the operas on his programme.

The soubrette has cheerful, mischievous, playful juvenile rôles. She belongs to opera buffa as the Heldentenor to Wagner; some examples are Serpina in Pergolesi's *Serva padrona*, Mozart's Bastienne and many characters in the operas of Lortzing, who was particularly fond of this type of voice and gave it a flavour of German romanticism. If the soubrette has distinct coloratura gifts, she may be called a coloratura soubrette or even coloratura soprano, whose range is much wider; Beethoven's Marzelline (*Fidelio*), Donizetti's Adina (*Elisir d'Amore*) and Norina (*Don Pasquale*), Flotow's Lady Harriet (*Martha*) and the typical Mozart rôles of Blonde (*Entführung*), Susanna, Zerlina and Despina – also Papagena, which needs extreme lightness of touch more than coloratura. This lightness in voice and acting is a general characteristic of all soubrettes and coloratura sopranos, which is why they are called the 'light' voices in all Latin languages. The achievements of seventeenth- and eighteenth-century singers in this respect are far greater than present-day practice allows; one main reason being that every singer of coloratura rôles could work out the decorative parts of the rôle according to her own judgment, or the judgment of her adviser, manager or conductor. This was the exact counterpart of the virtuoso instrumentalist's cadenzas in those times, where he had the right, indeed the duty, to present his own fantasies and give a display of hair-raising technical *tours-de-force*. Such ornamentation for both player and singer was naturally harder to perform than any composer would dare to put down on paper. The tradition of the great prima donnas, who had their proprietary rights in such things, lived on so strongly in the minds of many leading sopranos that as late as the 1920s one of the early interpreters of the Marschallin (Hempel) asked Strauss to let her put in her own decorations.

The great rôles for coloratura soubrettes include Ännchen in *Freischütz* (making a beautiful vocal contrast with Agathe, the young dramatic soprano part), Gilda, Manon, the flighty Philine in Thomas' *Mignon* (in contrast to the dark, emotional mezzo of the title rôle), Gretel in Humperdinck's opera (where Hänsel is sung by a darker female voice as a breeches rôle), Carmen's companion Frasquita, Nedda in *Pagliacci* and the Woodbird in *Siegfried*. In *Tales of Hoffmann* Olympia is usually cast with a coloratura voice, but a versatile soprano sometimes takes all three women's rôles in this opera. It works all right dramatically, but vocally means mastery of three different vocal specialities; she has to sing coloratura as

Olympia, be dramatic as Giulietta and lyric as Antonia. Rosina in *The Barber of Seville* is considered a coloratura soprano rôle, but as with many of his parts Rossini meant it for a mezzo with coloratura (his 'star' and future wife Isabel – Isabella Colbran); the combination was considered impossible for many decades, which gave sopranos the opportunity to take possession of this magnificent rôle. But in our time mezzos with amazing coloratura facility have been turning up again, to recapture this and other rôles – Teresa Berganza, to name only one of today's great singers. One of the last masters to write great rôles for coloratura sopranos was Richard Strauss; Sophie, Zerbinetta and – though artistically far removed – Fiakermilli in *Arabella*. More recent composers sometimes demanded the highest soprano registers from their characters – like Alban Berg from *Lulu* – but coloratura voices can scarcely be employed here, because the dramatic element in such rôles is usually more important than fluency in decorative singing.

Typical rôles for the warm, touching, lyric soprano include Cherubino and Pamina, Micaela in *Carmen*, Marenka in *The Bartered Bride*, Tatiana in *Eugen Onegin*, Liù in *Turandot* and – especially popular with beginners – the breeches rôle of Siebel in Gounod's *Faust*. The difference between the lyric and the juvenile dramatic soprano is hard to recognise or capture in words, and the two divisions often merge. Among the latter we have Mimì, Desdemona, Marguerite and Agathe, and also many rôles where the dramatic element is more strongly emphasised; *eg* Elsa in *Lohengrin*, Elisabeth in *Tannhäuser*, Eva in *Meistersinger*, Gutrune in *Götterdämmerung*, Lisa in *Queen of Spades* and Chrysothemis in *Elektra*.

The dramatic coloratura soprano is the voice for Bellini's Norma and several Mozart rôles; Constanze (*Entführung*), the Countess (*Marriage of Figaro*), Fiordiligi (*Così*), the Queen of the Night and Donna Anna – leaving it a vexed question whether Donna Elvira is for a juvenile dramatic or a dramatic coloratura soprano. The latter will also sing Salome and the Empress (*Frau ohne Schatten*), Madame Butterfly, Leonora in *Trovatore* and probably Violetta, though this too is debatable. The pure dramatic soprano sings Gluck's Alceste and Iphigénie, many Verdi rôles – Lady Macbeth, Amelia (*Masked Ball*), Leonora (*Force of Destiny*), Elena (*Sicilian Vespers*), Elisabeth (*Don Carlos*) and Aida – Wagner's Venus, Sieglinde and Brünnhilde (the last, with Isolde, Wagner's prototype of a dramatic heroine), Strauss's Marschallin, Elektra, Ariadne, Dyer's wife (*Frau ohne Schatten*), Moussorgsky's Marina in *Boris Godunov*, Puccini's Tosca and Turandot, and Mascagni's Santuzza (*Cavalleria Rusticana*).

Many opera-houses have a dramatic soprano for Ortrud in *Lohengrin*, others prefer a dramatic mezzo. Who can be dogmatic on which is right? Where does Carmen belong? Contraltos have always been particularly happy to sing this rôle, since the dark timbre of their voice produces that sombre, fateful sound which is so appropriate for the Spanish gypsy; all mezzos have Carmen in their repertory, but sopranos too have often coveted this wonderful rôle. This is one interesting case where the singer's personality may sometimes be more important than the nature of her voice.

Dramatic mezzos are much rarer than dramatic sopranos, but have some fine rôles, such as Dorabella in *Così*, three great Verdi parts – Lady Macbeth (sometimes sung by a dramatic soprano), Eboli and Amneris – in Wagner works, Venus (preferable to a soprano for the more sensual timbre), Brangäne, Fricka, sometimes Ortrud (as mentioned above) and Kundry, also sought after by dramatic sopranos. Richard Strauss gave mezzos three magnificent rôles, characters inhabiting completely different worlds; Klytämnestra, Oktavian and Amme (*Frau ohne Schatten*). Marina in *Boris Godunov* is also a part for mezzo voices. They have few leads, but these, besides Carmen, include Delilah in Saint-Saens's opera *Samson and Delilah*, Thomas's Mignon, the Countess in *Queen of Spades* and Hänsel in Humperdinck's opera. Other important mezzo rôles, which are sometimes sung by contraltos, are Adalgisa in *Norma*, who has to produce powerful high notes, Nancy in Flotow's *Martha*, the Countess in *Wildschütz* and Irmentraut in *Waffenschmied* (both works by Lortzing), Lola in *Cavalleria Rusticana*, which can be sung by almost all women's voices, Suzuki in *Madama Butterfly*, Maddalena in *Rigoletto* and Emilia in *Otello*, Mary in *Flying Dutchman* and Magdalena in *Meistersinger*.

What is the difference between a mezzo and a soprano? The former is by no means a soprano without a high range. As a rule she has high notes almost equal to soprano voices, except coloratura sopranos. The main thing is that she has a darker, 'velvety' timbre, with an exciting effect; this is even more so with the contralto. The mezzo voice has a lower register, three, four or five notes more than the soprano, and from there to the contralto it is only a short step. Fewer demands are made of the contralto in the high register, but in the low you can hear the real contralto timbre, which is very unusual and on the telephone or a record can sound like a man's voice (since a contralto's larynx has long vocal cords like a tenor's). Among the famous contralto rôles are Gluck's *Orpheus*, Erda in *The Ring* and three Verdi rôles – Azucena in *Trovatore*, Ulrica in *Maskea*

Ball (sometimes sung by mezzos) and Mistress Quickly, a typical character-contralto with her comic 'Reverenza'. Contraltos can also sing many of the rôles given above for mezzos.

Among the various classes of tenor, I will start with the *spieltenor* or tenor buffo, who needs a voice and body of great mobility, native humour and a talent for mime. His most important rôles are Jaquino (*Fidelio*), various Mozart parts such as Pedrillo, Monostatos, Basilio and Don Curzio – the last two or three requiring such skill in characterisation that they could also attract a character tenor – Vasek in *The Bartered Bride,* Bardolph in *Falstaff*, David in *Meistersinger* and perhaps Mime in *The Ring*, although this primarily demands dramatic expressiveness, four Offenbach parts in *Tales of Hoffmann*, Andreas, Cochenille, Pittichinaccio and Franz, to be taken by the same singer, some of the buffo figures in *Ariadne auf Naxos*, two of the comic ministers in *Turandot*, the Idiot in *Boris Godunov*, a psychologically complex part, Beppe in *Pagliacci* and the Bishop of Budoia in *Palestrina*; really a very extended range of characters.

The main thing we look for in a lyric tenor is beauty of tone. He will sing Almaviva in Rossini's *Barber*, Mozart's Belmonte, Don Ottavio, Ferrando and Tamino, Gounod's Faust, Flotow's Lionel (*Martha*), Donizetti's Nemorino (*Elisir d'Amore*), Thomas's Wilhelm Meister (*Mignon*), Massenet's Des Grieux (*Manon*), Puccini's Rodolfo (*Bohème*) and Pinkerton (*Butterfly*), Tchaikovsky's Lensky (*Eugen Onegin*) and Hermann (*Queen of Spades*), Verdi's Duke (*Rigoletto*) and Alfredo (*Traviata*), Strauss's Narraboth (*Salome*), the Italian Singer (*Rosenkavalier*) and Matteo (*Arabella*) – small parts these last three, but vocally important.

Notable rôles for the Italian heroic or dramatic tenor are Manrico, Radames, Otello, Calaf. The Germans have a class of 'young heroic tenors', a phrase which has nothing to do with age, only with dramatic expression; the Italians call them *lirico spinto*. Their rôles include Weber's Max (*Freischütz*), Adolar (*Euryanthe*) and Huon (*Oberon*), Florestan (*Fidelio*), although to be in harmony with the female lead, Leonore, this is often sung by a 'heavy' heroic tenor, Don José, Canio, Kienzl's Matthias (*Evangelimann*), Offenbach's Hoffmann (also possible for a lyric tenor), many Verdi rôles like Gabriel Adorno (*Simon Boccanegra*), Arrigo (*Sicilian Vespers*), Riccardo (*Masked Ball*), Alvaro (*Force of Destiny*) and Don Carlos. Jenik in *The Bartered Bride*, Laca in Janacek's *Jenufa* and Debussy's Pelléas sound best in the voice of a 'young heroic tenor', as do Turiddu (*Cavalleria Rusticana*), Pedro in d'Albert's *Tiefland* and the

Gluck rôles of Admetos (*Alceste*), Achilles and Pylades (both from *Iphigénie en Aulide*). Strauss parts for this type of voice include Aegisthus (*Elektra*), Bacchus (*Ariadne auf Naxos*) and the Emperor (*Frau ohne Schatten*). Herod in *Salome* is often sung by a character tenor, as is Melot in *Tristan*, but where such specialisation is not possible or desired, both are sung by 'young heroic' voices. Puccini's finest tenor rôles, such as Des Grieux, Rodolfo, Cavaradossi and Calaf, can be sung equally well by lyric or 'young heroic' voices, but the latter is preferable for Calaf, if only to complement the very dramatic Turandot.

The German heroic tenor's rôles, chiefly Wagner, of course, range in heaviness from Lohengrin and Stolzing through Tannhäuser and Siegmund to Tristan, Siegfried and Parsifal. Italian singers do not have this class, which partly explains the alarming lack of such voices, for it is extremely rare to find one coming from Italy or the operatic countries influenced by Italy. Caruso did sing Lohengrin, which may be considered the most lyrical of Wagner rôles, but apart from the younger Erik in *Flying Dutchman* and the seldom performed *Rienzi*, only Ramon Vinay from Chile, a magnificent Tristan, proved an exception, though for quite a short time.

The lyric baritone's rôles include the following; Mozart's Guglielmo and Papageno, the latter really a buffo character, but there is no real class of buffo baritone, Donizetti's Belcore (*Elisir d'Amore*) and Dr Malatesta (*Don Pasquale*), Figaro in *The Barber of Seville*, also with distinct buffo traits, Valentin in Gounod's *Faust*, Escamillo in *Carmen*, Tchaikovsky's Onegin, Schaunard in *Bohème*, Silvio in *Pagliacci* – he should form a strong vocal contrast with the dramatic Tonio, who sometimes has to produce the softest lyrical tone as well – three of the most important of Puccini's baritone rôles, Marcello, Sharpless and Scarpia, several great Verdi rôles, Count di Luna, Germont the elder, Renato (*Masked Ball*), Carlos (*Force of Destiny*) and Rodrigo (*Don Carlos*). A cavalier baritone – a term known only to German opera and hard to distinguish from the lyric type – is usually called on to sing such parts as the Count in *Figaro*, Don Giovanni and Mandryka in *Arabella*. Of the many Wagner parts for baritones the most lyrical is Wolfram in *Tannhäuser*, the rest are for heroic or else character baritones like Alberich, Donner and Gunther in *The Ring* and Klingsor in *Parsifal*. Rôles for character baritones in the works of other composers include Pizzaro in *Fidelio*, Mozart's Figaro, Verdi's Rigoletto and Iago, Puccini's Gianni Schicchi, Lindorff, Coppelius, Dapertutto and Doctor Miracle, the four rôles taken by the same singer in *Tales of Hoffmann*, Alfio in *Cavalleria*

Rusticana, Strauss's Faninal (*Rosenkavalier*) and the Music-Master (*Ariadne auf Naxos*).

Rôles for heroic baritones include two Orestes figures, in *Iphigénie en Tauride* and in *Elektra*, Handel's Caesar, and great Verdi rôles like Macbeth, Simon Boccanegra, King Philip, Amonasro and Falstaff. Some of these last are also sung by basses, and the same applies to Boris Godunov, and to the many fine rôles which Wagner gave to baritones with a dark, heroic timbre, the Dutchman, Telramund, Kurwenal, Hans Sachs, Amfortas, Wotan (and the Wanderer, which lies a little lower). Scarpia can be sung by a heroic baritone, as can two Strauss rôles, John the Baptist (*Salome*) and Barak (*Frau ohne Schatten*).

Buffo basses have a rewarding field in opera. Their most important rôles are the delightful Osmin and Leporello, both offering great scope, Bartolo in *The Barber*, the splendid Kecal in *The Bartered Bride* and Colline in *Bohème*, with his fine mock-pathetic farewell to his coat before it goes to the pawnbroker's. Gianni Schicchi, as already mentioned, may be a part for a character baritone, but is just as often sung by a buffo bass. Puccini thought of this type of voice also for the cameo rôles of the Landlord in *Bohème* and the Sacristan in *Tosca*, so did Verdi for the gloriously funny Fra Melitone in *Force of Destiny*, a rôle also possible for baritones. Daland in *The Dutchman* is sometimes considered a buffo rôle, but I would regard it as more for a 'serious' or 'deep' bass. The grotesque Beckmesser in *Meistersinger* is obviously Wagner's best offering for this class of singer, with Baron Ochs, it is the crown of such buffo rôles.

Rôles for character basses, or bass baritones, include Mephistopheles in both Gounod's *Faust* and Boito's *Mefistofele*, Masetto in *Don Giovanni* and Don Alfonso in *Così*, Sparafucile and perhaps also Monterone in *Rigoletto*, the Conspirator in *Masked Ball* and the Grand Inquisitor in *Don Carlos*, though this too may be sung by a deep bass. Whether Fasolt and Hunding in *The Ring* are given to a deep bass or a bass baritone is a matter of taste.

Among rôles for deep basses are Sarastro and the Commendatore, Rocco (*Fidelio*), in character also within the range of a buffo bass, Oroveso in *Norma*, the Hermit and perhaps also the villainous Caspar in *Freischütz* (the latter sometimes given to a bass baritone), Pimen the Monk in *Boris Godunov*, Prince Gremin in *Eugene Onegin*, Timur in *Turandot*, King Arkel in *Pelléas et Mélisande*, various Wagner rôles – the Landgrave in *Tannhäuser*, the King and the Herald in *Lohengrin*, King Mark in *Tristan*, Pogner in *Meistersinger*, Fafner and Fasolt in *The Ring*, Gurnemanz and Titurel in *Parsifal* – and various Verdi rôles – Banquo, Fiesco (*Simon Boccanegra*), Guardiano (*Force of Destiny*), Ramphis (*Aida*), Lodovico, and in *Don Carlos*, King Philip and the Grand Inquisitor, who have a long, extremely dramatic scene together, a rarity for two basses.

This is a bare summary, and does not claim to be anything like comprehensive. It does no more than suggest how operatic rôles are assigned, which includes a very fine sensitivity to the abilities of each singer, and also an appreciation of the demands of the rôles both vocal and psychological. Excessive specialisation can lead to miscasting; as a rule the singer's abilities extend beyond the range of a single type of voice, nor are dramatic suitability and voice always combined in the same type. Let us look a little more closely at these problems as manifested in Mozart's operas.

It would be a sad time for contraltos if the repertoire were entirely devoted to Mozart, since in his great operas (*Entführung, Figaro, Don Giovanni, Così, Magic Flute*) he uses only high voices for his female rôles. In theory sopranos could sing all these, except for the Third Lady in *Magic Flute*. But in character and in type of voice they are so different that a clever manager can produce striking effects from these contrasts.

To start with *Entführung*, this has two women, mistress and maid, according to the favourite design of that age. Constanze is a dramatic coloratura soprano needing great penetration, supreme technique and warm, feminine timbre; Blonde or Blondchen, the typical soubrette, also needs great vocal and coloratura accomplishment, typical of eighteenth-century German *Singspiel*, to which *Entführung* belongs.

In *Figaro*, there are five rôles for women, two of less importance. Of the other three, one is the breeches rôle of Cherubino, which is best sung by a dark soprano voice or a not too sensual mezzo-soprano. Here much depends on appearance, to carry conviction as a boy, and on acting ability – at least we expect this in opera today – earlier ages seem to have been much less critical. (There is a recording of Adelina Patti singing Cherubino's aria, which sounds lacking in musical precision and vocally unsuitable in our conception.) Mozart did not demand specially high or low notes from this rôle, which makes it within the range of any female voice expressive in the middle register, but the chances it gives can only be seen and heard when there is a first-class artist taking the part. The Countess is considered one of the most important lyric or young-dramatic rôles. She has to have very good breath control, an inherent nobility, the charm of a mature woman, rather like the Marschallin in *Rosen-*

kavalier, and great artistry. She is one of the true 'ladies' in opera, fine in bearing and voice, lending herself to a masquerade only in extreme psychological necessity, although with a truly feminine delight in feigning. There is a strong contrast to her in the simpler, more working-class, though far from coarse Susanna, used to defending herself in life with cunning, flirtatious, very conscious of her attractiveness, but capable of sincere love. We feel that Mozart was here immortalising his favourite type of woman. Vocally the rôle is more demanding than might be imagined; composers of that time, when writing music for their operas, had very concrete ideas for a particular singer, for whom the première was designed and whose strengths and weaknesses were clearly taken into account. Mozart expects of Susanna a vocal range of two octaves, although she is a soubrette with coloratura, her 'rose aria' in the last scene calls for lyrical tone and great control, as well as some surprisingly low notes.

In *Don Giovanni* there are three women's rôles, variously connected in the plot with the seducer – two noble ladies and one from the lower classes. It is remarkable how finely Mozart shows the psychological differences by purely musical means; how different the arias of the two 'Donnas' and those of the simple peasant girl sound. Anna and Elvira have a hard time of it, for Da Ponte's book makes them rather static characters despite their ardent emotions, the producer has the difficult task of giving them greater animation. It is much easier for little Zerlina, who wins the audience's sympathies from the start, and although Mozart has written brilliant music for all three, we can feel that he too is fondest of Zerlina. It is a fine touch that while he gives Anna and Elvira splendid, and extremely difficult, arias, he raises Zerlina for a moment to the status of Don Giovanni's real partner, giving her a love duet in which she is completely his equal, *La ci darem la mano*. Obviously these three rôles demand completely different vocal types, at best a dramatic soprano, a lyric soprano and a soubrette.

There are also three women in *Così*, two mistresses (sisters), and one maid. To distinguish Dorabella and Fiordiligi, they are usually cast with one a lyric or dramatic coloratura voice and the other a mezzo, which also serves to complement the voices of their partners in this opera buffa, which are similarly arranged. It is a bel canto opera of purest beauty, which only true bel canto singers can handle satisfactorily. Despina the maid has to be up to this standard too. Like Blondchen, Susanna and Zerlina, she is a lower-class girl, more experienced and with more real delicacy than her 'ladies', a typical soubrette well fitted, like the other three, for coloratura. So there are three characters providing a striking contrast through their different voices. It is almost as if Mozart, over a century before the invention of recordings and radio, had had in mind these media, where such differentiation is normal.

In *The Magic Flute* there are three important women's rôles, plus the Three Ladies and also the Three Boys, if women rather than children are engaged to sing them. Designedly, all these show extremely strong contrasts in both character and voice. Pamina is a lyrical creature in voice and action, innocent, accommodating, with deep feelings, great modesty and – especially in her difficult G-minor aria – perfect musical line. Her mother, on the other hand, the Queen of the Night, is conscious of her sovereignty, and exudes regal power; in her, Mozart created one of the most dreaded and exalted coloratura parts. Her staccati and runs in the highest range – sometimes beyond the high C – must glitter and sparkle, giving the impression of utter assurance, without becoming shrill or piercing. Pamina is by nature rather passive, and most producers leave the Queen of the Night completely static, but what these two rôles lack in dramatic nobility can perhaps be made up by the third, Papagena, in itself a small rôle, but with her *Pa-pa-pa-* duet capable of singing and acting herself into any audience's heart.

And what about the men's rôles in Mozart's most performed works? He has, of course, no heroic tenors, they did not become necessary until half a century later. His tenors are bel canto singers of the purest breed, when they are representing 'masters' – Belmonte, Ottavio, Ferrando or Tamino – lyrical tenors, in fact 'Mozart tenors', although no such technical class exists; but anyone familiar with good singing will at once understand the term. It means perfect intonation and breath control, uniformity of register, with no transition difficulties from low to middle, or middle to high, faultless legato and *mezzavoce* (half-voice, *ie piano*), beautiful timbre – and quite a lot more.

Pedrillo, Belmonte's servant, is a buffo tenor, but Mozart expects him, besides the obligatory merriness, to have considerable vocal gifts. In *Figaro* the composer does something unusual; he gives both male leads to baritones. But Count Almaviva and his valet are as different in voice as they are socially. The Count is a cavalier baritone, whose position must be unaffected even by the abortive adventure with Susanna. Figaro, on the other hand, rougher and craftier, does not need to be so concerned with image as his master, and this is expressed too in his voice, although it should not lapse into coarseness – of course no voice ever should, but least of all in Mozart. The

Count is the exact vocal complement to his wife, Rosina; as Figaro is to Susanna. Mozart conceived this with genius, and showed equal finesse in sustaining it. There is a cross-connection between the classes; the Count's love duet with Susanna – this is acting on her part (she knows the Count too well, unlike Zerlina with Don Giovanni, where the girl has an amazed glimpse of a wonderland conjured up before her). Then, musically and vocally, Almaviva does not descend to his wife's chambermaid; she rises, as with Mozart this type is always capable of doing, to cut a very good figure in a higher world as well.

In *Don Giovanni*, of course, Mozart created his most famous baritone rôle, though it is also a favourite for high bass voices. It has often been mentioned in this book, for it has remained until the present a showpiece for many great singers. The brilliant cavalier is every inch a man, a seducer of the most sensual radiance – even though Da Ponte shows him more in adventures and awkward situations than in conquests, and is vocally a brilliant part which requires personality, very good melodic line, erotic timbre, great skill and fluency (for the 'champagne aria' and the many recitatives which develop into the most rapid parlando), unusual range and a complete assurance in every situation. The other men are a big contrast to him; his servant Leporello, crafty, often playing the clown, can show a servant's malice, as in the Catalogue aria, is companion in action yet completely inferior – all of which can and should find vocal expression; Ottavio, cavalier, slightly pale and immobile in personality but glorious in song, a truly lyrical Mozart tenor; Masetto, farmer's boy with an understanding of nature, attractively simple, almost a simpleton, no match for either Don Giovanni or his own sweetheart, Zerlina – a baritone or bass-baritone rôle without too many subtleties.

There are some connecting points between Don Giovanni and the worldly-wise Don Alfonso in *Così*. Not in essentials, for the former is a passionate, restless, impulse-ridden hunter, the latter a man of reflection, not instinct. But the experiences which Don Giovanni will never be able to exploit as such, Don Alfonso has to a certain extent collected in life and now uses them to good account. Where Don Giovanni puts all his faith in the power of personality, Don Alfonso is a cynic weighing up the time-honoured rules of life with deep scepticism; a superb character, a rare type for Mozart, who should have the vocal superiority of all Mozart's 'masters', enhanced by a common sense attained by neither Almaviva nor Don Giovanni, which is due not only to age but to a cooler disposition. The two lovers, Ferrando and Guglielmo, are quite different from him. Mozart raises them far above the buffo figures they really are – puppets in the hand of Alfonso and strenuous seducers of each other's sweethearts, hoping their own will be entirely faithful – and gives them the purest bel canto singing which could ever be conceived. The libretto here really becomes secondary – disguises, mistaken identities, the whole arsenal of the good old opera-buffa – and what is left is singing; wonderful arias, duets, ensembles, of a lyrical tenor and a cavalier baritone.

Mozart's last baritone is a comic one, Papageno, who clearly, to both ear and eye, is one of his favourite characters; a child of nature, untouched by any higher spirit, enjoying life, good-natured in his primitiveness. But Mozart surely sees more in him than this. Together with hundreds of clownish tricks, he gives him a lyrical duet with Pamina in which there is even talk of high ideals; 'The man who feels love's sweet emotion', they sing, though it remains very doubtful whether they understand what they are saying; in his other duet with a girl, the 'Pa-pa-pa' with Papagena, things are different and far more down-to-earth. So there is an unusually wide emotional range in Papageno, and the merry bird-catcher is a more important rôle than appears at first sight. True, amidst so many more effective rôles, it is often he who repeatedly wins the most applause; but this presumably is due more to his delightful humour than to the smattering of philosophy which – almost by accident, it would seem – he has acquired.

Mozart still has something left for comic basses. In Leporello and Osmin he has provided two marvellous parts. Osmin, the simpler character of the two, is given specially wide intervals and the lowest of low notes, a figure who is amusing by his very absurdity. Leporello has a far greater range of expressiveness, reaching from exuberant complicity with the master he admires, despite all his disapproval of him, to his quaking animal fear when faced by natural or supernatural perils, such as in the cemetery scene and the appearance of the statue in the last scene. But there is another showpiece rôle for the serious bass; Sarastro, key figure in *The Magic Flute*, one of the most magnificent characters in all opera. Dramatically, he has very limited possibilities, but through the radiance of personality sheer beauty of sound should come over to the audience – with extremely low notes, though not quite so low as Osmin's, the noblest phrasing, perfect legato and a timbre reflecting wisdom, kindness and loftiness together.

To appreciate fully the performances of singers, such analysis of

Cesare Siepi as Don Giovanni, a role in which he is familiar to both stage and film opera-goers

Regine Crespin, Wagnerian soprano and an
unforgettable Marschallin in 'Der Rosenkavalier'

Leonard Warren as Rigoletto, one of his greatest
roles

Left to right: Claire Watson as Eva, Jess Thomas
as Walther von Stolzing and Hans Hotter as
Hans Sachs in Rudolf Hartmann's production of
'Die Meistersinger' at Munich

Risë Stevens the American singer as she appeared
in Mortari's 'La Figlia del Diavolo' at La Scala
in the 1953/54 season

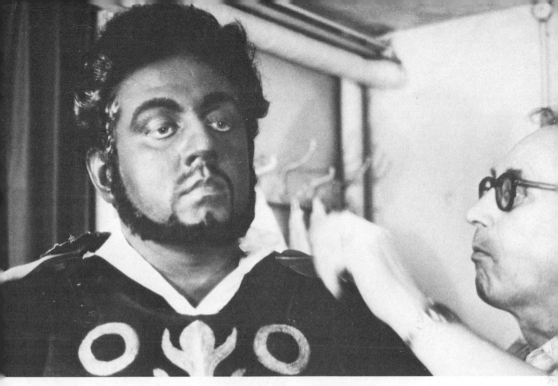

James McCracken having his costume adjusted as Otello, a role he has sung in every major opera house

A scene from the Munich production of Strauss's 'Capriccio' with (*from left to right*) Donald Grobe, Barry McDaniel and Claire Watson

Joan Sutherland as Norma, one of the bel canto roles which have become very much her property
since she achieved international status with her sensational singing of the title role of 'Lucia di
Lammermoor' at Covent Garden in 1959

Leontyne Price as Aida

The German lyric tenor Fritz Wunderlich and
Teresa Stratas in 'La Traviata'

Giulietta Simionata the great Italian mezzo-
soprano as Carmen

Nicola Rossi-Lemeni the Italian bass as Boris
Godunov

Cornell MacNeill as Verdi's Nabucco

Mario del Monaco as Otello, one of his most celebrated roles

Boris Christoff, a great bass of our time, as King Philip in Verdi's 'Don Carlos'

rôles can be extremely useful for the listener. They show him how the true artist 'gets into' his parts, and the way he perfects them intellectually and vocally, as well as musically.

'Outsiders' and 'Freak Voices'

Although quite a number of singers of world class have come from backgrounds outside that of opera or concert-hall, the two 'outsiders' I am concerned with in this section are men who acquired immense fame against all the odds – Joseph Schmidt and Mario Lanza.

On 29th March 1929 something remarkable happened in Germany. That evening many opera-lovers were sitting at their wireless sets to listen to a rare work, Meyerbeer's *L'Africaine*. The tenor lead of Vasco da Gama, which reaches its peak in the magnificent aria 'O Paradis', was sung by an unknown. At the end of the broadcast his voice was no longer unknown. Three hours were enough to make it a discussion point for amateurs and professionals alike – an irresistible, spell-binding voice, which had aroused tremendous admiration and enthusiasm. But there was still nothing known about its owner, except his name. Thousands of enquiries reached the wireless station the same night, tens of thousands in the next days, 'Who is this Joseph Schmidt? In which opera-house can we hear him?'

He could not be heard in any opera-house. With one unimportant exception, he never appeared on the stage; great though he might be as a singer, he was too small in stature, under five foot, and looking like a boy who would have been better in short trousers. But now he could no longer be hidden. He was dragged into the limelight by masses of fanatical supporters. He had to appear on concert platforms; in this way the managers at first tried to stop him being compared with people of normal height. Once, however, it did not work; at a concert in New York he appeared with the tall, dazzling prima donna Maria Jeritza, and she felt it better at the end not to take Schmidt's hand when acknowledging the rapturous applause.

To make up for his physical disadvantages, the public gave him twice as much devotion. In 1931 the 'radio singer' – an entirely new category – gave his first concert in Berlin's Beethoven Hall. A year later, in a competition organised by a Berlin evening paper, he was nominated 'the most popular singer'. On 30th January 1933 he was singing once more in a gala radio programme. It was the evening of an extremely eventful and fateful day, the full consequence of which very few guessed, and his voice calmed the waves of disturbance and fear. It delighted those who had voted for the Nazis that day, as well as their social democratic and communist opponents. In fact for a brief hour German listeners could forget everything but the magic of that voice.

On 9th May, Schmidt sang in person at the première of his film, *Ein Lied geht um die Welt* (A Song goes round the World), with several melodies which did just that, on hundreds and thousands of records. But it was his swan-song in Germany. He was first banned from public appearances and soon afterwards exiled, for he came from an orthodox Jewish family. He was born in 1904 in a village in Bukovina (Rumania), made his way to Vienna and Berlin when still a boy and as the beauty of his voice became more and more evident, thought of a career in a synagogue choir; as a midget he did not imagine anything else would be possible. But then some influential person happened to hear him on the wireless and gave him the chance to sing Vasco da Gama and win fame overnight.

Despite his boundless popularity, Schmidt's life was in a deeper sense at an end when he left Germany. Though a Rumanian Jew, he felt so closely bound to the circles of the German language and culture that this uprooting, this parting from his most loyal public, could scarcely have anything but a tragic ending. He was driven from place to place, both by the precipitous advance of the Nazis in the following years and through his own inner restlessness. When the war broke out, he suffered the same fate as millions of others. He finally escaped, at the fourth attempt, from a French internment camp into Switzerland. Here his life was no longer in danger, a threat he had faced every day for years, but he never felt at home. All he had wanted was to give pleasure to his fellow-men by his singing, and now this was no longer possible there was nothing for him to live for. On 16th October 1942, at the age of thirty-eight, little Joseph Schmidt died of a heart attack at a camp near Zürich.

His records were destroyed or pulped, and few dared to preserve them over the grim years. His films have also been destroyed, so that copies have a rarity value. Some of these, if not picked up by the Nazis, were lost in the air-raids. There is a peculiar charm in comparing his voice on the few remaining sound-tracks to those of the greatest singers of his time – let us say Gigli and Björling, the one rather older, the other younger. It is amazing to find that there is hardly any perceptible difference in quality. The lyrical timbre, the heroic high notes, the superb legato control, the effortless attack –

everything was completely in the same class. Poor Schmidt, with a midget's body and the voice of a Caruso! The voice did not, of course, have Caruso's power, for that is closely connected with physical size, but it had the melting sweetness possessed by only the finest tenors. A few years later Schmidt would have found not only a new world of freedom but the new mass media of long-playing records and television. As things were, before reaching its full brilliance, 'his star set', as it says on his grave.

To be measured against Caruso is the fate of all tenors of our century. But to be 'the great Caruso' on the screen, to represent this unique figure in a film designed to preserve his imperishable fame for posterity, this was the task that fell to Mario Lanza, whose life shows some parallels with Schmidt's. He did not perform in opera, and he too died of a heart attack, at the same age of thirty-eight; also, they both won much of their popularity at a distance, that is, through records, films and radio.

Mario Lanza, really Alfredo Cocozza, was born in New York's Italian quarter and trained as a singer in Philadelphia while earning his living as a removal man. In 1940 the distinguished conductor and patron Serge Koussevitzky heard him and brought him to the conservatoire at Boston, but then the United States entered the war, and Cocozza, just twenty, was drafted. When he returned home, there was at first no talk of singing, all the possible trades provided a very modest existence. Then a small company came together under the high-flown name of Bel Canto Trio. No one would have guessed at their appearance in small-town bars that two of them would become world-famous; Mario Lanza, who had now become a tenor, and a bass baritone called George London, who climbed quickly to international triumphs (the third in such a noble band deserves at least a mention – Frances Yeend). London became one of the great opera-singers, an unforgettable personality whose impressive power and affecting melancholy lives on superbly in many recordings. But Lanza went into films, and soon became very popular among the masses in America, so much so that an ingenious producer decided to shoot the film *The Great Caruso* with him in the title rôle. That was 1951, and afterwards the world waited eagerly for the appearance on the stage of this 'new Caruso'. Lanza had settled in Rome, and whether in morbid fear of such a confrontation or whether his head was turned by fame, he became involved in a fantastic personal drama which caused a sharp decline in his powers both physically and psychologically. He still pulled himself together for an occasional concert, until the heart attack which killed him in October 1959. He may not have been a great singer, if we judge by the highest standards of that word, but he was certainly an unusual phenomenon, with an unusual career, on the fringe of greatness.

Perhaps this is the place for a few thoughts on other extraordinary voices also on that fringe. From time to time voices turn up which especially in range go far beyond the norm. Sometimes nature seems to create abnormal larynxes, like the other natural 'anomalies' which often occur. Women with such a larynx may then produce amazingly high notes, or men amazingly low notes. There are, of course, no operatic rôles for such voices, just as you cannot buy clothes off the peg for abnormal bodies. In ordinary singing they can only be used if, besides their speciality, they have a good ordinary voice. But the temptation to exploit their speciality is understandably very strong.

There is nothing new in this. We do not know when and where such a thing first occurred. We know that Mozart enjoyed such curiosities (indeed he enjoyed all curiosities) and composed unusual pieces of music for unusual larynxes. He met the singer from Ferrara, Lucrezia Agujari, who was called La Bastardella; in Parma she sang coloratura for him up to C in alt (*ie* a whole octave above the so-called High C, which is already a nightmare for many singers), whereupon he immediately composed some pieces for her. Such things amused him. When he composed *The Magic Flute*, he designed the rôle of the Queen of the Night for an unusual larynx, that was why he several times gave her F in alt and other vocal acrobatics, which make this part the highest in the ordinary opera repertoire, and to reach these heights, as with achievements in sport, continual training is needed plus native ability. Another contemporary of Mozart's, Antonia Bernasconi, an Italian born in Stuttgart, is said to have had a range of four octaves, almost double that of a normal voice; there are three octaves between the lowest note of a contralto, which does not exist in the opera repertoire, to the highest note of the Queen of the Night. Could this lady really manage another whole octave?

Coming to our own times, I must mention three freak voices, all singers who have achieved great popularity. One, Miliza Korjus, was from the United States, though she had Slav blood, the other two are the German Erna Sack and the Peruvian Yma Sumac. Probably all three had an unusual larynx formation, but their origins are so different that this cannot be connected with questions of race or nationality.

As a student, Erna Sack sang contralto parts at the Berlin State

Opera, but in 1930 a radical change suddenly took place and an extremely high soprano voice broke through. Whether she should be accounted great as a normal singer is debatable, but she certainly became internationally famous for her ability to sing wide intervals, leaping into super-high regions. Understandably, she liked doing this, sometimes where it was artistically unjustified. It still had a big impact on a wide public, and she toured the world amidst general admiration, making records which sold better than those of many other well-known singers.

Did she illustrate a natural phenomenon or a technical accomplishment which can be acquired by training? The vocal cords may to some extent be compared with the strings of a violin. Just as a stringed instrument can produce 'pipe-tones' (overtones or harmonics), something similar may possibly occur with the voice too. It is well-known that male voices, with a little practice and without strain, can produce falsetto, a kind of speaking or singing which sounds unnatural, and there is much debate about the possibilities of its artistic use, especially in high registers, where it can be confused with very soft notes. There might surely be something like this with female voices as well, but as such tones can scarcely if at all be modulated, the artistic value of this kind of singing is again very doubtful.

I would quote again from Franzisca Martienssen-Lohmann's book *Der wissende Sänger* (The Skilled Singer), which under the heading 'Pipe-tones' says, 'In our century the singer's art is no longer assessed, as it was in earlier centuries, by the virtuosity of its trills, leaps and staccati. Today this side of singing is scarcely taken into account with male voices. For a particular type of high female voice, however, it is very much valued, especially as it represents a kind of rarity. For such ability must be combined with a real virtuoso mastery of the highest vocal range, for which today far too little training is given. That is why a "phenomenal" singer like Erna Sack is bound to acquire world fame. The heights here seem almost infinite, and the special technique required to produce a "pipe-voice" makes it also flawless in verve, tempo and certainty of intonation.'

So is it something which can be learnt, or a rare natural phenomenon for a particular type of high female voice? Many women's voices can surmount the barrier of their upper vocal limit, if they do not try to do so through a steep climb, but on the contrary by taking their voice right back to a pianissimo (just as when producing harmonics on a stringed instrument). But this super-high register is very different in sound from the rest of the voice – another point against its artistic value. For the great singer is above all one in whose voice all registers show the same sound and timbre, with no sort of break perceptible in transition from one register to another. Moreover, the pipe-tones of the super-high register cannot be associated with words; at best they form a staggering extension of coloratura, a *tour-de-force* – one might almost say a circus number – and as such to be highly respected, sometimes admired. Art, however, is more than a particular form of ability. Voices like these make no appeal to our aesthetic judgment, nor do they touch the heart.

Yma Sumac is probably the most interesting modern case of such a freak voice. From the age of fourteen she toured with a company of American Indians, conducted by the Peruvian Moisés Vivanco. More by instinct than intent he gave her vocal effects which, at least for the white public, were literally unprecedented. She was a very beautiful girl, her gleaming black hair setting off the bronze skin, and her warbling was as high and as lovely as the rarest song-birds in her native Andes. The fascinating thing was not only the height she reached – starting where Queen-of-the-Night voices end – but the sound too. You felt you were hearing some pristine sound from long-forgotten ages. Artistic considerations did not come into it, for Yma Sumac never sang anything from the classical repertoire, in fact she had probably never heard such singing. She did not distort or spoil anything, or sacrifice art to effect, she was equally far removed from both art and effect. She was a piece of Nature, as music can sometimes be in especially lovely moments; that is until Hollywood discovered the simple Indian girl, made her into a diva and dressed up her voice as artificially as its owner, so that nothing more was left of the age-old power of a primitive race and a mysterious world.

Singing Technique

The natural provisions of the voice can be read about in any anatomy book. A basic rule is that the length of the vocal cords determines the register – just as with stringed instruments (where there is the same thickness and the same tension) the lower sound corresponds to the longer strings. But this does not explain the most important thing, a voice's beauty. Again as with instruments, this depends largely on the number of overtones produced by the vibrations. For, as is well-known, when a sound is created, there is not only a basic note which vibrates, but with it a succession of further notes which have a precisely defined physical relation to it. They all merge to form a common sound, which the ear can no longer split up into its elements. A Stradivarius violin produces more overtones than an ordinary mass-produced violin, and there are more overtones vibrating in a beautiful voice than in an ordinary one. With the violin it is thus a consequence of human, artistic mastery, whereas with the voice it is a consequence of natural, innate differentiation. It is true that skilful and intensive study can also affect a voice's sound as well as its fluency and strength, but as a rule a beautiful voice is mainly an innate gift. It may have a little to do with the elasticity of the vocal cords – just in that part of them which is susceptible to influence – but more with the resonance conditions in the throat, the mouth, the head, the chest, in fact almost the whole body. For singing is more than setting in motion a vibration of the vocal cords; it makes almost the whole body share in a vibration process, the details of which remain mysterious.

This may be why there is no other sphere of music which has a doctrine and technique so surrounded with esoteric rites and complicated jargon as we find in singing. There must be hundreds of different books and manuals on singing methods, and there are very few singing teachers who do not develop a method of their own which they believe to be the best or most essential. Consequently it is also a sphere where quackery, bluff and dilettantism thrive – which, as the human body is involved, may lead to dangerous injuries.

But even among those who must be judged real authorities there are great differences of opinion on almost every question about singing – even on the elementary matter of breathing, which is a natural process, and the basis of singing; 'If you can breathe, you can sing,' an Italian saying has it. This has given many singing teachers the idea that for correct voice control the one thing needed is the maximum amount of breathing. If only it were as simple as that! 'Where a pupil is taught to take in an excessive amount of air, the vocal organs are in serious danger of being forced and becoming hard,' says F. Martienssen-Lohmann, and continues, 'There is scarcely any term in singing technique which is so much used and so little clarified as breath support. Everyone swears by his own form of it; stomach support, deep support, diaphragm support, flank support, chest support, back support, throat support and so on. There is no single meaning for the term.'

I do not want to delve very far into technical questions of singing. This book was not intended to be anything of a manual, and the confusion among teachers is too great. Still, if the amount of air breathed in is very important for the singer, its complete control by his will-power is even more important. Let us take a concrete

example. I have spoken of the great Mattia Battistini, the Italian
cavalier baritone, whom some of my older readers may have heard.
I have tried to explain the effect he had through his glorious voice,
perfect phrasing and the nobility of his personality. F. Martienssen-
Lohmann writes; 'The brilliantly youthful sound of Battistini's voice
when he was about seventy corresponded with the whole external
view of this master in the art of breathing. The sound demonstrated
the indestructible power of the roof of the stomach working inwards
from the abdomen, co-ordinated with the expansion of the broad
flanks and back; all this scarcely visible and yet clearly perceptible to
the sensitive listener through the steely resilience of the diaphragm –
though always combined with a complete immobility of the upper
chest and a regally casual bearing.'

Let us take note anyhow that even on breathing, the first point in
teaching singing, there are many kinds of methods, all having a
common end – the support of the voice, to some extent the foundation on which it rests. The essential thing is that every great singer is
complete master of the breathing technique which is right for him,
and that through it he can achieve his maximum potential. As there
are different training methods in sport, for instance, with the same
objective of achieving maximum potential, so in singing. No one –
even if he could – should slavishly imitate the note-production,
breathing support or resonance of an admired singer; the right thing
for that singer depends on his physical proportions, his resonance
conditions, his vocal timbre and – also important – his personality.
So at most only parts of it can be taken over as a singing method.

Correct breathing can lead not only to good singing, but far
beyond, to yoga-like strengthening of the will and powers of concentration. But as there are many different ways of breathing in,
there are also many different views on letting the air out of the body
in order to form a musical sound. Centuries ago the Italians were
already talking of a 'resonance' in the head. The French invented the
word 'mask' – used today by practically all singing teachers – within
which the ideal note-formation should take place. You do not
simply let the sound come out of the mouth when it comes out of the
larynx, you direct it into the head, let it vibrate there, become concentrated, gather overtones, and find support, before it escapes from
the body and is passed on to the audience.

There is much confusion on the subject of mouth position and
articulation. I have already mentioned that many bel canto singers do
not worry unduly about precision in pronouncing the words; they
will give a different 'colour' to vowels, with the evident aim of pro-

ducing an 'outflow' that is uniform and as sonorous as possible. The opposite school lays special emphasis on good and clear pronunciation, so that a high proportion of the text is intelligible. Obviously, different principles are being applied here, and the difference between representatives of the two schools can be seen merely by looking at their mouths. The bel canto singer's mouth shifts very little from a rounding which remains almost the same, and there are no abrupt movements, whereas you can lip-read the words of the other type of singer; he sings the text so as to give every vowel its very precise formulation and bring out every consonant sharply and clearly. The mouth position is therefore never static, but is determined at each moment by the words. There is little point in asking which of the two schools is the correct one. Obviously the former is suitable for the Italian, classical, bel canto style, the latter for music drama and for Lieder-singing. If there is a golden mean, again I would say that each individual singer has to try to find it for himself, and that there are many different paths which lead to the greatest singing.

Has great singing declined in our time, as many people assert and others as passionately deny? A crisis in singing might be caused by a lack of good voices or by too little training for the voices available. It is not unnatural that a larger number of beautiful voices should be produced at certain periods than at others. Man's mind and body, together with the conditions of life, have been especially subject in the second half of this century to rapid and violent change. Many of these changes might well have an effect on the voice; for instance, the new generation's increased stature and size due to better feeding, and so on, the decline in physical activity due to progressive automatisation, the increase in psychological stress, the accumulation of poisons of all kinds, such as tobacco, alcohol, drugs, air-pollution, poisons in foodstuffs and nuclear fall-out. The vocal capacity may have altered as a result of these and other environmental influences, but as we are only in the early stages of this development, it is too soon for any scientific investigation to be made on this subject, fascinating as it would be. At present, however, there is no evidence that the general level of singing in our day is inferior to that of past generations.

Music-lovers who heard Caruso and the other vocal giants of his age may talk nostalgically of the good old times, but as I have pointed out before, there is no objective standard by which to measure those good old times against ours. Certainly we have very many good singers, and some great ones. No one can say whether as a whole they reach the level of any previous age, even the age of

Caruso, because we cannot compare their singing on records made under absolutely the same conditions. Even if we could, the results might still be misleading, since appreciation of singing is no doubt just as susceptible to change as appreciation of beauty in general. Every age has its own singing ideal, which is not necessarily shared by other ages.

So we come to the second alternative; are voices less well trained? Have the secrets of the old bel canto style been lost in the very different conditions of our time? Are the last masters of this art dying off without being able to pass on their ability? That again seems plausible at first sight, perhaps paralleled by the decline in the teaching of the classical painting style, which today means only theoretical and historical knowledge. But the parallel does not really apply, for the reverse process has occurred; our age has discovered a new delight in baroque music and therefore in bel canto singing. We perform far more old operas than did previous generations in this century or the last; we are incomparably more occupied with works from the seventeenth and eighteenth century. That is because contemporary works are not good enough, it might be suggested, and we are simply making a virtue out of necessity. But this suggestion does not hold water either, and could not explain so strong a current of taste. Besides, where a bel canto singer with special talent turns up we go back to long-forgotten works in order to give him new opportunities, which scarcely indicates a rejection of the whole bel canto tradition.

Are there enough teachers in our world with adequate mastery of the rules of that tradition, and the powers of communicating them? Probably not. In its day bel canto was the only style, and everyone knew it, because it was the expression of the age. Today it is one of many styles which the future opera-singer must acquire. Consequently, the singing teacher's task, like most tasks today, is more complex and therefore more difficult. He has to prepare a young soprano with a high flowing voice for Mozart's Constanze, but also for Berg's Lulu!

In former times many singers who felt their own voice disappearing would devote themselves more and more to training the next generation. This was natural enough. Who should give the up-and-coming singer better counsel than the mature artist with stage experience, intellectual and musical superiority, and human understanding? But many teachers fall a long way short of this ideal. A great singer may not have enough teaching talent for such a task. In the course of a lifetime's practice he may have worked out a very individual technique which is right for his own voice, body and mind, but cannot be passed on, and might not even be useful if it were. A sign that we give this problem due importance is that there are now professional training institutes for singing teachers as well as singers.

Besides the difficulty of choosing the right singing teacher, the budding singer is likely to be distracted by the prevailing unrest and impatience among students. They are always in search of novelty, and need continual diversion of interest; constant pressure for quick success, publicity, the vastly increased opportunities for exhibiting talents (competitions, youth festivals, films, television and so on), and the possibility of amplifying the voice, indeed distorting it, through the microphone, all of which may well lead today's young student to break off his studies prematurely. But wait, did earlier generations of singers invariably pursue their studies for six, seven or eight years in stern determination? Far from it. In this book I have given a few examples of prima donnas who made their stage débuts at seventeen, sixteen or even fifteen. In general the rule still holds, as it always has done, that those who are best trained and prepared for their art have a relatively more secure future. But there is scarcely any field which can show so many exceptions as careers in the arts. Genius 'waives the rules', though not always with impunity.

To shed as much light on the subject as possible, and at the risk of repeating points already made, I would finally quote an article written soon after the war by Egon van Rijn, a singing teacher, who was incidentally grandfather of the prima donna Anja Silja:

'In Leipzig's "German Bookshop" before the Second World War there must have been 50,000 books and booklets about the scores of different methods of training voices in Germany. In Italy, many would assert, there were literally none ... Italian pre-eminence, covering about five hundred years, has been preserved up to the present day by the tradition of immense sensitivity. In Germany a whole number of heroic baritones with naturally magnificent voices have died of heart attacks on stage or in the wings; they had "supported themselves" to death with their diaphragm ... Old opera-goers in Vienna assert that the world stars of bel canto were not "supported" at all by the diaphragm but by an imagined top resonance point in the frontal cavity; it is as if they felt that the voice production needed for virtuoso singing was like continually taking a very fine thread through the tiny eye of a needle, while the diaphragm has only a secondary, purely automatic function. This mystery of the sublime "support function", which is so hard to work out, is the reason why up until today the celebrated seven years of study are obligatory ... Those concerned with German opera, unique throughout the world, are always complaining about the lack of new singers worthy to perform it. There are no more teachers, people say, and so many foreign singers are engaged that it brings protests from the theatrical unions. Perhaps much of the trouble can be attributed to obsolete ideas on the physiological foundations of singing ... The superstition really still exists ... that by an absolute biological law dramatic singing and stoutness go together ... No Isolde or Brünnhilde without a matronly figure, or the whole opera might collapse ... By an absurd taboo, no emotional rôles, let alone tragic ones, may be interpreted by young singers of an age at all corresponding to that conceived by the composer for the characters in question. For one thing, allegedly, even singers of thirty to thirty-five, male or female, are physically incapable of mastering the vocal demands of such rôles without disastrous over-strain; and for another, singers of that age are bound to lack the spiritual and psychological maturity. This is obviously complete non-sense. The volume, carrying power and "penetration" of a voice are determined by natural anatomical factors plus technically accom-plished handling of the organ – as with any other instrument. It has nothing to do with age ... Either a voice is properly placed, or it is not. If it is, there is automatically as much or as little dynamic-chromatic expression as corresponds to the human radiance of the singer's personality, no matter whether he is young or old.'

Many of the points in this deliberately controversial article have already been covered. It was written, of course, at a time when the generation starting their singing careers were clearly under the in-fluence of the war and post-war conditions in Germany and Austria, where tens of thousands had been killed in the war, and most of the population were hungry, homeless, cold and extremely poor. It seemed no time to take up so unprofitable a profession as singing. Opera, and musical life in general, had been greatly limited, and for the most part stopped altogether during the war years, and the laborious reconstruction going on still left opera-singing a very pre-carious livelihood. So it was no wonder that German-speaking opera was for a while short of good singers. The position has improved immeasurably since then.

As to the question of the 'German' and the 'Italian' singing methods, the more one thinks about it, the more improbable it be-comes that any polarity exists at all. The real difference has nothing to do with nationality. It is partly due to the contrast between bel canto and the dramatic-singer tradition, but also due to the language contrast; between Italian, so rich in vowels, where the words are thrown forward on the tip of the tongue and the lips, and German, which has more consonants and so makes the melodic line more fragmented. Despite these contrasts the difference is probably smaller than is generally supposed, and it can be surmounted. Many singers from German-speaking countries, and from Scandinavia, Holland, Britain and America, have fitted into Italian companies without the slightest difficulty; they can sing their own operas with complete verbal clarity and pronunciation of the consonants, while in Italian operas and in that language they go over completely to the bel canto style.

No one will deny that there must have been a highly developed 'Italian singing method', although, as Van Rijn rightly says, there are practically no manuals on it. True, there are collections of exercises, scales, arpeggios, coloratura passages, used by singing teachers all over the world, but they are not very important. For they can at most be considered a tool, and using the tool then becomes a new problem. Books on 'How Caruso practised' do not help students much either. The teacher needs a very sensitive ear, so as to maintain the strictest supervision over each note and connection of notes, and know at once what to improve, enhance and bring into the continuous line of a flawless melody.

In any case we should never forget that singing is a natural gift or ability and a natural human activity. Only what is developed from nature by natural means, however artistically, can be considered right. To be unnatural in singing is to be wrong.

'Le Physique du Rôl'

Vocal requirements are obviously the primary consideration in casting an operatic rôle; but nowadays the manager will pay almost as much attention to the physical attributes, what the French call *le physique du rôl*. The audience expects the young Siegfried, for instance, to look young, handsome, strong, brilliant, nonchalant and, if possible, he should be fair. A very short, insignificant or plain Tosca or Turandot is at a great disadvantage, however good a singer she may be, for one of the main features these two characters are meant to display is a strikingly attractive appearance. Beauty, of course, is only a relative term, and Tosca and Turandot must have something more than ordinary beauty – a special radiance which puts men under their spell. Only a Tosca with such a fascination can enthral a man of Scarpia's wide experience. Only a Turandot of dazzling sensual charm can make you understand why so many kings' sons should have destroyed themselves for her sake.

Until the First World War it was common for opera-singers of both sexes, especially in the highly dramatic rôles, to be decidedly corpulent. This is shown by portraits of the first Tristans and Isoldes and photographs of the early Brünnhildes. A sketch, from one of the productions of *Bohème* at the turn of the century, without any intention of caricature, portrays the lovers with such enormous bodies that it is hard to imagine how they embraced each other. Nineteenth-century audiences may not have been completely insensitive to such things, for we know that the world première of *Traviata* (Venice, 1853) was a failure, mainly because the first Violetta looked too robust, healthy and fat to be dying of consumption. Still, audiences everywhere seem to have tacitly accepted overweight singers in the most important rôles, so they must have somehow assumed it was a necessary evil.

We do not today consider physical size essential for vocal power, though physical strength and fitness are certainly prerequisites of vocal strength and stamina. It had been proved that an opera-singer in a leading rôle uses up as many calories as a lumberjack in Alaska, so he must be put in the category of 'heavy workers'. Although there is a big difference between the expenditure of energy by a Wagnerian tenor and by a Mozart soubrette, great physical demands are made on them both, and these can only be carried out by a healthy body which is trained for such tasks. Does such a training – in fact does studying singing – lead to abnormal physical capacity? This is by no means a ridiculous suggestion. Increased breathing activity, as with sportsmen, enlarges the chest. Combined with a singer's heavy work, it also causes an enormous appetite. Consequently, in times when there was little scientific knowledge about diet, singing almost automatically meant putting on weight. Today we know how to keep this within tolerable bounds, but it probably cannot be completely avoided except in cases where it is counteracted by unusually nervous and hypersensitive temperament.

The singer, again like the sportsman, must achieve and maintain peak condition. This demands not only physical strength, but also the power of mental concentration, strength of will and great perseverance. The leading singer, like the leading sportsman, has to be continually in strict training. He must make sure he gets enough calories, yet choose his food and drink carefully to give him strength without excessive fat. He will scarcely be able to remain very slim, however, the development of many of his muscles makes that impossible.

At any rate we can today come much nearer than former generations to the ideal of the *physique du rôl*, and it has become more necessary than ever. Films and television are more merciless in this context than very large stages at some distance from the audience. For vocal considerations the reverse is true; the stage is more merciless, for since there is no play-back process, singing and acting must be produced simultaneously. Audiences' visual demands have also become far higher today. In the past only the real opera-lovers went to performances; they went often, to hear their favourite artists, and were less critical of appearances. Today opera comes to the masses, especially through television, and the masses are always harsher and less discriminating in this respect. Having little appreciation of artistry and vocal gifts, they are mainly interested in an aspect which connoisseurs of former times considered superficial and secondary. If that interest is satisfied, they can gradually be educated to opera; if it is disappointed, an important opportunity has been lost.

Then there is the question, brought up in Van Rijn's article, of the relationship between the singer's age and the age of the character he is interpreting. This is a problem of all theatre, of course, and not only of opera. Van Rijn was not concerned so much with singers interpreting characters too young for them, but with the prejudice against giving certain rôles to very young singers, especially dramatic rôles of great emotional depth and physical strain. In earlier times it was thought that such rôles were physically too demanding for them, and even now there are authorities who still maintain this view. In the past a singer who perhaps began as a lyric soprano and only gradually grew into dramatic rôles, might not have sung Senta in *The Flying Dutchman* until she was over forty, although Senta has to say, 'I am a child and know not what I sing.' Of course this is not only a question of the *physique du rôl*, where miracles can be performed today, especially with the greater slimness that can be achieved; we find it more important that she should be psychologically right for the part, with the naïvety of one who is still a child. Isolde would ideally be older than this, though still in her twenties. But singers in the past were only given Isolde in full maturity. It was considered injurious and dangerous for younger women because of the immense physical strain, quite apart from the intellectual and psychological maturity needed, which was also thought too much to expect of them. Madame Butterfly gives her age as 'just over fifteen', a statement which should be cut out if the singer is too unsuitable in appearance, character and mobility, not just if she is older or even much older; it depends less on the actual date of birth than on the extent to which in body and spirit she can depict a teenage girl. Maria Jeritza still had a seductive charm when she was well over sixty, and her flexible body had lost none of its expressiveness, radiance and mobility. Although in her fifties, Elisabeth Schwarzkopf is a dazzlingly beautiful Marschallin, whose erotic effect on the young 'Quinquin' is immediately believable. There are many more examples, especially several Don Giovannis equally convincing as charmers of the ladies at a very advanced age; they still possessed the *physique du rôl*, which basically means much more than conformity of age.

Today we are trying to get away from the prejudice against young singers in dramatic parts. Van Rijn's remark that a voice is either properly placed or not, whatever the singer's age, may be right, although it does not remove all the problems of younger singers in particular rôles. This may be affected by the much earlier physical maturity of modern youth. Undeniably, however, only years bring experience; as a nice South American saying has it, the Devil is cunning not because he is the devil but because he is very old. The young of today are in many ways in advance of previous generations, but the *physique du rôl* certainly includes physical stamina, and we come back to the fact that singing and acting an important rôle means heavy work. So to interpret such a rôle, indeed for a singing career in general, you need to have attained maximum physical potential – instead of attaining it during your career, as often happened in the past. Consequently methods of training young singers are different today, with almost as much attention given to the physical side as if it were for sport, not singing.

The age when a singer is ready for important rôles depends on when his body has achieved the stamina to take such a strain without impairment, and also, of course, on when he has attained the necessary psychological maturity. Still, it does depend as well on when he has got his voice rightly 'placed'. (While this demands a healthy body, faulty singing methods may, conversely, incur damage to health and even lead to death, as Van Rijn mentions. Quite a number of singers have died on the stage or directly after a performance.) Badly placed voices – caused by poor training or being poorly adapted to the whole organism – quickly lose their brilliance, facility and power. At a surprisingly early stage they become brittle, uneven, incapable of soft legato – the criterion of good singing – and soon enough unserviceable. Well placed voices, on the other hand, even in decades of constant use, scarcely show any signs of wear and tear, so wonderful is the vocal apparatus nature has provided.

However, although having the voice rightly placed substantially reduces the physical strain of making it carry in large halls, that strain can never be eliminated altogether. In any case the really strenuous part of interpreting a rôle is not just producing the voice and making it carry, but the total concentration needed for 'living' the rôle with true creative empathy. And that brings us to the unique artist already referred to many times in these pages – Maria Callas.

Callas – and Tebaldi

In the fifties and sixties – if a questionnaire had been submitted to a random selection of people without any musical education, giving a dozen names of singers and asking them to mark the names of those they knew – all over the civilised world one name would have left the others far behind; Maria Callas. It was more than a name, it was a symbol.

Unlike all the other magnificent musical personalities of our time, who were read about only in the arts and review sections of the papers, Callas's name often filled the front pages of the world's press. Whereas the opera-lover became aware of other singers mainly when they appeared in his country, he would consciously or unconsciously follow her career from country to country, from opera-house to opera-house. With other singers, very little was known about them except professionally; but everyone heard details of Callas's private life, fact and fiction, anecdotes, scandals.

She was 'the last prima donna'. Since the war she has become a legend in her own lifetime, the true picture distorted almost unrecognisably by partisans' hatred or enthusiasm, a common topic for arguments even among those with no knowledge of opera or music. She was, in fact, a phenomenon like the prima donnas of the past, which might have seemed quite impossible in our time. She was attacked for 'maltreating' her mother, for making the President of Italy wait vainly in his box for her to continue a performance she had broken off, for obtaining the dismissal of a celebrated baritone from the Met, for collecting fantastic salaries, for carrying on an intensive war of nerves against her rival, Renata Tebaldi, for not keeping to contracts for guest performances because of quarantine difficulties over her dog, for getting a divorce from her husband and manager, Meneghini. Certainly Callas has never been an easy-going person, ready to put up with injustice, real or presumed, in a quiet consciousness of her own integrity, nor a person of carefully calculated reactions. She is impetuous, temperamental, hypersensitive in life as on the stage.

In her defence, if she needed defending, it could be said that since childhood there had been a growing hatred between her and her mother, and the faults were certainly not on one side only; that with the spectacular breaking off during performances, which have occurred strikingly often in her career, a subjective compulsion was involved, a sudden vocal breakdown real or imagined, together with a terrible crisis of nerves – so that there can be no question of mere temperament; that the baritone concerned had tried to win a petty personal triumph over her by behaviour both inartistic and unworthy of a colleague, holding the final note of a duet longer than she did, that the Tebaldi fans were almost as eager to hurt Callas as the latter's fans were to hurt Tebaldi, that tender affection for a dog in a very lonely woman is a positive trait, evidence of a loving heart not so often revealed in her life, that her divorce from the man whose millions had facilitated and accelerated her tumultuous climb to world fame, certainly did not occur when Meneghini's fortune was exhausted or even reduced, but on the contrary when it had been augmented a good deal further by her triumphs, and that the divorce was probably due to both the age gap and to an incompatibility of character and temperament, which could never have been surmounted.

It is Callas's fate to be compared with Tebaldi in everything, and Tebaldi, besides her *voce d'un angelo*, as Toscanini called it, has an 'angelic' disposition – she is gentle, good-natured, kind-hearted, radiating friendliness. After hearing about an interview in which Callas had called her 'a colourless woman', Tebaldi – who very rarely attacks anyone – said she had something else which Callas lacked; heart. But Tebaldi is exceptional. It is very unusual for a singer who needs to represent temperamental, desperate, vengeful, passion-crazed women on the stage, and can do so superbly, to show completely opposite characteristics in life.

In any case, when considering an operatic prima donna in this book, I am primarily concerned with what she was or is like on the stage; her personal character can be left out of account except where it affects her performance either positively or negatively. On the stage, then, has Callas the finest voice of her generation or of the century? Not at all. The quality of a voice's sound cannot be measured, but Callas's voice was certainly neither the most sonorous nor the most powerful among the opera-singers of her time. Did she sing better than her rivals? Again we cannot give an unqualified 'yes', for one thing because that too is not subject to measurement, and for another, because several other singers who were her contemporaries sang near enough perfectly, and there are no degrees in perfection. And yet Callas was the *prima donna assolutissima*, as Pasta, Grisi, Mara, Malibran, Sontag, Lind and Patti had been before her. Were they the greatest singers of their time? Nobody can judge. But they were the most fascinating, they bewitched their listeners to such an extent that objective judgment was out of the question.

It was the same with Callas. She fascinated like no one else in her age. She emanated a hypnotic power which cannot be explained, for which a glorious voice and a perfect technique were only means to an end. Even before she was famous – so that her name did not produce an immediate bias in her favour – when she came on stage as Norma, Bellini's Druid priestess, and slowly walked forward through the chorus – before she began to sing, in fact – the audience were gripped as if in a magnetic field. Thousands of people were under the spell of an unknown, indefinable force. If they had been asked to raise an arm, they would probably have found they could not move. Their will was paralysed, a stronger will than theirs had emerged and radiated its invisible force right to the furthest rows of the gallery. Probably a similar effect was produced also by Sarah Bernhardt, Eleonore Duse, by the prima donnas just mentioned and by Caruso; by the inexplicable power of personality, increased to its highest potency – a primitive phenomenon beyond singing or music.

Maria Callas is a magnificent actress, in the highest class as a tragedian. She lives so intensively every character she portrays on the stage that in each rôle she is literally a completely new and different personality. She has taken a very wide variety of operatic rôles with the consequence that it is hard to pick one out which has been more successful or more 'hers' than any others.

She was born in New York. According to the documents she is an American citizen, though Greek by blood. They give her birth date as 2nd December, but it may have been 3rd or 4th, and she herself prefers to consider it the last, which in Greece is sacred to Saint Barbara, a strong and pugnacious saint to whom she is specially devoted. She was christened Maria Anna Sofia Cecilia Calegeropoulos. Her father was a chemist in New York, but her mother, who did not settle down happily in the United States, returned to her native Greece in 1937 with the fourteen-year-old Maria. There she began studying singing in the Conservatoire at Athens. Her teacher was the Spaniard Elvira de Hidalgo, who at twelve had been a concert pianist, at sixteen had been Rosina in *The Barber of Seville* at Naples and soon after that had sung at La Scala, the Colón, the Met, Covent Garden and on a tour with Chaliapin. Maria Calegero-poulos made such rapid progress that by the time she was sixteen she had the opportunity to appear on stage singing the highly dramatic rôle of Santuzza in *Cavalleria Rusticana*. She was an unhappy girl, however. She asserted later that her mother had never loved her and had always favoured her young sister. She was also an ugly duckling, as all accounts agree, with an extremely big mouth, a massive nose and very fat. Psychiatrists afterwards declared that her extraordinary appetite and the equally extraordinary fat she kept putting on were attributable to psychological disappointments, a kind of love com-pensation for a girl who always felt herself rejected. Nevertheless, a number of rôles were given her at the Athens Opera, including Tosca, long before she was out of her teens.

The war seemed to put an end to this career, as to so many others. Maria had to work in many jobs, until in 1945, with the first oppor-tunity that came along, she boarded a steamer and went over to her father in New York. There people listened to her voice and found it 'not bad', but were deterred by her appearance. Nobody wanted to put her on the stage. Eventually she was engaged by a travelling opera company, but the tour collapsed before it had properly started. It entailed a law-suit in which an alleged 'discoverer' of her talents tried to claim a large sum of money, and this embittered her for many years afterwards.

At last a chance came. The Met showed an interest in her, but never gave her a début, no doubt luckily for the young singer who was to enter the 'Golden Horseshoe' years later as the most celebrated diva in the world. At the time, of course, she was very disappointed, but a slight sign of progress appeared. She was engaged, for a very small fee, to sing the title rôle in Ponchielli's *Gioconda* in the Arena at Verona. This surprising contract was probably attributable to the rumours of her possible connection with the Met. At any rate it proved a foundation for the later prima donna's meteoric rise and for an important chapter in her private life. For when landing in Italy, she made the acquaintance of the industrialist Giovanni Battista Meneghini, who was to become her fatherly protector, her im-presario and from 1949 her husband.

Meanwhile she had produced two changes, one easy enough to bring about – she simplified her name to Maria Callas – the other much harder, to come down to normal weight. She set about this with the same energy as she tackled every other problem, and in two years, according to some biographers, took off nearly six stone, from over fifteen to under ten; without losing or impairing her voice, one must add. Others say it was 'only' four-and-a-half stone; but whatever the amount, such rapid and drastic slimming clearly represented a dangerous experiment.

As explained above, every voice is, and must be, adapted to the physique of its owner, whose physical size and the resonance possibilities this allows play an extremely important part in singing. If a singer has geared her voice to the size of her body, and the basis of that voice, the resonance space, is suddenly reduced a great deal, the voice may well not find sufficient support any more. Also, drastic slimming of this kind may weaken the whole body, which indirectly will have a negative effect on the voice. As a result singers generally are loath to take slimming cures, and should only do so under the most careful supervision of experts who know something about both medicine and singing.

So in two respects this Callas section connects up with points I have already made; her unusually early début, at fifteen and in a dramatic rôle, and the complete change she brought about in her body. It is by no means out of the question that these two points have a bearing on the vocal difficulties she experienced with surprising frequency and eventually on the relatively early age at which her voice declined.

But to return to her rapid climb: Meneghini soon gave up his factory in order to devote himself exclusively to being his wife's manager. And another man, also much older than Maria, Tullio Serafin, one of Italy's most famous conductors and a leading figure in international opera, became her most enthusiastic promoter. This bond too did not endure to the end, which may be attributable to an instability in Callas, such as is often found in unique characters. One day, long afterwards, Serafin engaged Tebaldi for an opera, and in Callas's eyes that was high treason.

For Renata Tebaldi soon became her great rival. Tebaldi was originally a lyric soprano, Callas a dramatic, but between these two classes of voice, of course, there are a number of rôles which can be sung by both. And it was just these rôles on which the passionate Italian public became most fiercely partisan for the two singers, stirring them on and calling for blood, as in a bull-fight or a boxing match.

Such contests have occurred often enough before in the history of opera. Sometimes, when an impressario intent on business considerations brought two prima donnas on the stage together, they have even scratched and bitten, pulled each other's hair and spat at each other. There are also examples of more peaceful rivalry, as with Maria Malibran and Henriette Sontag, prima donnas of the highest class and tremendous popularity. This contest took place in Paris, and started with fees, for Malibran had a fabulous sum in her contract with the Opera, and Sontag demanded the same amount for a short appearance, in fact a higher fee. In *Don Giovanni* they had to appear together. Sontag chose her favourite rôle, Zerlina, so Malibran took over Donna Anna! Nothing sensational happened, and when the two met in a salon, they joined their voices in a Rossini duet and were so delighted with each other that they embraced and parted as friends. What would have happened if the manager of the Met or of La Scala had persuaded Tebaldi and Callas to appear together in an opera?

But these two glorious singers, the greatest women singers of their time, never did appear together. Perhaps Tebaldi might have accepted, being softer and more accommodating. It was not her fault if her singing performances were always being compared with her rival's. By no means to her disadvantage, incidentally, for professionals and amateurs alike agreed with Toscanini's verdict that she had one of the most beautiful, most angelic voices there can ever have been. In Desdemona's pathetic willow-tree song and intensely moving Ave Maria, in the soprano solo in Verdi's Requiem, especially the delicate, high, pianissimo passages, she produced moments of sublime enchantment through the human voice's expression of a heart's deepest feelings.

The careers of Callas and Tebaldi took remarkably parallel courses. They climbed the heights at the same time, fought for supremacy at La Scala and the Met, made records which were best-sellers all over the world. And when Callas retired, the voice of Tebaldi, who was a year older, showed the first signs of exhaustion, rather duller passages which marred the brilliance of those top notes so remarkably light before.

Callas reached her peak in 1951. She sang the *prima*, the opening performance of the season, at La Scala. Under Victor de Sabata's inspiring baton she interpreted Elena in Verdi's *Sicilian Vespers*. Callas the world star was born, amidst an exultation rare even for this opera-house accustomed to tumultuous enthusiasm. Tebaldi, however, had enjoyed a similar triumph under Toscanini at the re-opening of La Scala in 1946 after its destruction in the war. Now both aspired to the top positions in world opera.

Callas always preferred interpreting the great figures, the tragic heroines fated to despair, death or madness, often sweeping the victims of their love or revenge down with them to ruin – characters like Norma or Medea – but with a ruthlessness that sprang from the depths of a love betrayed. Callas was heard at La Scala in twenty-three different rôles, she was the first woman singer for many decades with an equally serviceable register covering three octaves. She was the first for a long time capable of singing the famous Bellini heroines, written by the composer for the most magnificent voices of his age – Norma, Amina (*Sonnambula*) and Elvira (*Puritani*). One of her records was a medley which had probably never been made before; it consisted entirely of operatic mad scenes. And her psychological, dramatic and vocal mastery shows in her almost incredible genius as an interpreter; for each madness is different, expressed differently, coming from different regions of shattered brains and ravaged souls.

In 1955 Callas made her first appearance in Germany, singing the mad Lucia di Lammermoor under Karajan in Berlin. The same year she made her début at the Met, eight years after that had first been a possibility. Now the Met lay at her feet, and she had a salary of such a giddy height that it put all previous figures into the shade. The problem was not how to pay it, but how to register it in the books, for the Met does not allow fees of over 1000 dollars an evening, an amount at which Callas could only smile. It took considerable skill, and the insertion of all possible clauses, to 'cook the books' over her salary, with the result that rumour pushed it up still higher than it actually was. But for these twenty-eight performances of *Norma* the Met would have made any kind of sacrifice.

In 1958 Callas sang at a gala performance at the Paris Opéra, with television companies from seventeen countries transmitting to millions the face and voice of the prima donna round whom so many legends had already been woven. As to her face, a real miracle had occurred there, for without any external aid Callas had become beautiful. Not only in appearance, such as plastic surgery might have brought about, but with a beauty radiating from within her. Just as she had a particular voice for each rôle, her compelling personality now produced for each rôle an expressive face full of the most authentic life. The ugly duckling had truly become a very fine swan indeed.

This reduces the significance of the incidents which seem to have occurred more frequently in her career than in others'. One of the saddening features of our time, which is often more interested in sensations than in real achievements, is that it was just these incidents, unnecessarily blown up into scandals, which brought her name on to the front page of the world's newspapers. No one could doubt her greatness as a singer, yet she became a protagonist in affairs which for the most part were artificially embellished, and which rarely had more than a marginal connection with her artistry. She was and is a strong personality, irritated by any mediocrities she may be obliged to have dealings with. She also lived by day in the highly charged atmosphere of the figures she would be interpreting in the evening, and for her they were more than a costume to be put on and taken off. She was more sensitive than ordinary people, for the deep emotions she expressed every evening through her singing also filled her daily life. She could not switch off when the curtain had fallen.

'Music is the supreme revelation for me,' she herself has said. 'Mediocrities in the artistic field are therefore intolerable for me. I cannot work in a second-class atmosphere. But if conductors and singers go about things with respect and real enthusiasm, then I too am prepared to work hard and give of my best. I do not want to have anything to do with inferior productions, conductors or singers. Above all, I never want to allow myself to give a bad performance. Everywhere I appear, I shall expect the best from myself and my colleagues. To all those, however, for whom quality means nothing, I shall appear capricious and temperamental – that is something I cannot help. At all places and times I shall be as "difficult" as is necessary for achieving the best results. But I never kick tenors on the shins, throw chairs at baritones, or drive conductors almost to distraction, as has often been said of me.'

Dr Herbert Graf, one of the best authorities on contemporary opera, who was for decades chief director of the Met, also director of Zürich and then Geneva Opera, has said of Callas, 'She is an artist to the last drop of her blood. I have seldom met a person capable of working with such concentration, such complete devotion and patience. She is a serious and hard-working artist pervaded by genius.' And the celebrated musicologist Friedrich Herzfeld wrote of her, 'Her singing is like a fresh wound in its outpouring of vital powers.'

The passionate demand for the best, the highest class, the absolute, has characterised her whole career. Merciless towards herself, she has achieved a perfection in her own field as complete as can be imagined for human capacity. This has produced a permanent and exceptional physical condition in her which is known by other outstanding artists, both executants and above all creative geniuses. Anyone in such a flight of spiritual exaltation, such a trance of ecstatic awareness, cannot be measured by the standards of ordinary mortals. In such an electric atmosphere, disturbances, like the inconsiderateness or importunity of a press photographer, the inattentiveness of a partner, whispering in the audience, can lead to real explosions. The average man who has never felt anything of this kind, who cannot attain such heights of intense experience, may then talk with a shrug, or even with indignation, of prima donna temperament and arrogance. As in *Ariadne auf Naxos*, two worlds meet (Ariadne's and Zerbinetta's) which can never understand each other, so the artistic genius suffers in his dealings with the everyday world, whether it is in his nature to complain of his suffering or keep quiet about it. He may even be smashed on that world, like a fine Japanese vase on an ordinary stone.

In her operatic life Callas's ruthless strictness with herself led to refusals to appear, which understandably would have been far less noticed in other artists. After all, thousands poured in from far and near for the unique chance of attending a Callas performance, often paying out sums which strained their resources to the utmost or even overstepped them (remember the satirical cartoon on Jenny Lind's American tour in 1850). And then perhaps Callas cancelled her performance. Was this sheer temperament or to show her power or obtain a still higher fee? All these motives can be completely ruled out. The explanation lies in her own words quoted above; always and on every occasion she wanted to offer the very best she could, as much for herself as for her audience, and if for some reason she thought this would be impossible, she preferred to withdraw. It is also conceivable that her hypersensitive disposition was so irritated by something which others would have found trifling, that it genuinely made her feel ill.

Her breaking off in the middle of performances, a phenomenon which is not very common in operatic history, needs further consideration. 'I will never interrupt a performance from rudeness or temperament,' she has said, 'I will never leave the stage while I can still sing.' So what of the evening at the Rome Opera, which caused such vehement debate, when the President of Italy sat in his box and the curtain could not rise for the second act because Callas refused to go on singing? Much worse conflicts must have taken place in her mind than in the auditorium after the announcement of the performance's premature end. 'That evening in Rome I could not go on singing,' she declared, and she was the only person who knew and should have been believed.

What can make an opera-singer break off a performance so abruptly? The case cannot be explained by ordinary hoarseness, which may sometimes set in unexpectedly and have a very nasty effect. On such occasions actors or singers generally save the performance, acting or singing until the end, after the audience has perhaps been asked for its indulgence, unless the loss of voice has been complete. Such cases have been known in opera-houses, cases, indeed, which ended in permanent loss of voice. They are among the tragic occurrences which are quite common in opera, even if only a fraction of them get into the papers. There have been singers who, during a great emotional or dramatic cantilena, suddenly felt they could not bring out another note. Only those who have been very near death can imagine such a moment; 'I'll never be able to sing again.' That is like dying – or worse.

Callas overcame two such crises. Twice she had to stop singing in the middle of a performance, and at those moments she may not have known whether it was temporary or permanent. But why did she have this traumatic experience which perhaps only 1% or even 0.1% of singers ever go through? That her voice was not rightly placed, and so could be overstrained, is something nobody has ever seriously asserted. As I have remarked, her drastic slimming cure may have been partly responsible, shifting the necessary proportions between physical size and vocal strength. But most probably the immense nervous pressure and tension caused a form of vocal paralysis. It is a medical fact that when the nerves 'snap' like this, the body is always attacked at its most sensitive point; the singer, therefore, at his voice.

Perhaps one needs to have seen Callas at least once in order to understand this. There were no uncaring moments; someone who seemed to consist entirely of exposed nerves and the most highly charged emotions, was experiencing the full drama of the stage character she portrayed, years of tragedy compressed into two hours. In fact it may be enough to hear recordings of Callas, even on records her extraordinary radiance can be felt. It is amazing, perhaps terrifying, to register the intensity with which she lived through everything she sang. Or suffered through it, one should say, for she was at her greatest in the portrayal of suffering characters – Butterfly, Lucia, Norma, Aida, Leonora (*Force of Destiny*). Besides the great tragedies which bring about the collapse of families, empires, epochs, she could depict small personal fates with such pathos that no one could remain unmoved – Mimì, Gilda, Violetta. It was marvellous how she could switch from the heroic gestures of a Medea to the deep passion of an ordinary girl sacrificing herself for love, and from such figures – as if she were putting on a different personality – to the delightful mischievousness of Rosina.

'When I sang, people suddenly loved me.' There are few more touching sentences from a singer's mouth than this remark by the young Maria Callas. She had discovered a magic charm to bridge the distance, real or imagined, which separated her from her environment. To be loved, that was her most secret goal, of which she was perhaps not always aware herself. She may have seemed hard in her stage career, where she often had to wrest victory from hostile circumstances, and heartless where externals were involved; but for the perceptive observer all this could not hide the existence of a heart capable of deep compassion which also beat in each of the characters Callas presented to the audience.

This warmth of heart radiated from Tebaldi in life as well – in that, she was comparable to Lotte Lehmann. Her path led her steeply upwards to the peaks of art and fame. A uniquely sweet voice of glorious timbre and unsurpassable deep feeling, flexibility and expressiveness, and a serene, affectionate, lovable personality, both contributed to her triumphs. Where there was a scandal about her, it was only a by-product of the rivalry with Callas, unsought by Tebaldi herself. The world's opera-houses filled on the announcement that she would be singing. Born in Pesaro, which was also Rossini's home town, she had an attractive open face, with no pretensions to beauty but down-to-earth, slightly rustic features and eyes that reflect kindness and understanding, and her movements had a simple, modest grace. Anyone who wants to hear pure singing can listen to one of her records. Whether she is singing Mimì or Tosca, Butterfly or Turandot, Manon Lescaut, Violetta, Aida, Leonora (in *Trovatore*), Desdemona, Madeleine in Giordano's *Andrea Chénier* or Cilea's half-forgotten *Adriana Lecouvreur* which was revived for her, there is always sheer delight in the flawless beauty of tone. As her biographer, Walter Panofsky, has written, 'This voice does not dazzle. It does not send out brilliant rays. It burns with a dark restrained glow. Tebaldi's voice does not electrify, but it touches the heart. It does not look for mere effect but for "affect".' And Friedrich Herzfeld, comparing two recordings from *The Force of Destiny*, makes the concise remark, 'Anyone concerned with Leonora's fate will prefer Callas. Anyone looking for beautiful singing will award the prize to Renata Tebaldi.'

The emergence of two singers like Maria Callas and Renata Tebaldi should reinforce confidence in the vocal and artistic capacities of our era. Who can talk of decline when there are singers of such quality, or even of a decline in taste and standards? For people pour in as much as they ever did to listen to beautiful voices. They go into raptures, like their fathers and grandfathers, their great-grandfathers and distant ancestors. They no longer harness the horses and draw the carriages themselves as their great-grandfathers did a century ago to express their ecstatic admiration, but they find other ways of showing such feelings. They even do something their grandfathers and ancestors could not do – they take home the voices of the artists they idolise, to enjoy them as often as they wish.

Callas, however, seems almost an anachronism! How can such an uncontemporary phenomenon as a prima donna turn up in the second half of the twentieth century? Renata Tebaldi, Elisabeth Schwarzkopf, Leontyne Price, Joan Sutherland, Gundula Janowitz, Anneliese Rothenberger, Mirella Freni, Victoria de los Angeles, Monserrat Caballé, Gwyneth Jones, Christa Ludwig and a good dozen more can be put into the highest class of great women singers; but Callas belongs in quite a different category, whether it is considered equal or superior to theirs, a category which is not comparable. For Callas is not only a prima donna, but, as the striking Italian double superlative has it, the *prima donna assolutissima* of our era.

Her last predecessors were Patti and Melba, half a century earlier, or perhaps Jeritza, a little later than that – for this blonde Czech had much in common with the Greek brunette, Callas. But she never achieved the popularity of Callas outside the world of opera and music; and this is perhaps a characteristic of the authentic prima donna, however foolish it may be. 'Logic and good sense have little to say in the world of prima donnas,' Kurt Honolka has written. 'The prima donna was always a creature of her environment, a social phenomenon in the highest degree. Her status did not rest on ability alone, but on the readiness of a society to offer its loyalty to the queens of song.'

So the emergence of a prima donna in the well-ordered operatic world of today, with its pension rights, unions and bureaucracy, is a sociological phenomenon of great interest. It is true that nowadays all stars travel ten times more than they did at the beginning of our century, yet opera 'business' is exactly regulated, established far in advance, guaranteed as far as possible against unexpected contingencies. But then a prima donna comes along and turns everything upside down. Programmes planned months before are altered at short notice for her benefit, dates are rearranged, rehearsals and opening nights fixed at her will, upper limits for salaries ignored, partners engaged only with her consent, conductors only commissioned if acceptable to her. It is a matter of course that she wears only her own costumes on the stage, although the rules of most opera-houses prescribe exactly the opposite; but beyond that, the costumes of others in the cast will often have to be adapted to hers. The papers are in a constant state of alert for news of the prima donna. She does not have a single quiet hour in any town, for their readers apparently want to know what she has worn, done and said, morning, noon and night. The deeper they can penetrate into her private life, the better, and if there is nothing sensational to report, then it must be invented.

There were prima donnas whose love lives would have filled volumes, and others who lived like modest, respectable court ladies in a puritanical environment. From this standpoint Callas was for a long time quite uninteresting to the sensational press. Meneghini was apparently the first man of any importance in her life. And their relationship – two years of close friendship and artistic collaboration followed by a perfectly normal wedding – scarcely corresponded with the romantic dreams of readers who liked their favourites to have adventures with mysterious princes and dashing film idols. It was not until much later that an extraordinary man came into her life, not a prince or a film star but more powerful, richer, more wrapped in mystery than Callas herself; a great tycoon and millionaire, master of empires without being king, controlling masses of people without having any public office – her fellow-countryman, Aristotle Onassis.

Anyhow, it is still astonishing that an age as businesslike as ours often claims to be can produce – and acknowledge – an authentic prima donna. But the power of personality has always been strong enough to rise above the crowd. The prima donna's magic is timeless. Even today the great soprano may be greeted with tumultuous applause, but the prima donna sends audiences crazy, as she did a hundred, two hundred and three hundred years ago.

Solo Song

The vast majority of great singers of modern times have spent most of their working lives, or at least a large part of them, in opera; but for the last century many have found song recitals an equally satisfying activity, while some have devoted themselves more or less exclusively to solo song or art-song – epitomised in the Lied. The

German word for 'song', this developed a meaning, accepted internationally, of ballads or poems set to music. Solo song flourishes
outside the German-speaking world, of course, and chansons, for
instance, or British and American ballads, have been the special
province of many distinguished singers. By a historical accident,
however, solo song as an art-form started with the Lied.

Strange as it may seem, art-song is much younger than opera.
Naturally there were chansons, madrigals, canzonettas and so on in
the Middle Ages before opera was born, but they provided only a
private diversion, a musical exercise in the intimacy of the home.
The *Minnesänger* were perhaps an exception; they had an audience,
albeit similar to that of a nineteenth-century Parisian salon, also, their
singing was based above all on improvisation and their own compositions. This was quite impracticable with the Lied as it afterwards
developed in the eighteenth century, still in a domestic framework
and without large numbers of outside guests.

Even Haydn's and Mozart's Lieder and the art-song of many
Italian contemporaries were rarely sung at concerts. They were
generally called ariettas (little arias), and many opera-singers sang
them while working at an *accademia*. Beethoven, too, still thought of
his 'An die ferne Geliebte' more in terms of music-making at home
rather than of concerts with professional artists. Near the end of his
life, when he got to know Schubert's Lieder, and exclaimed 'That
man has the divine spark', he perhaps recognised the true significance
of the genre. A new Romantic age had started, demanding musical
expression for the subtlest psychological impulses and emotions in a
stylised form accessible to a wider circle.

The Viennese opera-singer Johann Michael Vogl was probably the
first real interpreter of Lieder – those of Schubert, the first real
Lieder composer. Schubert made Vogl's acquaintance when he was
nineteen and the famous singer forty-eight. Three years later they
went off together on a romantic journey round Upper Austria. It
was far from being a tour in the modern sense, merely a matter of
stopping at various villages and giving a short song-recital. A friend
called Schober did a sketch, or caricature, of the two of them
'marching to battle and triumph', the little composer always at a
respectful distance behind the mighty court singer. Their 'triumph'
did not bring them great financial reward, but it was the birth of the
Lieder-singer, who without the aid of scenery or costume can express
in three or four minutes of words and music the deepest stirrings of
the human soul.

In his short life, with only fifteen years of creative activity,

Schubert wrote over six hundred Lieder, immortalising the words of minor poets like Müller and giving an extra dimension to the work of great poets like Goethe. He was followed in the new genre by Weber and other German romantics, by Mendelssohn and by Schumann – who was a fervent admirer of Schubert. The repertoire grew; and as with the opera repertoire, only a tiny fraction of the Lieder written remained in the memory of each succeeding generation. About 50,000 operas have been produced some time and somewhere, but fewer than a hundred are regularly performed today; and out of the hundreds and thousands of art-songs that have at some time been sung, only two or three hundred ever appear regularly on the world's concert programmes today. Yet even amateur composers, or professionals long forgotten today, have sometimes succeeded, perhaps with a single song, in capturing the mood of a happy hour, or more often a sad one.

Probably the first important singer to concentrate entirely on Lieder was Julius Stockhausen, born in 1826, almost sixty years after Vogl. He set out to be a concert singer, and did not come to it by way of the stage, as was usually the case. In fact he fulfilled the requirement set out by Franziska Martiennsen-Lohmann; 'One can never opt for a career as a concert-singer simply because one has not the range, volume or expressiveness required for the operatic stage.' Lieder-singing is a life's work. As the painters of miniatures or water-colours can co-exist with the masters of great frescoes, solo song and opera are accepted as being equally valuable art-forms. The demands they make, however, are very different. A powerful voice may be more suited to the stage; a softer one, capable of more delicate nuances, to the concert platform. But of course they are by no means mutually exclusive. Leo Slezak was not only an opera star, he was also a superb Lieder-singer. One evening he could conjure up the most intimate feelings in Lieder by Schubert and Wolf, the next night his forte notes would nearly shatter the ear-drums of the audience at the opera-house.

The Lieder-singer really needs an even finer technique than his colleague in the opera-house. His breath control must be flawless; the orchestra at an opera can help the singer to hide breaths between notes, but the piano accompaniment gives no such protection. The transitions between high, middle and low registers of the voice must function without 'joins' and almost imperceptibly, since a different colour for the voice at high and low notes, which might be acceptable in many operatic rôles, is completely out of the question in a short song. The concert singer must be more careful about his facial expressions than is necessary on the stage; for one thing, the distance between singer and audience is generally smaller than in an opera-house, and for another, the audience's attention is much more concentrated on the singer's face without the diversion of action on the stage. The concert singer must have a more concentrated power of vocal and psychological expression, because he cannot even use movements or gestures to suggest dramatic action.

But he does have the advantage of being able to adapt each rôle to his voice. In opera the singer must sing in the key decided by the composer, whereas the Lieder-singer may choose the key he finds best through transposition, which can be done with every Lied without in the least affecting its structure. Transposing in opera is exceptional, though the first act finale in *Bohème* and the tenor's 'Di quella pira' in *Trovatore* (to avoid the repeated High C) are both normally put down a semitone or a whole tone, and – as mentioned earlier – Toscanini once allowed a favourite singer, Lotte Lehmann, to sing the *Fidelio* aria a tone lower. But transposition is an integral part of Lieder-singing. Each singer should be able to experiment and choose which key is most comfortable for his vocal resources, not so much to avoid extremely high or low notes as to give him the maximum freedom for expressiveness. This is a consideration which does not, as in opera, affect many other people – partner, conductor, orchestra – it merely demands an arrangement between him and his accompanist; usually, in fact, it is the accompanist who acts as adviser. Opera-singing can often be mainly a question of power; Lieder-singing is pure expression.

Another pioneer in the Lied was Raimund von zur Mühlen, one of the first to give recitals exclusively of Lieder, *ie* without operatic arias and other additions common at the time. The great Wilhelmine Schröder-Devrient, long after she had retired from the stage, was persuaded by Stockhausen to take up concert singing. The most celebrated Leonore of her generation now sang Schubert, Weber and other contemporaries with the same deep feeling. Schumann dedi-cated to her his magnificent 'Ich grolle nicht'.

Amalie Weiss and Hermine Spiess were closely associated with Brahms. He probably loved them both, though he certainly never told them of his love; as usual he expressed his feelings only in immortal Lieder – which they would sing. Amalie Weiss married Joseph Joachim, Germany's best-known violinist of the time, who collaborated with Brahms on his violin concerto. In the late 1880s, when Brahms used to stay at Lake Thun, Hermine Spiess came to visit him and helped to keep him young in heart.

The famous opera-singer Eugen Gura, a leading Wagner baritone at Bayreuth, was much occupied with the ballads of Karl Loewe, a composer unjustly neglected today. As a Wagnerian, Gura also took up the cause of Hugo Wolf and his then scarcely known Lieder. Ludwig Wüllner, a little younger (born in 1858), won an almost unique position in Europe's concert-halls. Tall and handsome, with long white wavy hair, even in old age he still radiated power and dignity. He was an actor in prose drama, and came late to singing; he started as a baritone, became a tenor and remained a sort of 'middle-man' between speech and singing, who could perhaps explore more deeply a Lied's poetic content than its musical qualities.

Accounts of Stockhausen say he showed a profound knowledge of psychology in his interpretations and brought out very movingly every different mood suggested by the Lied – although he was really a bel canto singer, ie one who considered the melodic line more important than the shades and stresses to be put on syllables and words. He was, after all, a pupil of Manuel Garcia, son of Rossini's friend who had brought opera to North America. Stockhausen was perhaps one of the first to fuse Italian technique and German expressiveness in interpretation.

The turn of the century, last period of late Romanticism, saw a splendid blossoming of the Lied. Such immense numbers of Lieder were written that the singer could easily arrange an impressive evening's recital. The line which had started with Garcia by way of Stockhausen was now continued in dozens of pupils brilliantly trained by him. One of the finest was Johannes Meschaert, memorable above all as interpreter of Schubert, and in many respects he had his female counterpart in the very sensitive Alice Barbi.

Within ten years six great women Lieder-singers were born, in different Central European countries. Significantly, they were all mezzo-sopranos or contraltos – a consolation for the fact that nearly all great women's rôles in opera were for sopranos. The concert-hall has always belonged mainly to the dark registers; their velvety beauty of tone comes out fully here and they are in their element for the moods of the romantic song, which are predominantly nocturnal and melancholy.

Maria Philippi was born in 1875 in Basle, and started her studies there. She then went to Stockhausen at Frankfurt and finally perfected her art with Pauline Viardot-Garcia in Paris. The concert platform was her objective from the outset, Bach and Mozart were her idols. Lula Mysz-Gmeiner, born at Kronstadt (Hungary) in 1876, had outstanding teachers too, in Gustav Walter, Lilli Lehmann and

Etelka Gerster. Her sister and brother, Ella and Rudolf, were both prominent concert singers like her. Julia Culp, born at Groningen (Holland) in 1880 and also trained by that wonderful teacher, Etelka Gerster, made a brilliant career throughout Europe and the United States, and her Lieder concerts were held up as models well beyond her own time. Ilona Durigo, born at Budapest in 1881, possessed a dark contralto of velvety tone and great interpretive power, who besides singing Schubert and Wolf Lieder was impressive in concert works with orchestra. For many years she was an almost unmatched soloist in Bach's *St Matthew Passion*, and when she sang the last words from Mahler's *Lied von der Erde* (Ewig ... ewig ... ewig ...) the audience felt the breath of another world stealing over them. Elena Gerhardt, born at Leipzig in 1883, conquered Europe's concert-halls with superb renderings of classical and romantic Lieder. In 1912, with the great conductor Arthur Nikisch, who also accompanied her at the piano hundreds of times, she made a triumphant tour of America. In 1933 she left Germany, and at seventy she was still singing in London for recordings. Emmi Leisner, born in 1885 in Flensburg on the Baltic, was equally fine in Lieder and in oratorio, though periodically to be heard on the stage as well, preferably in rather passive but vocally rewarding rôles like Gluck's Orpheus.

Many male singers of that age, though mainly operatic, also did a great deal of Lieder-singing. Some of the most prominent names were Karl Meyerhofer, Karl Scheidemantel, Franz Betz, Theodor Reichmann, Alexander Heinemann. I have already talked of Karl Erb who, after his accident and at the age of fifty-three, became a most sought-after soloist for the Evangelist in Bach's *Passions* and a Lieder-singer of the first rank as well. The baritone Friedrich Brodersen, also discussed earlier, was a vivid interpreter of Schubert Lieder in the first decades of this century.

Until the First World War Vienna had a real sanctuary for Lieder in the old Bösendorfer Hall, with its own highly cultivated audiences, who listened several times a week to the greatest Lieder-singers of the day, like Meschaert, Julia Culp, Elena Gerhardt, Lula Mysz-Gmeiner. The programme always carried the phrase; 'at the piano, Richard Pahlen'.* Known throughout Europe as an outstanding Lieder accompanist, he died young, and was succeeded by Ferdinand Foll, then Carl Lafitte, later Erich Mella, Franz Miltler, Otto Schulhof, bringing us to the masterly Erik Werba. After the building's destruction, with war and post-war difficulties, the delicate art of Lieder-

---

* *Translator's note:* The author's father.

singing also suffered in Vienna; but artists who could maintain the tradition continued to emerge – Franz Steiner, Viktor Heim, Anton Tausche, Oscar Jölli, Gustav Fukar, Marianne Mislap-Kapper.

Whereas today the overwhelming majority of opera-singers appear very rarely on the concert platform, it was quite common two generations and even one generation ago. Claire Dux and Henny Wolff were excellent Lieder-singers; Tiana Lemnitz, an outstanding interpreter of many very different rôles in opera, also specialised in Lieder recitals and was magnificent in her renderings of Hugo Wolf. Among the really great artists Lotte Lehmann was an extremely sensitive Lieder-singer. Elisabeth Schumann's memorable recitals with Richard Strauss at the piano have already been mentioned; Erna Berger had a high voice of light joyous timbre and a natural playfulness which she used to full effect in gay songs, though she also shone in serious ones. Among male Lieder-singers, Paul Bender remained in the front rank over many years, as did Heinrich Schlusnus, who gave well over 2000 concerts. Hans Hotter proved a worthy successor, as expressive and deeply reflective an interpreter on the platform as on the stage. Gerhard Hüsch had the intensity required for the greatest songs; Helmut Krebs especially in Bach, sang with supreme accomplishment; Fred Drissen was highly regarded for his Lieder singing; Tauber, of course, was superb in this genre as well; and Julius Patzak's intellectual sensitivity enabled him to sing as wide a variety of Lieder as Tauber and with the same depth of feeling.

Marga Höffgen, who on the stage captured the mystical quality of Erda in *The Ring*, gave most of her finest performances in oratorio. Maria Stader, heard in opera chiefly as Pamina – she had a fine Mozartian bel canto voice – made an immense impact in Lieder and oratorio. Else Scherz-Meister devoted her lovely soprano to her fellow-Swiss, Othmar Schoek, one of the last composers of Lieder in nineteenth-century form. Among the Swiss, I must pick out Helene Fahrni, Dora Witz-Wyss, the sonorous bass Felix Loeffel: of the younger generation Ursula Buckel, Margarethe Furrer-Vogt, Clara Wirz, and the famous tenor Ernst Haefliger, as much in demand for Lieder concerts and oratorio as for Mozart operas.

For a long time the art-song was considered an exclusively German genre. Even composers from other countries, like Liszt, Dvořák and Grieg, either set German texts to music or were used to hearing their melodies sung in German translations. But then with Fauré, Duparc, Debussy and many other French composers, the chanson made its appearance, closely associated with impressionism, and demanding a completely different kind of interpretation. Among its early 'master-singers' I would mention Charles Panzéra from Geneva, who launched many of these songs, often accompanied by the composers, several of whom (d'Indy, Roussel, Milhaud, Honegger) he inspired to intensive song-writing. Today's leading authority on the French chanson, Pierre Bernac, was another who specialised in this field, particularly in the songs of Poulenc, his accompanist. Ravel's remarkable *Chansons hébraiques* were first sung by Madelaine Grey, and Ninon Vallin became the ideal interpreter of Debussy's iridescent melodies. Maggie Teyte, the English singer who lived in Paris for much of her working life, was generally recognised throughout the world both as the true Mélisande in Debussy's opera – successor of Mary Garden – and as a supreme interpreter of French song: Berlioz ('Nuits d'été'), Fauré, Reynaldo Hahn, Debussy and others. She was made a DBE by Queen Elizabeth, and has for some years, in her old age, lived again in London.

The Geneva Prize festival of 1947 brought into prominence a young Spaniard, Victoria de los Angeles. A resplendent operatic career won her the highest acclaim, but she also gained general acceptance throughout the world for the rarely heard songs of her native land, especially those of Manuel de Falla. Her unusually wide range and equal facility in different registers give her as much command of dark mezzo notes as of brilliant soprano heights, so that her repertoire has an unusual variety both in opera and in chamber singing.

There are two outstanding British tenors who specialise in art-song; Peter Pears and Alfred Deller. Pears first worked in small ensembles, until he made his début with Sadler's Wells Opera, and had leading rôles written for him in the operas of Benjamin Britten, with whom he was to form a very close friendship. They often went on concert tours round the world, reviving old British folk-songs in new arrangements by Britten, and also rendering Britten's own beautiful songs; their joint association with the Aldeburgh Festival has already been referred to. Alfred Deller is a counter-tenor, a rare class akin to the coloratura soprano among women's voices. But since the repertoire for this voice is extremely limited, it has necessitated the rediscovery of long-forgotten works or the performance of modern compositions, which have sometimes offered rewarding tasks for Deller, for example Orff's *Carmina burana* and Britten's *Midsummer Night's Dream*. The tragic early death of Kathleen Ferrier robbed the world of one of the loveliest voices for art-song of every kind, and other notable British concert-singers have been mentioned earlier in the section on oratorio, where they also shone: Heather Harper, Janet Baker, John Shirley-Quirk, Benjamin Luxon. Fine Lieder-singers also emerged from Holland: Agnes Giebel, who found her way on to international concert platforms through the Bach cantatas which she sang with such intense feeling on the Berlin radio, is one of the few world-class singers today who perform exclusively in oratorio or art-song. The younger Elly Ameling has followed a very similar path with equal success.

After the devastation of the Second World War the quiet Lied may have found a special rôle in bringing comfort and serenity. At any rate solo song has since then reached a new peak, with a generation of extremely sensitive interpreters, who through the mass media have gained an extraordinarily wide audience for this art-form. As I have said, lower voices are particularly expressive in it, so it is not surprising that four baritones are among the greatest names for our own age; the Frenchman, Souzay, Fischer-Dieskau and Prey, both from Berlin, and Angel Mattiello, an Argentinian who is largely unkown in Europe.

Gérard Souzay was the first to begin giving song recitals round the world soon after the war. His linguistic skill made him as capable of German classical and romantic Lieder as of French impressionist, Russian, Spanish, British and Italian songs. His *Dichterliebe* (Heine-Schumann) can scarcely have been sung with more authentic German romanticism, and he brings out just as completely the spirit and melody of Verlaine's and Baudelaire's poems set to the inspired music of Duparc and Fauré, Debussy and Ravel, to whose world-wide popularity Souzay has made a substantial contribution. In distant countries which had scarcely heard any European singing except Italian opera, he succeeded in attracting massive audiences for the far more intense, quieter and more intimate art-form of solo song.

Dietrich Fischer-Dieskau has created a new style. He is the thinking singer *par excellence*. No previous singer has illuminated with such analytical clarity the thought behind every word of a song. Not that he lacks vocal power, his performances in opera show he has plenty of that. But in Lieder he gives priority to the content, much to the satisfaction of the audience, who enjoy the rare pleasure of understanding the words. The technique of over-articulated syllables, which is largely his creation, has its critics and opponents as well as its supporters and imitators, but certainly no one else has achieved such world-wide fame as a Lieder-singer. In this he surpasses not only his contemporaries but all predecessors, thanks to the immense sale of his records. With his intellectual ardour, Fischer-Dieskau is always searching for new fields to master, and this is as admirable as his linguistic versatility. He leaps the barriers of language with as much ease and elegance as Souzay, one more expression of the growing internationalism of musical life today. For some while it looked as if Fischer-Dieskau might be wholly absorbed in opera, but an accident, though it did not at all affect his voice, brought him back to the concert hall as his main source of activity; here he has set standards which will surely last for a long time. In the unsurpassable 1972 Salzburg Festival, however, he made a brilliant operatic come-back as Don Alfonso (in *Cosi*), and at the same Festival sang the tenderest of Hugo Wolf Lieder to an audience of 2300 who listened with breathless attention.

Hermann Prey, a little younger, is like Fischer-Dieskau in many respects, though more extrovert, so that delight in singing and sheer beauty of tone come over more strongly; his artistry is always on a high level, but it leaves behind a heartening impression of carefree simplicity. He too brings out the full content of the Lieder he interprets, but there is much he finds less fraught with problems, less melancholy, than Fischer-Dieskau. In 1952 he won a competition on the Hessian radio in Frankfurt, and directly afterwards started rising fast in an operatic career. By 1960, after singing in many of the great opera-houses in Central Europe, he was already at the Met, where he was splendid as Wolfram in *Tannhäuser*. But he can also make a delightful Papageno, and anyone who has heard him in different operas can testify to his versatility as well as the attractiveness of his personality. His Lieder recitals are treasured all over the world as feasts of sensitive interpretation. Like Callas and Tebaldi in opera, Prey and Fischer-Dieskau are two giants in Lieder-singing who have breathed enormous new vitality into this noble branch of music.

In Buenos Aires, one of the three or four cities with the finest and most intensive musical life, Angel Mattiello has long played an important part both as leading baritone in the famous Teatro Colón and in oratorio and the art-song. He is another singer with a complete mastery in language and style of the German, French and Russian song repertoire, and sings in English and Italian as well as his Spanish mother tongue. His Schubert song-cycles show such deep emotional projection that the audience feel they are on the banks of the Danube or Rhine instead of the Rio de la Plata.

Besides these four baritones there are a great many excellent concert-singers today. Among them I would pick out three artists who are mainly operatic stars but who often delight large audiences in the concert-hall as well: Elisabeth Schwarzkopf, Erika Köth, and Peter Lagger – whose black-toned bass is extremely moving in Schubert, and in Russian songs gives audible expression to the grimness of the steppes at night.

I must also say something more about accompanists, without which no discussion of the art-song would be complete, for the finest concert-singing needs perfect harmony between singer and accompanist. We do not know how Schubert accompanied his Lieder, but Brahms by all accounts had a sensitive, accommodating touch with faultless technique at the piano. Strauss too made a perfect partner, as many still alive will remember, both in his own lovely and often stirring melodies and also for the compositions of others. Germany's most famous accompanist in recent times has been Michael Raucheisen, Maria Ivogün's second husband. Ivor Newton partnered many great singers between the wars, and among outstanding modern accompanists I would mention Gerald Moore, prolific in the recordings he has made, author of the delightful Memoirs called *Am I Too Loud?*; Geoffrey Parsons, widely regarded as Moore's successor; Dalton Baldwin; Günther Weissenhorn; Paul Ulanowsky, who left Austria for the United States and was there accepted as a valued adviser and accompanist to leading singers; and the young English pianist Irwin Gage, distinguished for his superb musical sense and his complete empathy with the singer he is accompanying.

It is the art of these pianists to encase a jewel of song so as to give it an added beauty. Forgoing the glory of solo performances, they have the inner satisfaction of teamwork, and although the uninitiated may see them as merely 'at the piano' to give necessary backing, for the real music-lover they are as important as the soloist. Teamwork is rarely found in musical life in such pure form as in the accompaniment of a singer, and I hope these few lines may suggest to some readers how much it can mean to the singer in guidance, support, confidence and inspiration.

There is a special type of 'art-song' which emerged in the USA after the First World War and caught on like a forest fire to spread over the world; the negro spiritual. This may be a new symbiosis between folk-lore and music as art, and a few of the great singers of spirituals certainly deserve some attention in this book.

Black Singers

The tall Negress on the platform is singing Schubert's *Ave Maria*. It streams from her mouth like the sound of a mighty organ. Her eyes are closed, and this is no affected pose, for everything about her is simple and sincere. Her thoughts are concentrated on the words of deep, primitive faith and on the ethereally pure melody. Directly she has finished, the audience start clapping frantically; it seems almost a sacrilege. They are stirred to an extraordinary degree, as if they had received some mystical revelation. At the end of the concert, when she sings spirituals and blues, there seems no conscious art; song simply flows out of her.

Toscanini, with typical Italian exuberance of expression, said that a voice like Marian Anderson's appeared 'only once a century', and perhaps it was not such an exaggeration. That voice embraced the mezzo's dark-blue, velvety sound, a tremendous power, true religious fervour, intense capacity for love, the unconscious pride of an old race, compassion for her brothers and sisters of all nations. With each note, she penetrated to the hearts of those listening, while the sound soared to the infinite heavens.

I remember very vividly when I first heard Marian Anderson. I was a student conductor at the Vienna Conservatoire. We were sitting round the piano when the door opened and the director came in with a young negress. That was unusual in itself, for very few negresses were seen in Central Europe in those days, least of all in classical music circles. She had an air of distinction about her, and gave an impression of modesty combined with firmness of character. The director introduced her, but her name meant little to us; we did not realise that in a few months' time it would be world-famous. Then he asked us to accompany 'the young singer from the United States' in a few Schubert Lieder. Her glorious voice with its strange outlandish beauty left us dazzled. While she sang, her face had a rapt, exalted, very beautiful expression. Voice and face combined the melancholy of Schubert and of her own race. Her mastery of the classical Lied was complete; she sang *Ave Maria* and *Death and the Maiden* with a perfection Schubert might have heard in his dreams.

Born in the Negro quarter of Philadelphia, Marian Anderson sang in the church choir, but there seemed little chance of a real singing career. She gradually gained a reputation, however, although at her early concerts in American cities audiences were assembled with the aid of many complimentary tickets; they could not really credit that a black singer should be anything extraordinary. Once they heard her in a single concert, they were spellbound, whether she was singing Lieder or spirituals, and very soon she was one of the most sought-after and celebrated singers in the world. Year after year her concerts were sold out, and ended in ovations usually reserved for star conductors, virtuoso pianists and violinists, operatic tenors and prima donnas. She remained modest, restrained, concerned only with the quality of her performance. On the platform she was like a priestess immersed in her act of worship, no singer has surpassed her as a symbol of Afro-American religious tradition in song. When she sang of her home in a distant land, of the infinite kindness of Jesus, of the pure joys of Paradise, her listeners were carried away from the every-day world, as she was herself, borne on the wings of that dark, lovely, soul-stirring voice.

It had been superbly trained, of course, and she kept up an un-remitting training so as to preserve the utmost flexibility; throughout her career she could call on deep organ notes like those of a great cathedral and the joyful high notes of an angelic choir.

Marian Anderson's triumphs included many world tours; a recep-tion by President Roosevelt at the White House, a thanksgiving recital on VE Day before a vast audience, her début at the Met as Ulrica in Verdi's *Masked Ball* – the first time a black singer had appeared there – which won her an immense ovation, and being sent to the United Nations Congress as her country's delegate. Long before any signs of age or exhaustion were perceptible, she retired to her small estate, deeply unhappy about the racial hatred and conflict in a world to which she had always preached brotherly love through the reconciling power of music. She is still living in the peace of the countryside, with her friendly animal companions, amidst a solitude of her own choosing.

For centuries, probably since the Arab occupation of Spain, Europe had remained sealed to invasion by any alien musical tradition. But now Negro music broke down the barriers, and through many others besides Marian Anderson. Three of the earliest invaders were William Warfield, Roland Hayes and Paul Robeson. Warfield toured the world as Porgy in Gershwin's opera. Hayes, the son of former slaves, had to overcome terrible disability and illness before fighting his way to fame. He too, sang Schubert and Mozart as well as spirituals, with his very melodious, supple voice of exotic timbre, and he toured the world successfully for over thirty years, until 1954.

Robeson's parents were also former slaves. He started as a lawyer, became an actor in 1921 (his most splendid part was Othello), and in 1925 gave his first concert, entirely of spirituals. For a time he alter-nated between appearances as actor and as singer. Frustrated by many setbacks, he turned first to Britain, and then with increasing frequency to Soviet Russia, whose political ideas appealed to him. For his audience in America, however, this only served to add to the ill-feeling aroused by his militancy as champion of his own race, and for a time he even had his passport taken away. Robeson's powerful,

melancholy bass, ideally suited to proclaiming the Negro's longing,
religious fervour and also drive for freedom, thrilled the millions from
many countries and of all colours who listened to him in rapt enthusiasm. One song from Jerome Kern's *Show Boat* has earned him
immortality; surely no one will ever sing 'Ol' Man River' as Robeson
did.

Casualties and Curiosities

Throughout this book I have been concerned mainly with singers
as artists, but naturally this has very often involved biographical
items. I would like to end the chapter with sundry facts about
singers' lives – and deaths. Many references have been made to the
strenuous nature of singing as a profession, so we will start with the
casualties.

Luise Schick, a favourite singer of Mozart's, burst a main artery in
her neck and died during a concert in Berlin. In 1883 Hedwig Reicher-
Kindermann, when she was only just thirty, died of a heart attack on a
Wagner tour which over-strained her both physically and psychologically. Schnorr von Carolsfeld barely survived the première of
Tristan, which for a tenor in those days meant excessive strain in every
respect. In 1910 Leopold Demuth collapsed and died on a concert
platform in Czernovitz. In 1921 Joseph Mann, at the age of forty-two,
collapsed during a performance of *Aida* at the Berlin State Opera. One
of the greatest baritones of our time, Leonard Warren, died on the
Met stage, also during a Verdi opera – *Force of Destiny* – in March 1960.
There are many more examples of what may be considered a happy
fate, being carried away at a moment when the voice has soared
triumphantly through space. Conductors too, incidentally, have quite
often collapsed at their stand, dying in full activity.

Suicide among singers, unfortunately, has also been no rarity. I have
already spoken of two who killed themselves in fits of melancholia:
Adolphe Nourrit, greatest French tenor of his time, the first to make
Schubert's Lieder popular in Paris; and Marie Wilt, the famous
soprano, target for Viennese caricaturists because of her unfortunate
figure. Other great singers have been murdered, from the legendary
Alessandro Stradella, who was stabbed in 1682 during one of his
love affairs, to the Rumanian tenor Trajan Grosavescu, shot dead by a
jealous wife, and the soprano Gertrud Bindernagel, shot by her husband.

Several great singers have lost their voice during a performance; a
fate almost worse than death! Such was the end to the operatic careers

of Alois Ander, first Viennese Lohengrin, while he was singing William Tell in 1864, and in the nineteen-thirties of Gotthelf Pistor, who sang leading roles at Bayreuth. The latter, however, continued to work as a singing teacher for many years afterwards, whereas Ander went mad and so was spared the full realisation of his unhappy state.

There have naturally been a great many victims of the concentration camp and the Second World War. Ottilie Metzger-Lattermann, who before 1914 had sung in all the important opera-houses and at Bayreuth, died in Auschwitz; the baritone Richard Breitenfeld, also a Wagner lead, in Theresienstadt. Karl Hammes, another very successful baritone at Vienna, Salzburg and Bayreuth, an extremely lovable Schwanda in Weinberger's opera, served in the Luftwaffe and was fatally wounded in an air battle over Warsaw. The Scala baritone Armando Borgioli was killed in an air-raid on Milan; Lina Cavallieri, partner of Caruso and Titta Ruffo, who had a film made of her life, called *La donna più bella del mondo*, died in an air-raid near Florence, though in her case at an advanced age.

Many great singers have been unexpectedly torn from a promising career. Gina Cigna, half French and half Italian, one of the most sought-after sopranos in the world, once a very powerful Tosca and Turandot, had to give up her starry career owing to an accident. The young Australian Marjorie Lawrence, after sensational triumphs, contracted polio at the age of thirty-two during a guest performance in Mexico. With wonderful persistence she managed to return to opera, and in 1943 sang Venus in *Tannhäuser* – the director agreed to keep her lying down throughout. She even sang Amneris again, but it remained, in the words of the title of her autobiography, an 'Interrupted Melody'. Axel Schiötz, one of Denmark's most popular singers (he was also very active in the Danish resistance movement during the war), became internationally famous as a tenor after the war. In 1950 he had a brain tumour, and the operation which saved his life caused a paralysis of the vocal cords and visual nerves. By superhuman efforts he regained his powers of speech and singing – now as a baritone – and continued to give fine performances for many years. Fritz Wunderlich, one of the most superb lyric tenors of our time, was only just thirty when he died, falling out of a window in a friend's house. Grace Moore, famous Met diva and film-star, was killed in an air crash.

Other great singers have unexpectedly retired in mid-career: as I have related, Maria Ivogün (according to common report) was keeping a vow to give up the stage if her eyesight was saved, and it was also because of a vow that the Mexican tenor José Mojica, tremendously popular in Latin America through opera and films, abandoned his career at the age of forty-seven. He had promised his dying mother to become a priest, and was accepted as a missionary among the Indians in the Peruvian Andes. He left his monastery only a few times, and in his monk's robes sang religious music in many American countries to collect money for his distant protégés.

Now for a few coincidences and curiosities. We have seen how two leading sopranos, Maria Barrientos and Mercedes Capsir, were both born in the same house in Barcelona. Three Met stars each had an unlikely start to their future prominence: Rosa Ponselle as cabaret artist (a double act with her sister as the Ponzillo Sisters), Helen Traubel in cabaret, and Richard Tucker in a synagogue choir. The brilliant Portuguese coloratura singer Regina Pacini was once told during a world tour that she would marry a head of state. She laughed at this prediction even when she married the Argentinian diplomat Marcelo de Alvear – until he became president of his country. She left the stage, occasionally appearing in charity concerts, and survived her husband by many years as the modest inhabitant of a home for retired actresses and singers in Buenos Aires.

In our century three brilliant careers began with 'understudy' appearances. In 1900, Mary Garden, still completely unknown, had to appear at short notice as Louise in Charpentier's opera of that name and became famous overnight. Astrid Varnay, one of the best Wagner singers of the post-war period, was discovered when she took over as Sieglinde from Lotte Lehmann, who had fallen ill. In 1959, when Callas refused to appear at the Met as Lady Macbeth, Leonie Rysanek had to take her place, won a terrific ovation, and was catapulted into fame – which often seems to depend on seizing a lucky chance.

Some of the great singers have had remarkable gifts outside music. Caruso did splendid caricatures, with subjects including himself, and so does Tito Gobbi. Paul Bender painted a very interesting self-portrait, which today hangs at the Munich State Opera. Among actor-singers there were Ludwig Wüllner, Franz Höbling, Paul Robeson, and among singer-conductors Richard Tauber, Hans Duhan and Julius Patzak.

I have already touched on singing families like the Garcias and the de Reszkes. Lilli Lehmann had a tenor father, a soprano mother and a sister Marie, who was also a very distinguished singer. Gustav and Leo Schützendorf were the most prominent of six opera-singer brothers. Titta Ruffo had a sister with a big reputation as a singer. Astrid Varnay's parents were both singers, so were Adelina Patti's, and she had two sisters who sang in opera. Christa Ludwig, also the child of two singers, probably inherited the lovely dark sound of her voice from her contralto mother.

She and Walter Berry provide one of many examples of marriages in which both partners are famous artists. Such marriages are subjected to great strain with the immense amount of travelling imposed by the international circuit; but many of them have been very happy ones, and it is natural enough for artists to come together in their own sphere and to find likely partners where there are similar interests, aims and ideals. For the record I give a few of the most celebrated couples in this century: Claire Dux – Hans Albers; Maria Cebotari – Gustav Diessl; Maria Ivogün – Karl Erb and Maria Ivogün – Michael Raucheisen; Barbara Kemp – Max von Schillings; Paula von Ahna – Richard Strauss; Lucille Marcel – Felix Weingartner; Eva von der Osten – Friedrich Plaschke; Berta Kiurina – Hubert Leuer; Fritzi Massary – Max Pallenberg; Meta Seinemeyer – Frieder Weissmann; Viorica Ursuleac – Clemens Krauss; Sena Jurinac – Sesto Bruscantini; Maria Olczewska – Emil Schipper; Leonie Rysanek – Ferdinand Grossmann; Irmgard Seefried – Wolfgang Schneiderhan; Virginia Zeani – Nicola Rossi Lemeni; Pia Tassinari – Ferruccio Tagliavini; Sandra Warfield – James McCracken; Evelyn Lear – Thomas Stewart.

IX

Opera In Our Time

Repertory or Stagione

Before taking a last look round at the music centres of today, let us consider some aspects of the performance of opera in the modern world. Opera-houses are sometimes accused of being purely 'museums of sound'. Disciples of the *avant-garde* believe that our age, which aspires to new forms in every sphere, should find a musical form more up-to-date than the eighteenth-, nineteenth- and early twentieth-century works on which the repertoire is based. Even if there is any validity to their arguments, it would obviously be absurd to abandon classical and romantic opera to oblivion. There is no reason why the present system should not continue, while at the same time the innovators experiment with modern forms as they think fit.

Assuming opera does survive in its present form – and it surely will, considering the enthusiasm it still generates among very large numbers of people – it is much more important to decide which is the better of the structures I mentioned earlier, repertory or *stagione*.

Only a permanent company can keep a repertoire going with many standard works always ready for performance. This kind of repertory company has been the aim of the opera-houses in North and Central Europe since the second half of the last century. A homogeneous group of the best singers that can be found is collected for one year or more to perform together as a permanent team. With a large number of operas in the repertoire (between twenty and sixty according to the importance of the opera-house), the manager or

director can arrange a varied programme of three, four or five different works a week – and even six or seven. Of course there will be
changes of cast due to illness, holidays, retirements, or for various
other reasons, when a member of the company, or a guest may have to
take over a rôle without benefit of rehearsal. In the course of time
these repertory performances, especially if the original well-rehearsed
première cast is no longer together at full strength, will begin to suffer
from signs of staleness. The term 'repertory performance' may become
a mere synonym for mediocrity. But with this system many subscription tickets can be sold, thereby guaranteeing a viable business
and a good use of the whole company.

Italy has never had the system. Every Italian season offers a certain
number of new productions, for which the best possible casts are
assembled from everywhere. Each opera is performed for a few
evenings, and is then replaced by a new première, and no opera will
be repeated during that season. The level may be high, since an
outstanding 'specialist' can be called in for every rôle, and with only
a few performances staleness is always avoided.

In our day the repertory system, at least in the larger opera-houses,
has come up against an insoluble problem. Besides constant activity
at his home theatre, so far as such a thing still exists, every well-known
singer has a great many other commitments to fulfil; festivals,
appearances at other opera-houses, making records, giving concerts on
the radio, taking part in films and television programmes. A top singer
may belong to several leading opera-houses at once, appearing twenty
evenings at the Met and as many again at the Berlin, Vienna, Hamburg
or Munich Opera, Covent Garden, the Colón, La Scala, the Fenice,
Genoa or Rome, perhaps a Swiss opera-house – all of them as 'member
for the year', partly on tax grounds.

Despite this difficulty many responsible directors especially in
Germany, Austria and Switzerland – notably Rolf Liebermann, for
many years Hamburg's very successful manager – defend the repertory
system, not only to preserve a worthy tradition but because a pure
stagione system means an impoverishment of the repertoire; a *stagione*
opera-house cannot offer more than ten or fifteen works in a season.
Karajan, on the other hand, prefers to rehearse an opera with the best
cast he can possibly get and perform it for a limited number of
evenings. He believes that even then there will be slight flaws showing
by the third evening, so that further performances cannot be artistically justified. When he was director of the Vienna Opera, he was
criticised for giving his best performances before a few favoured
thousands, not to the great mass of opera-lovers. To meet this criti-

cism and make up for the few performances of each work, he is becoming involved more and more closely with the mass media, and hopes to 'immortalise' outstanding productions on record and television film.

The *stagione* system also corresponds to the specialisation which is advancing in all fields today. Consequently singers concentrate increasingly on a particular type of singing; there are specialists for individual rôles, summoned to interpret them on many different stages. Schröder-Devrient, of course, was a specialist a hundred and fifty years ago, travelling from opera-house to opera-house with her interpretation of Fidelio. The public in every city preferred to see the great singers always in the same rôles, the rôles where those singers could exhibit their talents most brilliantly and which were therefore inseparably bound up with their fame. But the repertoire of all those singers was very extensive, whereas today's specialists are not so interested in versatility and universality; they prefer to develop the smallest item to perfection.

Still, with the greatly increased numbers of young singers emerging, the repertory system seems likely to last for a good while yet; it is firmly anchored at least in Central European opera-houses, where it is still considered the ideal training-ground. Other countries will keep or adopt the *stagione* system. In any case the supremacy of the singer will not be shaken. Contemporary opera may attach more importance to dramatic factors than to beauty of tone and the melodic line, but fine singing as well as fine acting is still necessary to preserve our 'museum of sound'.

The Peaceful Invasion

For centuries, composing, producing and singing in opera was a purely European business, mainly Italian to start with, until gradually a French sector was added, then a German-speaking and later a Russian one. From about 1830 production of opera spread to America; composition of new works started there about half a century after that. The first North American opera-singers who went to Europe did not attract much attention; except in Britain itself, they were taken for British. The same sort of thing happened to the Latin Americans, who soon found their niche in Italian opera. But at the beginning of this century singers from the New World still formed a very small minority in European opera-houses.

With the end of the First World War the proportions began to shift. The United States, more strongly involved in Europe through

their presence on European battlefields, began to penetrate its cultural life as well; generally the opera-singers were white, the jazz
and spiritual singers, of course, coloured. But soon coloured singers
were taking an interest in opera and showing talent for it. At first
they were given rôles like Otello – which fitted the *physique du rôl* –
although Negro heroic tenors were a rarity. There were more negro
sopranos, in their element as Aida, the Ethiopian princess. There are
also attractive rôles for mezzos; for instance, Amneris the Egyptian
princess, Saint-Saens's Arabian Delilah, Strauss's Salome. The characters in Bizet's *Pearl-Fishers* and even his gypsy, Carmen, are well
suited to coloured singers. Negresses were widely accepted, too, in
rôles where all the scenes are played in less strong lighting, as with
Azucena in *Trovatore* and Ulrica in *Masked Ball*. The characters of
Porgy and Bess were naturally the domain of coloured singers from
the outset. But beyond that – a mixture of races very soon developed
in opera.

As I have mentioned, Wieland Wagner caused a sensation by giving
the role of Venus in *Tannhäuser* to the Negress Grace Bumbry. In some
ways this was highly appropriate, for the inaccessible goddess of love
embodies Tannhäuser's erotic dreams; at the time of the Crusades,
when medieval Europe was coming into contact for the first time with
people of darker skins, such dreams might well have been of a dark-
skinned Venus. Directors were soon giving characters like Titania
and Oberon (both in Weber and in Britten) to coloured singers;
again, there was nothing in writing to say they had to be white.

Finally considerations of colour were dropped altogether. Since
anyhow the idea of realistic opera had ceased to be important, nobody
even bothered about 'convincing' make-up. Young Negresses with
their sensual attraction and often extreme physical suppleness were
engaged for Alban Berg's *Lulu* (Felicia Weathers), or even for the
typically Viennese Sophie in *Rosenkavalier* (Reri Grist) and Lisa, the
young Russian aristocrat in *Queen of Spades* (Annabelle Bernard).
In short, race barriers were down in opera, as in sport, and the Negroes
pouring in from America gained full equality and top positions.

But they formed only a part of the peaceful invasion of highly
talented American singers who swept over Europe after the Second
World War, and provided the biggest access of new blood to European opera-houses. When Dr Herbert Graf, quoted in an earlier
chapter, became director of the Zürich Opera and wanted to re-
juvenate and rebuild the company there, he brought with him a
dozen American singers. In the opening performance a new heroic
tenor, James McCracken, made a great impact. Afterwards ten of

these young Americans sang in the brilliant première of Britten's *Midsummer Night's Dream*. Graf could easily have had it sung in the English original, but he wanted it in German for the benefit of his audience, and also perhaps to show the linguistic facility with which his new members could adapt themselves everywhere. Many of those he imported have since attained considerable success; McCracken, Sandra Warfield, Reri Grist, Glade Peterson, Robert Kerns. Many others were already prominent in European opera, and climbed quickly to world class; Jess Thomas, James King, Jean Madeira, Leontyne Price, Thomas Stewart, Evelyn Lear, Vera Little, William Warfield, Gloria Davy, Lawrence Winters, Regina Resnik, Blanche Thebom, Risë Stevens, Grace Hoffman, Barry McDaniel, Ella Lee, Eleanor Ross, Shirley Verrett, Jerome Hines, Robert Merrill, Sherrill Milnes, Martina Arroyo, Beverly Sills, Jan Pearce, Richard Tucker, Cornell MacNeil, Marilyn Horne – and Grace Bumbry, Annabelle Bernard, Felicia Weathers, mentioned above. Such a host of outstanding singers from one country can rarely have appeared at the same time.

We could add American-born children of Italian parents; Dusolina Giannini, Anna Moffo, Virginia Gordoni – and why not Callas too? This is also the place to list some of the singers who played a decisive part in the rise and expansion of American opera; appearing at the Met, the New York City Center Opera House or other important operatic centres; Jeannette Scovotti, Joann Grillo, Phyllis Curtin, Eileen Farrell, Dorothy Kirsten, Patricia Brooks, Rosalind Elias, Judith Raskin, Barry Morell, Frank Guarrera, Robert Weede, Norman Treigel, Giorgio Tozzi and Eugen Tobin.

The young American singers bring not only healthy and 'trouble-free' voices of great brilliance, but also, for the most part, striking good looks, physical mobility, the stamina and energy associated with sportsmen, an unaffected ingenuousness, and a tough determination to learn. Whether they have reached near perfection at home (more often the case than we care to think in Europe) or want to finish their studies over here, whether their acting is based on sound technique or natural ability, they form the most amazing reservoir of singers anywhere in the world.

Today's 'Greats'

When the Vienna Opera rose again out of the rubble, the spirit of Maria Cebotari must have hung sometimes over this her last opera-house, where she had reached unforgettable peaks of performance.

In 1942 she made a film about the fantastic life of Maria Malibran. She did not guess that she too would only be granted a short stay on the summit. It was almost the last time that her Slav-based voice was to be heard climbing effortlessly to coloratura heights, although she maintained until her death the lyric timbre which had enabled her to sing Bohème so gloriously with Gigli. Max Lorenz's heroic and intelligently-handled voice survived the war; he was celebrated throughout the world, no only for his Siegfried and Tristan but also for his Otello and Florestan, which became legends to all opera-lovers. The king of Wagner tenors for many years, he had a worthy successor to his crown in Wolfgang Windgassen. Born in France, the son of a tenor and a coloratura soprano, Windgassen made his Bayreuth début in 1951 as Parsifal, and since then has made an ideal Wagner singer in all the greatest opera-houses, extremely skilful in diction and interpretation, a fascinating actor.

Among his successors, Ramon Vinay started as a baritone, making his début in Mexico as Count di Luna in *Trovatore*; six years later he had become a heroic tenor, progressing from Otello (under Furtwängler at Salzburg in 1951) to a Tristan as perfect as can be imagined. After ten years of glory, in this most taxing of all rôles, he ended as a baritone again. Jess Thomas and James King had meanwhile taken over as Tristan, sharing the inheritance with the Canadian, Jon Vickers, one of the most triumphant heroic tenor voices of our day. Two other outstanding heroic tenors are Hans Beirer and Ludwig Suthaus. The latter, who sang Siegmund, Stolzing and Loge at Bayreuth was, after the war, the first German singer to be invited to Moscow's Bolshoi Theatre.

Of the magnificent heroic baritones to be heard in our time, first mention must be given to Hans Hotter, perhaps the greatest of them all. His powerful Wotan and his recitals of Schubert Lieder yielded two types of emotion that were equally compelling. By the time he retired, after a long and illustrious career, several younger rivals had come to the fore. Theo Adam showed a remarkable maturity for his age in the rôles of Sachs, Wotan and Baron Ochs. Franz Crass had the dignity for Sarastro and the humour for Nicolai's Falstaff, with a mellifluous voice of rare beauty. Walter Berry (born in 1929, the same year as Ghiaurov, Wächter, Prey and Kmentt) will be remembered for many performances, perhaps most of all for his Wozzeck, which paved the way for heavier rôles such as Sachs and Wotan. These he studied with Paul Schöffler, who was a dominating stage personality until well into his sixties. The great Hotter-Schöffler line is being continued by the American, Thomas Stewart. During the long years of his climb to prominence Stewart dreamed of Sachs and Wotan, thought the rôles through again and again, moulded them within himself. His chance came when Karajan cast him as Wotan in the Salzburg Easter Festival, when he presented a Lord of Valhalla of great intellectual power, painfully accepting renunciation. Norman Bailey became the first English Sachs at Bayreuth; Donald McIntyre, a New Zealander, is much in demand for the major Wagner rôles and is also noted for his Klingsor.

Let us turn to the ladies. In 1958, when Munich's Cuvilliés-Theater was re-opened, the wonderful voice of an American girl was heard as the Countess in *Figaro*. Five years later, when the city's National Theatre was re-opened, Claire Watson was an ideal Eva in *Meister-singer*. Has there ever been a Marschallin to match Lotte Lehmann? Four singers can possibly make that claim: Hilde Konetzni, Maria Reining, Viorica Ursuleac and Elisabeth Schwarzkopf – four very different interpretations, each perfect in its own way. And more recently we have had another outstanding Marschallin, Régine Crespin, very 'Viennese' although she lives in Paris. Born in Mar-seilles of French-Italian parentage, she is surprisingly involved with German music, and sings a Brünnhilde such as Wagner himself might have wished.

There are not many great Wagner heroines in our time. But there is one who fulfils all the wishes of both composer and audience – Birgit Nilsson. She travels all over the world, turning productions of *Tristan* and *The Ring* into festival performances. Her voice soars effortlessly over vast orchestras in full flood. She is a Swedish girl, brought up on the land, and singing was something really without precedent in her family. But she thrust herself into this career, starting in Stockholm, then brought over by Busch to play Verdi's Lady Macbeth and afterwards (1951) Electra in Mozart's *Idomeneo* at Glyndebourne. She had already sung the usual dramatic heroines – Donna Anna, Turandot, Tosca, Aida – and then at Covent Garden she heard the mature Kirsten Flagstad, undisputed queen of Wagner singers. It was a mystical moment; the world diva nearing the end of her glorious career and the young singer who was to step into her shoes. In the following years Nilsson took enormous strides towards this position; at Vienna in 1953 she was Elsa in *Lohengrin* and Sieglinde in *Die Walküre*, made her début a year later at Bayreuth, in 1955 sang the whole *Ring* Cycle at Munich, in 1956 gave a Wagner concert before an audience of 20,000 in the Hollywood Bowl, and the year after realised her greatest ambition – Isolde at Bayreuth. Ernest New-man, Grand Old Man of British music criticism, wrote then: 'I am glad I have lived long enough to have seen and heard a young Wagner singer of such perfection.'

Since then she has achieved even greater perfection, not only as Brünnhilde and Isolde, but as Turandot and Salome. In 1966 at the Met she undertook the task of being both Elisabeth and her antagonist, Venus, in the same production of *Tannhäuser*; truly a challenge taken up only by an artist of Nilsson's rank. She is capable of portraying completely these two extremes of female character and so shedding tragic light on Tannhäuser's dilemma caught between heavenly and earthly love; Nilsson's performance points the connection between them, showing them to be two facets of the eternal woman inseparably linked despite their distance from each other. And Nilsson has found a harmonious balance between two other extremes, Italian and German singing: 'I believe bel canto is a great help for Wagner. Today there is a widespread idea that one is bound to become a Wagner singer provided one develops a powerful voice. But it is Wagner of all composers who demands beautiful singing.' Who will one day accede to Nilsson's crown, and carry on the dynasty of Flagstad, Varnay, Mödl, Nilsson? Among the favourites are Amy Shuard, Anja Silja, Gladys Kuchta, Dvorakova, Dernesch, Kniplova, Janku, Ligendza.

Stuttgart is fortunate enough to possess in Gerhard Stolze one of the most remarkable performers of our time; to see and hear him is a tremendous theatrical as well as musical experience. He is a tenor, who made a splendid Pedrillo in a televised performance of *Entführung*, but also a baritone; the register is quite unimportant, it is completely subordinate to the figure he is interpreting. At Stuttgart under Rennert's direction Stolze has taken two baritone pa 's, Wozzeck and Shishkoff (in Jánack's opera *From the House of the Dead*), that almost defy classification. When he is on the stage as Loge, you suddenly understand this twilight figure, unloved half-brother of the gods, superior to them all and yet an inferior by birth. Stolze should be seen, too, in Orff's *Oedipus* (with vocal demands which scarcely any tenor voice has had to master before), as the grotesque in Egk's *Revisor*, and as the Painter in Berg's *Lulu*. Whatever he sings becomes a leading rôle.

A few years ago the Hamburg State Opera was touring the United States, with six contemporary works. One of these was American, Schuller's *Visitation*, and it had a wonderful coloured baritone of extraordinary power in McHenry Boatwright, who brought an almost personal terror to the nightmare vision of being lynched. With him as 'singer-actors' were Kerstin Meyer, Felicia Weathers and

Erwin Wohlfahrt. In the same tour, Anneliese Rothenberger, one of the leading German sopranos, a successor of Schwarzkopf with strong personality and keen intelligence, an oustanding Constanze in *Entführung*, appeared as Lulu. A strange, and 'commercial' idea of manager Liebermann to cast Rothenberger as the original 'vamp', unless it was a quite deliberate reinterpretation of this ambiguous part – 'a vamp with angelic features' – conductor Rennert is said to have called her. From Rothenberger's very wide repertoire another unusual character-study sticks in the memory; in Poulenc's *Dialogue des Carmelites* two nuns are talking of the death which lies inexorably ahead for them, one is full of quavering animal fear, the other joyful through the faith with which she awaits everything sent by God. The first was Rothenberger, the second Irmgard Seefried, at the peak of her career.

Anja Silja also caused a stir as Lulu, but then she has done that ever since 1951, when she was eleven, and Heinz Joachim in *Die Welt* greeted her as 'a new Ivogün'. Aders van Rijn, a music-teacher I quoted in an earlier chapter, then made her learn rôles like Butterfly and Tosca – against all the rules and traditions. At twenty she was singing Senta at Bayreuth, with five years in opera already behind her: Rosina (*Barber of Seville*), Zerbinetta (*Ariadne auf Naxos*) and Micaela (*Carmen*) at Brunswick; the Queen of the Night and the *Trovatore* Leonora at Stuttgart; then at Frankfurt, Constanze and Fiordiligi, Santuzza (in *Cav*) and the four women's rôles in *Tales of Hoffman*. From 1961 to 1965 she sang only in Wieland Wagner's productions; he cast her as Elsa, Isolde, Salome and then Brünnhilde, when she was only wenty-two. At twenty-four she was a young Elektra such as Strau· always wanted but did not live to see. Her sensuous Lulu had an erotic intensity seldom experienced on an operatic stage, yet she brought the same empathy to Turandot, the 'iceberg' princess. So she was a born character portrayer, but, more astonishing still, a born singer, with a larynx which even as a small girl could be exposed to the heaviest burdens. According to her biographer, Heinzelmann, when she was having her opera rehearsals in Brunswick, she asked her grandfather 'May I play a little football, grandpa?' an unusual request from a future Isolde! It remains to be seen how her voice will stand up to such precocious development.

A few years ago the new Met arranged a celebration for Richard Tucker's quarter-century of leading rolcs: he sang the first act of *Traviata* with Joan Sutherland, the second act of *Gioconda* with Renata Tebaldi, the third act of *Aida* with Leontyne Price; three of the greatest sopranos of the moment, perhaps of the century. Almost the same age as Tucker, Jussi Björling had to retire many years earlier, one of the most glorious tenor voices became prematurely muted. But it still has an almost unparallelled radiance on records, and purely as a singer this Swede was unsurpassed. A few evenings before the Tucker anniversary concert Joan Sutherland had sung her peak rôle, Norma, with a partner who was one of the great discoveries of our day – the mezzo-soprano Marilyn Horne. The wheel turns, bringing up new voices over and over again. It seems only last year that Callas and Stignani were so fully inside these rôles that you could not expect anything like them ever again.

As I said in the section on Callas, her magnetic personality was unique, and in that respect Joan Sutherland cannot be mentioned in the same breath. But for sheer vocal expertise, to judge by this Norma, Sutherland could claim the rank of a *prima donna assoluta*. Except that there are a whole lot of claimants to the throne of Callas; Leontyne Price, Martina Arroyo, Renata Scotto, perhaps Raina Kabaivanska, Hanna Janku. In the Callas era her most important contemporary in German opera (if such distinctions can be made at all) was probably Elisabeth Schwarzkopf. Magnificent in demeanour, with a superbly controlled, warm, lyric-dramatic soprano, her international career began with the end of the Second World War and brought her innumerable triumphs. Recordings have preserved wonderful moments of her stage life, especially as the Marschallin, and also in a colour film of *Rosenkavalier* made about the same time. A truly great singer, she has also given very many Lieder recitals.

In Caruso's day the tenors were the real kings of the operatic stage. Who has maintained their dominance during the last two and a half decades? Helge Roswaenge kept his fine lyric tenor with pleasing high notes until he was quite an old man. Franz Völker was the best Lohengrin, Siegmund (*Walküre*) and Florestan (*Fidelio*) of his time, but that noble voice too is now silent. Peter Anders stepped into their place, and after the war became one of Germany's best-loved tenors. Although the timbre of his voice was really lyric, he sang a superb Otello, but died in 1954 after a car crash, only forty-six years old. Fritz Wunderlich, as we have seen, after making himself a great name as a Mozart and bel canto singer, died even younger.

Rudolf Schock's father was an artisan, his mother was wardrobe mistress in the Duisberg City Theatre. Through her he got into the children's chorus there, eventually becoming a minor opera-singer, and in 1936 he joined the Bayreuth chorus. Then, despite war service and a period as a prisoner of war, his progress was rapid. In 1949 Tauber, his greatest idol, had just died, so Schock took over Tauber's

Australian tour. He appeared at the Edinburgh and Salzburg Festivals, sang the tenor solo in Beethoven's Choral Symphony under Furt-wängler, and in 1959 Stolzing at Bayreuth. He has recorded forty-eight operas, Italian as well as German, leads and also smaller rôles like the Shepherd in *Tristan*, and twenty-eight operettas. His immense success, however, may derive even more from his popular songs and from television and films, which have given him entry into the widest social strata. In New York he celebrated what was perhaps his greatest triumph as Danilo in a spectacular production of *The Merry Widow*. At the last moment Schwarzkopf could not appear with him; instead his partner was Rothenberger, who was just beginning her career. And there was also a very young tenor, moving towards world fame, Nicolai Gedda.

Today Gedda is one of the greatest and most sought-after of artists. His first name comes from his Russian father, and he took his surname from his Swedish mother. Discovered in 1952 in the Stockholm Conservatoire, he achieved a swift rise, largely through records, for which he possesses the ideal voice. In a very short space of time he sang a surprising number of rôles, and in many different languages, for he has equal facility singing Italian, German, French, Russian or Swedish. In 1953 Karajan cast him as Don Ottavio (*Don Giovanni*) at La Scala. Then came Rome, Paris, Vienna, London, in quick suc-cession. 'The poet among the lyric tenors,' a leading New York paper called him, while *Die Welt* said he was 'the best lyric tenor singing today' and the proverbial comparison with Caruso was 'all there was left to make'. But as I have remarked often enough in this book, living singers cannot be compared with the dead; Gedda is a great tenor, and that should suffice. Like his fellow-countryman, Jussi Björling, he husbands his resources skilfully; he commits himself to only seventy-five stage appearances and to making about five re-cordings a year. With something like eighty rôles at his command, a good dozen in almost unknown operas, he has the intellectual agility and artistry to be adding continually to his repertoire.

Giuseppe di Stefano is a 'people's tenor', rather like Schock in Germany. Born in Catania in 1921, he was a newspaper seller and knife-grinder, was captured during the war and escaped from a German P.O.W. camp to Switzerland, where his voice aroused great interest. In 1946 he made his début in Reggio Emilia as Des Grieux in *Manon Lescaut*. This started a lightning career, only pos-sible with the *stagione* system, for in a single year he stormed through Venice, Bologna and Rome to La Scala and soon to the Met. In 1955 he sang as Callas's partner in *Lucia di Lammermoor* under Karajan, but the evening ended in a scandal. Callas appeared alone for the curtain call, di Stefano refused to take part in other performances and made disparaging remarks about his partner's artistry. Yet he remained the leading Italian tenor. Then in 1963 Karajan rejected him for Rodolfo in *Bohème* at La Scala, choosing instead the young and as yet unknown Gianni Raimondi, whose performance – after an initial battle with the many di Stefano supporters in the audience – finally won tumultuous applause. Di Stefano then went to Vienna, and with three artists of world class in the cast (Jean Madeira, George London, Hilde Güden) sang a much-praised Don José in *Carmen*. After that he tried to recapture La Scala. With the wonderful young singer Mirella Freni, one of the sweetest voices in Italy today, he showed in Donizetti's *Elisir d'Amore* that on his good days he could still match any tenor in the world. But the critics remained unfavourable. The ebullient Sicilian went to America, then in Berlin sang in a long run of Lehar's *Land of Smiles* – without Tauber's charm or vocal delicacy – and finally turned his back on opera for good, saying it was 'so commercialised it had nothing to do with art any more'.

His relatively early retirement cleared the way for several Italian tenors. Carlo Bergonzi was chosen in 1951 for most of the leads in a radio opera cycle for the fiftieth anniversary of Verdi's death. Since then he has come to rank as one of the finest lyric-dramatic tenors in the world, a splendid Radames and a Manrico with superb high notes. Franco Corelli from Ancona had little interest in singing until he was twenty-six, when he won a competition, and in 1954 started a world career in Vienna. It was studded with sensational triumphs; in 1955 he sang at Naples in the *prima* – the opening of the summer season – which is accorded special honour in Italy, in 1957 he was at Rome, the following year at both Rome and Naples, in 1960 with Callas at La Scala. A year later he was at the Met, where on one of his most brilliant evenings he partnered Nilsson in *Turandot* and with the aria 'Nessun dorma' gained an ovation that lasted for several minutes.

Flaviano Labó began as a lyric tenor in Italy's minor opera-houses. One day, at a guest production of *Bohème* in Zürich, he stood in for di Stefano, and although partnering the highly acclaimed Virginia Zeani, achieved a sensational success with his own performance. He may perhaps have gone over too early to heroic parts, with the handicap of rather short stature. Then there was Mario Filippeschi, with an unusually sonorous voice; but all the same, compared with the days when Gigli, Schipa, Martinelli, Pertile and half a dozen other beautiful voices were rivals, the supply of good Italian tenors seems to have dropped off. In any age, however, the magnificent voice of Placido Domingo from Mexico would have stood out as a tenor in the highest class, sending millions into rapturous enthusiasm. The same goes for Alfredo Kraus from Spain, who has a stupendous high register. Two others who are given leading rôles today are Adolf Dallapozza, who matured in the chorus of the Vienna Opera, and the Hungarian, Robert Ilosfalvy. Richard Lewis, who has often delighted Glynde-bourne audiences, must be considered one of the great tenors of today, especially in Handel operas, and of Charles Craig, Covent Garden's dramatic tenor for many years, Sandor Gorlinsky, leading international agent, is reported as saying: 'There are opera-houses on the Continent who wouldn't put on *Otello* without Craig.'

Heroic tenors are not in great supply either. In 1961 James King won a big competition in Cincinnatti, after training in order to change from baritone to tenor. He made his début in the Teatro della Pergola (Florence), was chosen by Karl Böhm in Berlin for increasingly dramatic rôles, till in 1965 he reached Wagner, as Siegmund in *Die Walküre*. His countryman Jess Thomas was suc-cessful in German opera-houses, and sang Verdi and Puccini in many German cities; then in 1961 Knappertsbusch tried him out at Bayreuth as Parsifal and so revealed the powers of one of today's most brilliant Wagnerian tenors. He has since sung Siegfried at Karajan's Easter Festival, and Tristan all over the world. Sandor Konya, the Hun-garian, became famous throughout the world especially as a mar-vellous Lohengrin.

Among 'German' tenors, the American Donald Grobe has been prominent since the mid-fifties. He sang Ottavio at the opening of the new German Opera in Berlin, and the title rôle in *Tales of Hoffman* is one of his finest interpretations. Horst Laubenthal, with a bel canto talent seldom heard today, seems a natural successor for Dermota and Wunderlich. Waldemar Kmentt has a glorious voice for both Mozart and young dramatic rôles. After a brilliant Hoffman he came to Don José and will surely develop into a top singer of lighter Wagner heroes like Lohengrin and Stolzing. Peter Schreier has recently risen to the highest class as a lyric tenor; in fact he is now one of the best singers in the world. His Evangelist in Bach's *Matthew Passion*, his Mozart interpretations, his Lieder recitals, all show a perfection both in voice and musicianship that makes them a sheer delight. He finds time to concern himself with unknown and forgotten works, and is a stylist of rare quality.

Helmut Melchert has a position all his own. Despite his melodious tenor he does not care much for conventional opera-singing. The key rôle in his career was Aaron in Schoenberg's posthumous work *Moses und Aaron*; he interpreted this so superbly that one cannot imagine it better sung or acted. In the Zürich world première, Moses was Hans Hermann Fiedler, in Berlin and in many other cities it was Josef Greindl – a great Wagnerian and for thirty years one of the leading basses in German opera. He made a remarkable impact in the *Sprechgesang*★ of Moses, and created an utterly convincing patriarchal figure.

So we come to the basses. From the previous generation, Ludwig Weber probably the last of those born in the nineteenth century to be still singing, was a guest artist all over the world, won triumphs at Bayreuth but also, despite his powerful voice, interpreted Lieder with great delicacy. Gottlob Frick was equally fine in Wagner and in Verdi's bel canto rôles, which he sang at La Scala and the Met. Kurt Böhme, both a Wagnerian and a comic bass, sang a delightful Baron Ochs, which was celebrated for decades. Gustav Neidlinger, guest artist at all the big opera-houses, presented a masterly Alberich both vocally and as a character study. Among younger basses Peter Lagger stands out, a glorious dark voice controlled by splendid intelligence and musical sense, already heralding future greatness with a wonderful interpretation of Boris Godunov. He is as capable of comedy as of tragedy, and shines in oratorio and all branches of solo song from Schubert Lieder to folk-songs. Karl Ridderbusch had triumphantly revealed his unusual powers as Boris Godunov, Sarastro and Hagen, when Karajan brought him into the first rank of singers at the Salzburg Easter Festival. Other fine basses to be mentioned are Manfred Schenk, William Dooley, brilliant interpreter of the Dutchman and Wotan as well as rôles in Roger Session's opera *Montezuma* and in Stravinsky's *Rake's Progress*, Arwed Andtncr, a Beckmesser magnificently sung and acted, David Ward, who has achieved international fame in Wagnerian bass rôles, and Michael Langdon, particularly in his element as Baron Ochs.

A tour of the world's opera-houses should certainly take us to Felsenstein's Comic Opera in East Berlin. It has perhaps the finest company that exists today, with Rudolf Asmus, a wonderfully versatile artist, its leading baritone, and Melitta Muszely as prima donna. One of the greatest singers of her generation, a lyric soprano with crystal clear coloratura, she sings a most moving Violetta in *Traviata*, which brings out the full pathos of tragic love and renunciation.

★ *Translator's note:* Literally 'speaking-singing', a method of writing music for the voice to follow its natural inflections but without a defined pitch.

Another magic carpet might waft us across to South America, to hear Teresa Berganza on the mighty stage of the Colón singing *The Italian Girl in Algiers*. Who can match her in such mezzo coloratura up to the effortless High Bs and Cs? She is also extremely pretty and graceful, with a natural playfulness and unfailing musicianship. With her is a splendid tenor for such Rossini rôles between lyric and comic, Renzo Casellato. The next evening *Sicilian Vespers* gives full scope for a dramatic soprano of tremendous power and radiance, claimant to real prima donna status for her magnificent control and beauty of voice, the American Negress, Martina Arroyo. Yet she is not concerned with stardom, only with service to her art. Once in Mannheim when an over-enthusiastic partner actually broke her arm, she went on singing Santuzza to the end, and she is so completely inside every rôle that she may not have felt the real pain until she had sung the last note. Her baritone colleague in *Vespers* is another American, Sherrill Milnes, with the majesty and sonorous power of Leonard Warren, if not quite his softness in transitions and melting beauty of tone. The bass that evening, delighting the audience especially with his aria 'O tu Palermo', is also a name to be reckoned with – Bonaldo Giaiotto. The third evening offers *Die Frau ohne Schatten* with two sopranos of the highest rank, the Yugolsav Danica Mastilovic and the Norwegian Ingrid Bjoner. Two nights later Bjoner is singing Leonore in *Fidelio*, a performance very hard to match.

But the night before that, the opera was Donizetti's *Anna Bolena*, which like Norma has two immensely demanding rôles, a soprano and a mezzo. The former was sung 140 years before by Giuditta Pasta, the *prima donna assoluta*. On this occasion too it was designed for a world star, who could not appear, however, and was replaced by the Greek girl Elena Souliotis – partnering one of the greatest mezzo voices of our time, Fiorenza Cossotto. Souliotis, though already an initiate of La Scala and with an international reputation, was faced with the assignment of her life and was extremely nervous. The first act passed with false notes and without applause. There was an interval of over three quarters of an hour, suggesting the performance might be stopped; eventually it was announced that the soprano was continuing, though seriously indisposed. Then came the surprise. From minute to minute the singer grew to a splendour far surpassing all her previous achievements. The wonderful duet with Cossotto burst forth triumphantly, to be greeted by the packed audience with an avalanche of surging applause; until at the end of the evening an almost unprecedented frenzy was reached, both on the stage and in the auditorium. A very good singer had responded to a challenge, and in the process turned into a great singer.

For our next stop on this world tour, there is no curtain to go up, for we are at Verona, part of the crowd of twenty thousand whose eyes are riveted on the vast stage, as we wait for the opening of Puccini's *Manon Lescaut*. Then we listen spellbound to the voice of Raina Kabaivanska, effortlessly filling the huge arena, soaring into the starry sky and leaving a glorious exhilaration in our hearts. Karajan had already cast the beautiful young singer as Santuzza in his television production of *Cavalleria Rusticana*; now she conquered the masses 'live' and will surely do so in the future all over the world. It was the same with Mirella Freni. When she achieved her triumph in *Bohème* at La Scala, television had carried her fame in advance to the world's opera-lovers. After that she had to follow in person, summoned from everywhere, achieving in the process new standards in vocal artistry. While Kabaivanska was setting Verona in a frenzy, Freni moved the audience at the Salzburg Festival with a deeply affecting Desdemona. Despite their enthusiasm, after her 'Ave Maria' in the fourth act, not a hand moved. It was the finest homage to her and Verdi – 'a Requiem', said one of those who heard her that night.

A few decades ago comparatively few opera-lovers had the chance to hear most of the finest voices of their time. How different it is now, when recordings offer almost an *embarras de richesse*. For instance, there is one of *Lucia di Lammermoor* with Callas, di Stefano and Gobbi. Unbeatable, you might think. Yet there are other recordings just as magnificent, with Renata Scotto, di Stefano and Bastianini; Callas, Tagliavini and Piero Cappuccilli; Antonietta Stella, Cesare Valetti and Renato Capecchi, or Lina Pagliughi, Giovanni Malipiero and Giuseppe Manacchini. That does not by any means exhaust the choice, for there are excellent non-Italian casts to compete: Erika Köth, Rudolf Schock and Josef Metternich; Roberta Peters, Jan Peerce and Philip Maero; Joan Sutherland, Renato Cione and Robert Merrill; Lily Pons, Richard Tucker and Frank Guarrera. Who would dare to say 'these and no others'?

It is the same with *The Force of Destiny*. We can choose between the older and still highly rated performance with Maria Caniglia, Galliano Massini, Carlo Tagliabue, and the newer versions with their galaxy of stars: Callas, Tucker and Tagliabue; Tebaldi, del Monaco and Bastianini; Zinka Milanov, di Stefano, Warren; Milanov, Jan Peerce and Warren. So one can listen to the famous duet between Alvaro and Carlos on the battlefield, perhaps the most moving duet between tenor and baritone in Italian opera, sung by two ideal lyric voices (di Stefano and Warren) or the more dramatic del Monaco and Bastianini.

These recordings have included many illustrious names for which I have found little or no place before. Lily Pons, for instance; to the young opera-lover today she will mean very little. But this graceful French singer was one of the most triumphant coloratura divas in all the big opera-houses, a Lucia and a Lakme of extraordinary virtuosity, member of the Met for thirty years, star among stars. Mario del Monaco, one of the most mighty Otellos of all time, an inspiring Radames, was unmatched in his day for heroic characters, and an actor who fulfilled the ideals of the great dramatists. Rather older than del Monaco and for years his keenest rival as a lyric tenor, Ferrucio Tagliavini had a bel canto voice which deserted him all too soon. The Yugoslav Zinka Milanov found a path to fame opened to her by Toscanini, who in 1937 gave her the soprano solo in the Verdi *Requiem* at the Salzburg Festival. Renata Scotto, the Italian prima donna, one of the finest Violettas, was in competition with another Italian, born in America, the beautiful Anna Moffo, who made a very individual character out of this rôle, singing it also in a film. Antonietta Stella's name was high-lighted in the *stagioni* of the big Italian cities. Since 1959 she has also been a member of the Met, a splendid Leonora in *Trovatore*, an Elisabeth of rare perfection in *Don Carlos* and also – like all Italian sopranos of whatever type – a Violetta.

There are three sopranos who have been particularly associated with the Queen of the Night. Wilma Lipp made a name for herself when she sang the rôle in Vienna at the age of nineteen, since then she has risen to the highest class, but has remained loyal to Vienna. Lucia Popp, another coloratura soprano, makes a speciality of this rôle, which set her on the road to fame. The same applies to Erika Köth, who sang it in 1953 when first engaged at Munich, and in 1956 at Salzburg under Fürtwangler. In 1958 at Munich, in the rebuilt Cuvilliés-Theater, she was Susanna in *Figaro* and in 1961 Zerlina at the opening of the West Berlin Opera-house. Two other sopranos of a similar type are Rita Streich, who enjoys popularity all over the world both as an opera-singer and as a wonderful interpreter of Lieder, and Ruth-Margret Pütz, who shows her vocal brilliance to full effect as Zerbinetta in *Ariadne auf Naxos*, but integrates the action as well with great dramatic intensity.

Hilde Güden is almost unrivalled in three extremely different rôles, Richard Strauss's Daphne, Johann Strauss's Rosalinda (*Fledermaus*) and the Countess in *Figaro*. Evelyn Lear might be considered an

American equivalent to Anja Silja; she too, while still a girl, attracted attention all over the world, and today her Lulu combines uncanny psychological penetration with seductively beautiful singing. In the première of Werner Egk's *Betrothal in San Domingo* she and Fritz Wunderlich portrayed the bloody racial conflict with shattering effect. Teresa Stratas, a Greek born in Canada, achieved great renown after appearing at La Scala in Manuel de Falla's posthumous work *Atlantida*, where she conveyed an unforgettable visionary quality singing Queen Isabel's dream. Mady Mesplé, with her unusually sweet voice and dazzling runs, may justifiably be called a successor of Lily Pons, and we should remember another French singer – indeed one of the greatest French singers of this century – Ninon Vallin. Her wide register allowed her to sing an enchanting Manon as well as the mezzo rôles of Carmen and Mignon; she was nearly sixty at the end of the Second World War, but long after that was still giving excellent recitals.

Among the young sopranos of today, Constanza Cuccaro, an American, though discovered in Zürich, has already had a tremendous impact. Ingeborg Hallstein, an operetta star of extraordinary charm, made the jump to opera very successfully, and sang the Queen of the Night flawlessly under both Klemperer and Karajan. She shows her fine musicianship in modern works (by Henze, Menotti, Fortner), and has become one of the most heavily committed singers – a remarkable Violetta and a delightful Lieder interpreter. Edith Mathis has an exceptionally well-trained soprano of light and pleasing timbre, and her rapid advance from Lucerne and Zürich by way of Cologne took her to Berlin and on world tours. She is now growing out of the soubrette rôles, which she has sung so brilliantly, and her voice has gained a glorious lyric timbre, so that she can be expected to enjoy international fame for a long time. Edda Moser, another very industrious artist, finds no task too hard for her (as she proves by her singing in modern operas) and no aim too high; in her swift rise she won herself a place in Karajan's Easter Festival, a star début at the Met, and an extremely successful tour of the Soviet Union. She has worked so tirelessly on her sonorous voice that she is now a most delightful Mozart singer. She comes from Berlin and is the daughter of a distinguished musicologist; in 1969 the *New York Times* ranked her among the best sopranos in the world.

There are several others today at the zenith of their powers: Lisa della Casa, Anneliese Rothenberger, Hildegard Hillebrecht, Helga Pilarczyk, Claire Watson, Leonie Rysanek. Lisa della Casa has perhaps stamped herself most strongly in the mind of audiences everywhere as an ideal Arabella; she has a rare combination of physical and vocal beauty. Through television Anneliese Rothenberger has become a prototype of stylish singing, and not only for connoisseurs; she has won her way into the hearts of thousands of ordinary viewers. She has never exploited this position for her own kudos, easy as it would be for her with such attractive looks and personality; instead she earns the high approval of all artists by modestly talking about professional conscience and the sacredness of art. Hildegard Hillebrecht's soprano shines in a wide repertoire, perhaps most radiantly in the cantilenas of Chrysothemis in *Elektra*. Helga Pilarczyk will go down in operatic history for her performances in contemporary works; two of her favourite rôles are Alban Berg characters, Marie in *Wozzeck* and Lulu, and two are from Schönberg, in *Erwartung* (Expectation) and *Von heute auf morgen* (from Today to Tomorrow). Of her interpretation of Prokofiev's *Fiery Angel* a critic wrote, 'For driving force and keenness of intellect, acting and voice, none of the world-class operatic sopranos would be as well suited to this operatic vision as is Helga Pilarczyk.' Leonie Rysanek was Sieglinde at Bayreuth in 1951, then a guest artist in important rôles elsewhere, until her fortunate stand-in performance as Lady Macbeth at the Met.

More and more names still spring to mind. A young Lotte Lehmann seems to have appeared in Gundula Janowitz, to judge by her singing of Sieglinde at Salzburg, partnered by Jon Vickers. Reri Grist has travelled a long way; from Cindy-Lou (Micaela) in the Broadway production of *Carmen Jones* and Bernstein's *West Side Story*, by way of *Fledermaus* and the soprano solo in Mahler's Fourth, to Zerlina, Despina, Susanna, on to Rosina and even Queen of the Night, at important opera-houses. Also from New York to Vienna (where she was miscast as Sophie in *Rosenkavalier*), to Milan and Salzburg, and triumphantly back to the Met, as one of the most perfect and spellbinding coloratura singers of our time. Helen Donath, another American, had three fine achievements in 1970; the soprano solo in Mozart's *Requiem* under Karajan at Salzburg, Marzelline in *Fidelio* at Rome under Bernstein, and Pamina under Kubelik at Munich. Leonore Kirschstein acts and sings a splendid Countess in *Figaro*. Pilar Lorengar, a wonderful voice from Spain, superb in everything from Mozart to Verdi and Debussy, shows her mastery in that real test of technical ability, the G-Minor aria from *The Magic Flute*. Catherine Gayer, a young American from Los Angeles, although extremely accomplished in the classical repertoire, has become a supreme interpreter of the most *avant garde* music. She sings Nono's

Intolerance and Zimmerman's *Soldaten* as if they were Mozart or Verdi, the way this kind of music should be sung. In a television production of the Martinu opera *Julietta* she was enchanting as an ethereal dream figure, ideal in appearance, singing and acting. She was also a valued contributor to Henze's *Elegy for Young Lovers* and Dallapiccola's *Odysseus*. An English girl, Elizabeth Harwood, has advanced to the highest world class with two magnificent Mozart performances at the Salzburg Festival, Constanze in *Entführung* and the Countess in *Figaro*.

Two examples will show how far specialisation has gone in modern singing, as in every field of modern life. Silvia Geszty, with her quite astonishing coloratura – there is something almost dreamlike in the virtuosity with which she masters some of the most difficult rôles in the repertoire – sings the Queen of the Night during a single season in Berlin, Dresden, Frankfurt, Hamburg, Hanover, Munich, Rome, Salzburg and Vienna. Ludmila Dvorakova sang Isolde fifteen times in a season, a rôle comparable in physical strain to at least a marathon race, demanding immense intellectual and musical concentration as well as psychological involvement; she sang it six times at the Met, five times at the Colón, three times at Genoa, and once at her home opera-house, the Linden Opera in East Berlin. She is still very young for this tremendous task, which justifies great hopes for her future.

Annabelle Bernard, born in New Orleans, won a singing prize in Munich, made her début at Berlin under Böhm, rose quickly to the top class of young dramatic sopranos, gave a concert in the Vatican, and brought many rôles to exciting life. The Dutch girl Gerry de Groot, a worthy successor of her countrywoman Gre Brouwenstijn, that most moving of *Fidelio* Leonores, is endowed with unusual vocal powers and a compelling though very pleasing personality. She makes a fascinating Minnie in *The Girl of the Golden West* – a character study of marvellous intensity – partnered by a radiant tenor Glade Peterson, an artist with a wonderful technique. The world will hear much more of Gerry de Groot, who achieved a sensational success with a powerful yet deeply feminine Turandot.

The lovely voice of the English soprano Heather Harper first attracted international attention through her soprano solo in Britten's *War Requiem* at its première in Coventry Cathedral; Beverly Sills, an American, is almost unrivalled in Handel's dramatic coloratura as well as in Verdi and Donizetti. The young Greek, Antigone Sgourda, already an extremely good Donna Anna, Tosca and Violetta, seems slowly but surely to be moving towards high dramatic rôles and perhaps Wagner. She has a natural musicianship and a powerful voice, from which great achievements can be expected.

Renate Holm, an enchanting soubrette, offers an Ännchen (*Freischütz*) and a Marzelline (*Fidelio*) rarely surpassed on German stages, and with an effectiveness which grows rather than declines even in huge opera-houses like the Colón. Lotte Schädle has already become very well-known internationally; in a short time she has sung in all Europe's musical centres, and won special tributes for her Susanna in *Figaro*. She is a little like Lisa Otto, one of her most celebrated predecessors in Mozart opera, but shows an equal accomplishment in Bach oratorios under Karl Richter. Nadezda Kniplova is a fine singer from Czechoslovakia; among many splendid Italian women's voices I think first of Bianca Maria Casoni, Margheritha Guglielmi and especially Ilva Ligabue, with her heart-warming soprano in the great tradition of Tebaldi. Carla Spletter, after a number of successful guest appearances, became a member of the Hamburg Opera, and in 1953 sang Germany's first Lulu with an extremely sonorous voice and riveting acting. A few months later she died, in her early forties.

One evening towards the ends of 1970 a Munich production of *Così* was televised and won admiration for the superb singing; Lilian Sukis and Brigitte Fassbänder, combining charm, talent and vocal brilliance, competed with their counterparts, Barry McDaniel and Adolf Dallapozza, in purest bel canto – as if it were not 1970 but 1790.

Brigitte Fassbänder is one of the young generation of remarkable mezzos. Her father was the memorable Berlin baritone Willi Domgraf-Fassbänder. She made her début in 1961 and is destined for a world career. Lilian Benningsen, less luxuriant in sound but a very sharp portrayer of character, has given outstanding performances as Herodias, Klytämnestra and Baba the Turk in *Rake's Progress*. A few years ago, in a lovely production of *Rosenkavalier* at Wiesbaden, Gisela Litz sang her way to the top as a passionate Oktavian with a dark melodious voice. At Hamburg Opera she developed into a mature, very human, creative artist with glorious beauty of tone. Julia Hamaris, a young Hungarian, widely sought after as a contralto Lieder-singer, made a sensational stage début as Carmen at Stuttgart. Elisabeth Schärtel was a magnificent Amme in *Frau ohne Schatten* at Cologne, with a brilliant company including Ingeborg Exner, Helga Pilarczyk, Herbert Schachtschneider and Franz Crass.

Oralia Dominguez, the exotic contralto from Mexico, has in recent years been called to important assignments, for instance by Karajan to sing Erda in *The Ring*. The American, Grace Hoffman, who studied with Friedrich Schorr, after her début at Zurich in 1952 climbed rapidly, reaching the Met and the Colón in 1959. She sang a Brangäne which for years has been unsurpassed, and there is a fine recording of excerpts from *Tristan* under Knappertsbusch with her and Nilsson. Kerstin Meyer, from Sweden, a brilliant Carmen, is also in great demand all over the world as a Wagner singer. Erika Wien, at home in a wide repertoire including Italian and comic opera, perhaps had her most notable achievement as an imaginative Magdalena in *Meistersinger*. One of the most distinguished mezzos of our day is the American Vera Little, who won several prizes in Germany, and became well-known in Switzerland and Belgium. In 1958 she came to Berlin, where she started her international career, as Amneris, Eboli, Ulrica, and also as Venus, Erda and the Countess in *Queen of Spades*. Rita Gorr from Ghent has, since 1958, sung many times at Bayreuth, above all as Ortrud and Kundry, though she cultivates the Italian mezzo rôles at La Scala as well. From 1962 she has been a member of the Met. The great mezzos and contraltos who reached their glorious peaks in the post-war period were Anny Helm, Elisabeth Höngen, Georgine von Milinkovic, Herta Töpper, all near retirement now. They remain unforgettable, as does Jean Madeira, one of the most dazzling Carmens of our time.

There seems to be no limit to the ability of Christa Ludwig who, after conquering almost the entire mezzo repertoire, now aspires towards the high dramatic field; her most notable rôles are Leonore in *Fidelio* and Oktavian in *Rosenkavalier* – though she is also a superb Marschallin – and as a seductive Carmen she proves she has not lost her contralto depths. Regina Resnik has gone the other and more unusual way; after winning an important competition, she made her début as Santuzza at the New York City Center, in 1948 sang the first American Ellen Orford in Britten's *Peter Grimes* and in 1953 Sieglinde at Bayreuth. Then she developed her lower register and became a much admired Marina (*Boris Godunov*), Eboli and Fricka, three mezzo parts to which as her peak rôle she added Carmen. Janet Baker, born on Teesside, sings music of all periods, from Monteverdi and Cavalli at Glyndebourne to modern pieces written for her, of all types – opera, Lieder and concert works – all round the world; in 1968 the New York Times critic called her 'the greatest British import since wool'. Her most important single triumph was as Dido in Scottish Opera's 1969 production of *The Trojans*, in which rôle, afterwards repeated at Covent Garden, she received ecstatic praise. Josephine Veasey has also achieved considerable success in this rôle and in 1972 actually alternated between Dido and Cassandra for several performances. Her mezzo colleague from New Zealand, Yvonne Minton, is also a popular guest artist throughout the world.

Grace Bumbry, whose sensational Bayreuth début I have discussed, has grown into one of the greatest of mezzos. Trained by Lotte Lehmann, she made her first stage appearance in Paris, as Amneris. A year later, in 1961, she sang Carmen thirteen times in Brussels, with a break for that Venus at Bayreuth. In 1964 she was Karajan's Lady Macbeth, later his Carmen, at Vienna and Salzburg. In 1965 she made a compelling Eboli at the Met, and a year later she was rapturously received at La Scala in two of her Italian rôles, Amneris and Santuzza. The many competitions she won include the Marian Anderson prize, which establishes a deep relationship between this generation of all-conquering black singers and that 'once-in-a-century' voice. Two other mezzo talents from the United States are Carol Smith, a moving and impressive Eboli, and Tatyana Troyanos, born in New York of a Greek father and German mother; she developed a wide repertoire at the City Center Opera, started her international career from Hamburg in 1964, and sang Carmen at Munich and Oktavian at the Salzburg Festival.

A few years ago various Italian cities had productions of *Don Carlos*, and opera-lovers in Italy had a chance to hear an amazing number of outstanding baritones. Apollo Granforte, who in his youth worked as a cobbler in the Argentine, was still going strong after being a leading baritone between the wars. Giuseppe Taddei had his career interrupted by the war, but a few years afterwards reached the top and was called to the Met in 1951; among his many rôles he was a Rossini Figaro of the highest class and a Don Giovanni to rival Pinza and Siepi. Tito Gobbi won a competition in Vienna in 1938, a year later he sang the elder Germont (*Traviata*) in Rome and in 1942 he went to La Scala. I have already talked of his Scarpia and his Salzburg Falstaff. There is a wonderful recording of *Otello* conducted by Tullio Serafin, with Gobbi as Iago, Leonie Rysanek as Desdemona, Jon Vickers as the Moor. Aldo Protti, an equally great Iago, sang the rôle with Renata Tebaldi, probably the greatest Desdemona of the last decade, and Mario del Monaco. Protti, who made his début at Pesaro in 1948 and went to La Scala in 1949, seems in his vocal power to have resurrected the glorious times of Scotti, Ruffo and Stracciari. Giuseppe Valdengo was Toscanini's choice for Iago, which is enough honour in itself; others would prefer Ettore Bastianini, who started as a bass and since 1953 has given countless master performances – Maggio Musicale (Florence), La Scala and the Met in the same season. While Valdengo sings on records with Vinay, and Taddei with the

Argentinian Carlos Guichandut, Gino Becchi, another splendid baritone, can be heard with Gigli! Rolando Panerai, from 1951 at La Scala, 1955 at the Met, 1957 at the Salzburg Festival, was in 1958 the first Italian Mathis in Hindemith's opera. And Piero Cappuccilli has a powerful and yet perfectly controlled bel canto voice, which still sounds quite exceptional to anyone who hears it.

The New World has a big challenge to offer in the baritone field. The first who comes to mind is George London, born in Canada in 1919, an almost unique personality on the operatic stage. The demonic seems to be his special domain, Méphistophélès (in Gounod's *Faust*), the Dutchman and Boris Godunov – he is the only non-Slav singer to interpret Boris at the Bolshoi Theatre, where he received as immense applause as everywhere else – but he is also a tragic Amfortas, a passionate Wotan, a self-sacrificing Wolfram, and no one can appreciate his full range without having heard him sing Brahms's *Four Serious Songs* and songs by Moussorgsky. Against this dark baritone with bass depths, Leonard Warren's lyric voice sounded light and high; Warren was so supreme in his field that when he died of a heart attack the Met had to fill his rôles with no less than five different baritones. Robert Merrill was born in New York in 1919. At the end of the war he made his début at the Met, where his voice held an honourable place beside the two stars Licia Albanese and Jan Peerce. He was commissioned to sing before the US Congress at the memorial service for President Roosevelt. The warmth and vibrance of his voice, especially in Verdi operas, are preserved on many records. Cornell MacNeil, born in Minneapolis in 1925, studied with Friedrich Schorr (like Grace Hoffmann) and found fame in 1950 as a thrilling Consul in the première of Menotti's opera; since 1959 he has made his artistic home at the Met. Lawrence Winters, notable in Lieder and other solo song, has also given fine operatic performances, as recordings with Maria Stader and Ernst Haefliger show.

Fischer-Dieskau and Prey are only two of the many splendid baritones from German-speaking countries. Josef Metternich, starting in the chorus at Bonn and Cologne, reached the front rank at La Scala and in Vienna, at Covent Garden and the Met. In 1957 at Munich he was the first Kepler in Hindemith's *Harmonie der Welt*. Vladimir Ruzdak, of Slav origin, developed at Hamburg into one of the most outstanding character singers of our time. His Golaud in *Pelléas et Mélisande*, his Prisoner, the title rôle in Dallapiccola's opera, are among the imperishable creations of the musical theatre. Otto Wiener, who had made a name for himself as a concert and radio singer, appeared on the stage in 1953 and in a few years became a leading opera-singer;

the joviality of his Hans Sachs was in sharp contrast to the harshness of
his Gunther and the melancholy of his Dutchman, demonstrating the
range of his characterisation as well as his voice. Otto Edelmann was
also Sachs at Bayreuth and at the Met. He took his amusing Baron
Ochs all over the world, and in Karajan's recording is immortalised
in this rôle with the finest of partners. Gerd Feldhoff, a Flying Dutchman full of intense yearning, shows a great sensitivity in operas of the
baroque period. Karl-Christian Kohn, a bass baritone like Feldhoff
and long regarded as an admirable singer, embarked on an international career after his well-deserved triumph as Mozart's Figaro at
the opening of the restored Cuvilliés-Theater. The Argentinian
Carlos Feller, a character singer of real vocal accomplishment, is one
of the most delightful comic basses in German opera today. Tom
Krause, another baritone of international status, interprets Mozart
and Rossini with great verve, and is a highly rated Lieder-singer. His
Hamburg colleagues Heinz Blankenburg and Toni Blankenheim are
brilliant character actors and singers, both with a talent for hilarious
comedy. It takes a very serious artist to be irresistibly funny on the
stage!

Zoltan Keleman, considered a model Alberich, is also Klingsor and
Leporello, Don Alfonso and Gianni Schicchi. Geraint Evans is a
masterly Figaro, Falstaff and Leporello, a singer-actor of world class,
and also a highly impressive Wozzeck. Peter Glossop, another
British baritone, has crowned his rapid career with a wonderful Tonio
in *Pagliacci* under Karajan. Raimund Grumbach is an excellent,
vivacious Figaro at Munich, which also gave scope for Kieth Engen,
a noble singer and interpreter. Armin Weltner was for many years a
pillar of several big opera-houses, a fine bel canto cavalier baritone.
Ralph Telasko has made a considerable impact in Europe and America
with his powerful voice and gift for characterisation. Willy Ferenz
remains in the memory as a deeply tragic Wozzeck and in countless
other deeply convincing character studies.

Benno Kusche, one of the most notable successors to the great
Schmitt-Walter as Beckmesser, after being an excellent Figaro for
years, now makes a delightful Dr Bartolo; he is also an impressive
Shadow in *Rake's Progress*. William Wilderman, born in Stuttgart,
a naturalised American, is a bass of the highest quality. So are Arnold
van Mill from Holland and Fernando Corena, an Italian (though
born in Geneva), whose gift for characterisation comes across remarkably on many records; his energetic international activity has
made him a leading comic bass. Otto von Rohr and Deszö Ernster,
two magnificent basses, are both oustanding as Sarastro and King

Mark, and in all other rôles demanding noble beauty of tone. Giulio Neri, their Italian equivalent, has achieved his most magnificent portrayal as the Grand Inquisitor in *Don Carlos*. Ivo Vinco, a wonderful baritone, has been a worthy partner of world stars on many records. Murray Dickie should perhaps be mentioned here as a fine comic tenor. The Hungarian Endre Koreh, who died young, will be remembered by any who saw his superb performance in *Entführung*, justifying one critic's description of Osmin as 'a tragic figure in the deepest theatrical sense'. Paul Kuen's light tenor is associated in the memory with Orff's *Carmina Burana*, which he has preserved on records with the sonorous baritone Marcel Cordes and the splendid Agnes Giebel.

Loren Driscoll, a young tenor who not long ago was still a cowboy in the Middle West, became in 1965 Henze's first Young Lord, and has since shown great accomplishment in the high bel canto range. Ernst Kozub, almost a Franz Völker voice with all its bel canto brilliance, makes an especially compelling Florestan. Nigel Douglas, a pupil of Piccaver's, creates a little masterpiece, both vocally and psychologically, with his Robespierre in von Einem's *Danton's Death*. Marilyn Zschau gives a remarkable performance as Jánaçek's Cunning Little Vixen, and she is very moving as the composer in *Ariadne*. As Donna Elvira she makes a fine counterpart to the wonderful Don Giovanni of her young fellow-American, Howard Nelson, with a really delicious Leporello from the Hungarian Joszef Dene.

The very gifted English baritone Benjamin Luxon, born in 1937, achieved renown in the past few years with the title rôle in *Owen Wingrave* on television and at Covent Garden, brilliant performances as Monteverdi's Ulysses and as Death in *Taverner*, also recording Delius's *Mass of Life* in place of an indisposed Fischer-Dieskau. Before this, however, he had taken many British rôles with the English Opera Group, touring as far away as Russia and Australia. His unusually wide range embraces the Bach *Passions*, and Lieder, and not very long ago he won high praise for his recording of Moussorgsky songs in Russian.

As my book draws inevitably to its end, I find hundreds of reviews and memories with performances and personalities that simply must be brought in. Clara Petrella's portrayal in *The Consul* of the revolutionary's tragic wife is unforgettable. Patricia Johnson and Barbara Scherler in Rossini's *Cenerentola* have mezzo coloraturas which almost reach the standard of Teresa Berganza. Jaime Aragall, a Catalan with a magnificent lyric tenor, was partnered in *Bohème* by a very touching Mimì, the young Mietta Sighele, who looks set for a prodigious career. The same applies to Alfredo Sanchez Luna from Venezuela, a radiant tenor who quite lately won his first laurels in the fine opera-house at St Gallen (Switzerland). One of the most lyrical Lohengrins of recent years is the Swede, Sven Olaf Eliasson, who almost matches Patzak and Erb in Pfitzner's *Palestrina*, partnered by the wonderful soprano of Gerlinde Lorenz. The Canadian baritone, Norman Mittelman, who started in Zürich, is now rising fast.

At the Hamburg première of Paul Burkhard's *Ein Stern geht auf aus Jaakob* (A Star goes up from Jacob) there were two remarkable sopranos, Elisabeth Steiner and Arlene Saunders. In Berne there was a really magnificent Otello, on loan from Sadler's Wells, Hugh Beresford. That the young Italian Rita Lantieri received equal tributes as Desdemona, shows her class. Vienna provided an unsurpassable cast for *Don Carlos*: Corelli in the title rôle, Ghiaurov as King Philip, Gundula Janowitz as Elisabeth, and – perhaps the most inspiring of all these wonderful voices – Shirley Verrett as Eboli. London in 1970 had a splendid production at Covent Garden of *Arabella* under Solti, with the Swedish baritone Ingvar Wixell as Mandryka; a performance which equalled the finest previous interpretations and confirmed the high promise of Wixell's Rigoletto.

The audiences at Frankfurt's opera-house have often been richly rewarded; when the dazzling Anny Schlemm sang Orff's 'Die Kluge' and Jánacek's Jenufa; when Willi Wolff offered a fascinating Don Giovanni and an intense portrayal of Dallapiccola's Prisoner; when Jean Stern, Bella Jasper, Wolinsky and others established an *Ariadne* quintet of rare perfection; when Leonardo Wolovsky gave a regal display as Boris and Khovantchina, but was also, in complete contrast, a Rocco of extreme simplicity in *Fidelio*, when Ernst Gutstein was Dr Schön in the hands of the wild-cat Lulu, terrifyingly portrayed by Pilarczyk.

In Berlin – and at many guest performances – the magnificent and sombre bass baritone of the Yugo-Slav, Tomislav Neralic, can still be heard, a Boris and Prince Igor of the greatest intensity, an Iago and Scarpia from such spiritual abysses, that one experiences a double delight and amazement at his Falstaff. There are two new baritones who sound extraordinarily promising: the Finn, Kari Nurmela, and the German, Wolfgang Anheisser. Lucretia West sings spirituals with moving fervour, and the fine voice and delightful personality of Ina Dressel have given an extra charm to Viennese operettas.

Indeed I have almost passed over the singers of light music. Surely Fritzi Massary was as great an artist in her way, for instance, as Madame Pompadour. Who would deny Judy Garland this rank, or her talented daughter Liza Minelli? Should not Edith Piaf come into the book, or Julie Andrews (for her enchanting *Sound of Music*); should we not take in Yvonne Printemps, Yvette Guilbert, Barbra Streisand? And there are so many others to mention, acknowledge, admire, and to astonish us with the inexhaustible supply of superb singers in our century.

How did that sentence run about Callas? 'Her singing is like a fresh wound in its outpouring of vital forces.' She is one of hundreds of great and dedicated singers to whom it would apply. In an age like ours which is apparently so indifferent to art and yet so hungry to experience it, thousands of people devote themselves to singing; not to earn a fortune, but from a true vocation, with a readiness to aspire to the highest realms of art, even though it should cost them their peace, happiness or even life.

The world began with song. It has been a blessing and delight for mankind till the present, and surely until the end of human history, song will never die away.

Index

COLLEGE OF MARIN

3 2555 00122777 1